CW00405462

Managing Volunteers
in Tourism

Managing Volunteers in Tourism: Attractions, Destinations and Events

Kirsten Holmes and
Karen Smith

AMSTERDAM • BOSTON • HEIDELBERG • LONDON • NEW YORK • OXFORD
PARIS • SAN DIEGO • SAN FRANCISCO • SINGAPORE • SYDNEY • TOKYO
Butterworth-Heinemann is an imprint of Elsevier

Butterworth-Heinemann is an imprint of Elsevier
Linacre House, Jordan Hill, Oxford OX2 8DP, UK
30 Corporate Drive, Suite 400, Burlington, MA 01803, USA

First edition 2009

Copyright © 2009 Elsevier Ltd. All rights reserved.

No part of this publication may be reproduced, stored in a retrieval system,
or transmitted in any form or by any means, electronic, mechanical, photocopying,
recording or otherwise without the prior written permission of the publisher

Permissions may be sought directly from Elsevier's Science & Technology Rights
Department in Oxford, UK: phone (+44) (0) 1865 843830; fax (+44) (0) 1865 853333;
email: permissions@elsevier.com. Alternatively you can submit your request online by
visiting the Elsevier web site at http://elsevier.com/locate/permissions, and selecting
Obtaining permission to use Elsevier material

Notice
No responsibility is assumed by the publisher for any injury and/or damage to persons
or property as a matter of products liability, negligence or otherwise, or from any use
or operation of any methods, products, instructions or ideas contained in the material
herein.

British Library Cataloguing in Publication Data
A catalogue record for this book is available from the British Library

Library of Congress Cataloging-in-Publication Data
A catalog record for this book is available from the Library of Congress

ISBN: 978-0-7506-8767-6

For information on all Butterworth-Heinemann publications
visit our Web site at www.elsevierdirect.com

Typeset by Macmillan Publishing Solutions
(www.macmillansolutions.com)

Printed and bound in Great Britain

09 10 11 12   10 9 8 7 6 5 4 3 2 1

Working together to grow
libraries in developing countries

www.elsevier.com | www.bookaid.org | www.sabre.org

ELSEVIER   BOOK AID
            International   Sabre Foundation

To
Steven and Gwen
Simon, Sam and Ben

Contents

List of Boxed Examples

List of Figures

List of Tables

List of Further Examples – Available Online at www.elsevierdirect.com/ 9780750687676

Preface and Acknowledgments

Volunteers are an essential part of tourism, whether they are volunteering in their local museum, at a sporting mega event, as an airport ambassador, or traveling the global as a volunteer tourist. Recent years have seen an explosion in research on tourism volunteering but this is still piecemeal and has tended to examine only one form or setting for volunteering, such as attractions or volunteer tourism. The motivation behind this book was to bring together the diverse forms of tourism volunteering within one framework. We focus on four settings: attractions, destination service organizations, events and volunteer tourism; and three forms of volunteering contributions: ongoing, seasonal and episodic. We take an organizational approach in order to understand the phenomenon of tourism volunteering more holistically.

This book is not a 'how to' guide to managing volunteers; there are a wealth of publications and online sources that do that and these will be highlighted throughout (e.g. see Part B Introduction). Rather, we review research and good practice to highlight the key management issues and relate them to the tourism volunteering context. We examine trends in volunteering and ethical issues and deliberately include under-researched forms of tourism volunteering, such as meet-and-greeters, surf life-savers, conservation, festival and information center volunteers and VolunTourists.

This book is divided into three parts. Part A begins by introducing the concept of volunteering and considering the variety of volunteer forms and settings within tourism. This Part also reviews the key trends impacting on tourism volunteering worldwide and analyzes the benefits and costs of volunteering to a range of stakeholders including volunteers, organizations, visitors, communities and society. Part B picks up the organizational approach and examines volunteer program design and planning, volunteer motivation, recruitment and selection, training and development, reward and retention and diversity management. A concluding chapter reflects on the future for tourism volunteering and considers some of the ethical issues inherent in tourism volunteering and its management. The management themes are carried through to Part C, with ten invited case studies from international researchers and practitioners. These examples of attractions, events and festivals and volunteer tourism from around the world provide an in-depth examination of the challenges facing those managing tourism volunteers in a range of settings. Parts A and B also include shorter boxed examples to illustrate how tourism organizations approach the management of volunteers, and resources for further information and best practice. Further examples are available online at: www.elsevierdirect.com/9780750687676

This book is designed for researchers, practitioners and students. Researchers will benefit from the comprehensive review of extant research in this field; practitioners can use the numerous examples and principles for good practice to inform the design and evaluation of their volunteer programs; and students can use the case studies and discussion questions to aid their learning. We hope this text is of value to its readers and enables the advancement of this important field of study.

Volunteering has been an important part of our own lives. While our doctorates examined the management of volunteers in heritage attractions, we have since investigated settings including events and festivals, meet-and-greet programs, visitor information centers, zoos, sports and volunteer tourism. We have also been volunteers ourselves and involved in managing tourism volunteers so we have first-hand experience of the highs and lows of volunteering.

Kirsten would like to thank the organizations who have supported her volunteering research to date, most notably Curtin University, the National Trust for Places of Historic Interest and Natural Beauty, United Kingdom and the Botanic Gardens and Parks Authority, Western Australia.

Karen acknowledges the value of her volunteering experiences at The Wordsworth Trust and with British Trust for Conservation Volunteers (BTCV), among others, and the support for her volunteering research from Victoria University of Wellington, the Centre for Tourism and Services Research at Victoria University in Melbourne and Nottingham Trent University.

We both recognize the support of current and past colleagues, not least coresearchers Tom Baum, Deborah Edwards, Leonie Lockstone, Marg Deery, Alix Slater, Geoff Nichols and Peter Taylor.

Lastly, we, of course, thank our families for their encouragement and support in this and earlier projects: our partners and children, Steven, Gwen, Simon, Sam and Ben and our parents, Jean, David, Joan, John, Adrian, Jill and Heather.

Kirsten Holmes and Karen Smith
March 2009

Currency Converter

The case studies and examples we use in this book use a number of different currencies. This table shows the exchange rates for these currencies in March 2009.

	Australian Dollar	Canadian Dollar	Euro	New Zealand Dollar	UK Sterling	US Dollar
Australian dollar	1	0.84	0.51	1.24	0.47	0.66
Canadian dollar	1.19	1	0.60	1.48	0.56	0.79
Euro	1.94	1.67	1	2.39	0.93	1.36
New Zealand dollar	0.80	0.67	0.42	1	0.38	0.53
UK sterling	2.14	1.79	1.07	2.66	1	1.41
US dollar	1.51	1.27	0.74	1.88	0.71	1

Contributors

Tom Baum is Professor of International Tourism and Hospitality Management at the University of Strathclyde in Glasgow, Scotland. Tom is a specialist in the study of people and work in hospitality, tourism, leisure and events, including human resource management, education and training and has researched, consulted and published in this field in many parts of the world. Tom is past President of EuroCHRIE and a former Board Member of International CHRIE. He was also the 2001 winner of the John Wiley Award for outstanding contribution to research. He is a Fellow of the International Academy for the Study of Tourism.

Peter Burley, Director of Sport Guidance Ltd, has a history of involvement in sport and leisure delivery spanning 25 years. As a senior academic staff member in the CPIT Business School in New Zealand he teaches leadership, management and event management having set up a number of tertiary education courses notably the Diploma in Applied Recreation, CircoArts and the Graduate Diploma in Event Management.

Deborah Edwards is Senior Research Fellow at the Sustainable Tourism Cooperative Research Centre in Urban Tourism in the School of Leisure, Sport and Tourism at the University of Technology, Sydney, Australia. Deborah's research interests are in sustainable tourism management, urban attractions, tourism planning, volunteers in tourism attractions and the impacts of events.

Beate Elstad is Associate Professor at Oslo University College, Faculty of Business, Public Administration, and Social Work in Norway. Her PhD thesis was on volunteers at the Kongsberg Jazz Festival. Her research interests are volunteers, festivals, freelancers, and cultural management from an organizational behavior point of view.

Carmel Foley is a Lecturer and Chair of the Teaching and Learning Committee in the School of Leisure, Sport and Tourism at the University of Technology, Sydney, Australia. Carmel's interests are in communitarian leisure, social capital development, leisure history, event theory and diversity management.

Jennifer Fresque completed her Master's in Applied Health Sciences at Brock University, Canada, where her thesis examined the role of collaboration in nonprofit environmental organizations. She is a PhD student at

Wilfrid Laurier University, supported by the Social Sciences and Humanities Research Council of Canada. Her current research interests include community-based resource management, environmental governance, and environmental change and adaptation in northern Canada.

Kirsten Holmes completed her PhD on museum volunteers at the University of Leeds and has since lectured in leisure and tourism at the Universities of Sheffield and Surrey in the UK. She is currently a research fellow at Curtin University, Western Australia. She has nearly 15 years experience of researching volunteerism and has presented her work at international conferences and published widely in journals. She is also a member of Volunteering Western Australia's research committee.

Andy Jefferies has worked since 2004 as one of the few nonvolunteer members of BTCV's international team. He has lots of letters after his name including BSc, MSc and MIEEM earned through a mix of ecological and development disciplines. None of them are as valuable as his extensive time spent volunteering in the ecological development field in the UK, Nigeria and other parts of the world.

Leonie Lockstone is a Lecturer in Event Management at Victoria University, Melbourne, Australia. Her PhD thesis was titled 'Managing the volunteer workforce – Flexible structures and strategies to integrate paid and unpaid workers'. She was a recipient of an Australian Postgraduate Award Industry scholarship involving industry partners the Melbourne Museum and the National Museum of Australia (Canberra). Leonie is an Associate Member of Volunteering Australia.

Alison McIntosh is Associate Professor at the Department of Tourism and Hospitality Management, The University of Waikato, New Zealand. Her main research interests are in tourists' experiences of heritage and culture, especially the personal, subjective and spiritual nature of tourism, hospitality and volunteer tourism experiences.

Geoff Nichols is a Senior Lecturer at the University of Sheffield, UK. His research has included national studies of sports volunteering; the needs of volunteers in netball clubs; a review of the contribution of the voluntary sector in sport; the support that local authority lottery officers give to voluntary sector sports clubs; the recruitment and retention of Guide leaders; and the impact of child protection legislation on sports club volunteers. Geoff is an invited member of the Sports Volunteering Research Network in the UK.

Ryan Plummer is an Associate Professor in the Department of Tourism and Environment at Brock University, Canada. His teaching and research broadly focuses on the human–environment interface. Environmental governance, comanagement, and integrated water resource planning are specific subjects of focus. His research is supported by Brock University Chancellor's Chair for Research Excellence, the Canadian Water Network and the Social Sciences and Humanities Research Council of Canada

Karen Smith is a Senior Lecturer in Tourism Management at Victoria University of Wellington, New Zealand. She has been involved as a volunteer with tourism and event organizations since her teens and has researched and published in this area since the mid-1990s, completing her PhD on the management of volunteers in literary heritage attractions at Nottingham Trent University, UK. Recent research for Sport and Recreation New Zealand has focused on sport event volunteering.

Diana Stewart-Imbert graduated from Vancouver's highly acclaimed Studio 58 Theatre program in 1980. After working as a Production Manager in the Street Theatre component of Expo 86, Diana moved to Lyons, France, where she taught English as a Second Language and worked with her late husband's French traditional music group, Lo Jai. Back in Canada Diana formed the Vancouver World Music Collective in 2000. She is currently Education and Volunteer Coordinator at the Vancouver International Children's Festival.

Siobhan White is a graduate of the University of Surrey's BSc International Hospitality and Tourism Management program. She spent her third year on placement with Greenforce, having first come across them during her gap year when she joined the Bahamas project. Siobhan is now furthering her interest in volunteer tourism by returning to Greenforce's Andros Marine Project as Expedition Leader for 2009.

Izumi Yasuda holds an MA in Arts and Heritage Management from the University of Sheffield, UK. Her study and volunteer experience in the UK led to her interest and research on the differences and similarities in volunteer philosophy between the UK and Japan. Izumi has worked for the World Bank office in Tokyo since 2007.

Volunteering and Tourism

INTRODUCTION

Volunteering is a widespread but complex phenomenon and Part A of this book provides an overview of volunteering, the roles of volunteers in tourism and the outcomes of tourism volunteering for participants, organizations, visitors, communities and society. We discuss key trends in volunteering and tourism volunteering and draw on research to provide a context for the volunteer management issues discussed in Parts B and C.

Chapter 1 introduces the concept of volunteering, its meaning across different countries, cultures and settings and the key factors which influence an individual's propensity to volunteer. We also review the major trends which are impacting on volunteer programs globally and the growth of different forms of volunteering including: international volunteering; volunteer tourism; episodic (as opposed to regular and ongoing) volunteering; virtual or online volunteering; family volunteering; and corporate or employee volunteering.

These trends are linked and impact on tourism volunteering in different ways. Previous research has tended to focus on volunteering in only one tourism setting or consists of case studies; this book brings together research and practice on a range of forms and settings for tourism volunteering. Chapter 2 builds toward a model of tourism volunteer engagements (Table 2.1), which combines four tourism settings and three volunteering time contributions. We use the terms 'tourism volunteer' and 'tourism volunteering' to mean any or all volunteers who are involved in tourism settings, namely attractions, destination service organizations, events and volunteer tourism. The first three settings most frequently involve residents as volunteers and we call these host settings. The fourth setting, volunteer tourism, involves some form of travel by the volunteer to a destination and we call this guest volunteering. These tourism volunteers contribute on an ongoing, seasonal or episodic basis. We note commonalities and differences across tourism volunteering and also reflect upon the blurred boundaries between different settings and contributions.

Chapter 3 focuses on the outcomes of tourism volunteering. While the benefits for the volunteers themselves have received most attention to date, we also examine the outcomes for the organization, the clients (visitors and communities) and wider society. We examine the positive outcomes, such as personal development for the volunteers, financial savings for the organization, a better service for visitors and increased social capital for a community, but recognize that volunteers are not free labor and so also examine the costs and some of the drawbacks of volunteering for all involved.

CHAPTER 1

Introduction to Volunteering

INTRODUCTION

Volunteers make valuable contributions across tourism. Whether monitoring marine life off a tropical island, guiding visitors around a historic castle or marshaling an Olympic marathon, volunteering enables people to make a difference. Some volunteers are tourists and travel great distances to volunteer and contribute to the environment and societies around the globe. Others volunteer in their own local community and contribute to the experiences of visiting tourists. Without volunteers many tourism organizations, particularly those in the not-for-profit sector, would have to reduce their activities or may even cease to operate.

This opening chapter provides an overview of volunteering before we focus on volunteerism in tourism settings. We begin by discussing what is meant by volunteering, a concept that is actually quite complex and takes on different meanings in different contexts. The section 'The language of tourism volunteering: a note on terminology', p. 6 discusses the language of volunteering to explain the terminology used in this book. The proportion of the population who volunteer differs between countries, and in the section 'Global participation in volunteering', p. 7 we examine briefly some of the factors that influence participation in volunteering and the barriers volunteers can face. Traditionally volunteering has involved an ongoing and regular contribution to a role and organization, but in the section 'Trends in volunteering', p. 10 we review six emerging types of volunteering that reflect the demand for more flexible and collective opportunities. Of particular importance for this book are the growth of volunteer tourism and episodic volunteering and these will be further discussed in Chapter 2.

CONTENTS

Managing Volunteers in Tourism
Copyright © 2009 Elsevier Ltd. All rights reserved.

WHAT IS VOLUNTEERING?

At its most basic, volunteering is a discretionary activity which is essentially a donation of time. Volunteering is quite complex and there is no consensus on what the term means. Internationally, different historical, cultural, political, social and religious contexts also add to the complexity of understanding what volunteering is. There is agreement that volunteering is a multi-dimensional concept, and well-cited work by Cnaan, Handy, and Wadsworth (1996, p. 371) presents four elements of volunteering definitions, each with a continuum of dimensions:

1. free choice (free will, relatively uncoerced, obligation to volunteer);

2. remuneration (none at all, none expected, expenses reimbursed, stipend/low pay);

3. structure (formal, informal);

4. intended beneficiaries (benefit/help others/strangers; benefit/help friends or relatives; benefit oneself (as well)).

Together these build into volunteering what Cnaan et al. term 'pure' to 'broad', depending on where on the continuum they sit. This results in a spectrum of volunteering ranging from models over which there is general agreement, to more debatable forms of volunteerism. These include volunteering involving monetary payments (e.g. internships where volunteers receive a stipend, or volunteer tourism where there is a payment to take part, see Chapter 2) or obligation (e.g. students volunteering for academic credit, or work for the dole programs for the unemployed).

Despite these variations, it is useful to look at a couple of examples to illustrate how the volunteering sector and governments define and measure voluntary activities. The UK Government's National Survey of Volunteering and Charitable Giving (published as *Helping Out*) defines volunteering as:

> *Any activity which involves spending time, unpaid, doing something which aims to benefit someone (individuals or groups) other than or in addition to close relatives, or to benefit the environment (Low, Butt, Ellis Paine, & Davis Smith, 2007, p. 10).*

More specifically, it defines formal volunteering as:

> *Giving unpaid help through groups, clubs or organisations to benefit other people or the environment (p. 11).*

In contrast, informal volunteering is defined as 'giving unpaid help as an individual' (p. 11). Levels of informal volunteering are usually higher than formal volunteering rates. For example, in the latest Canadian *Survey of Giving, Volunteering and Participating*, 45% of adults had volunteered formally through an organization, whereas 83% had volunteered informally at least once during the previous 12 months (Hall, Lasby, Gumulka, & Tryon, 2006).

This book focuses on formal volunteering carried out through the structure of an organization. Definitions and statistics presented by national volunteering bodies and governments tend to focus on formal volunteering. For example, Volunteering Australia (2005, p. 1) defines formal volunteering as:

An activity which takes place through not-for-profit organisations or projects and is undertaken:

- *to be of benefit to the community and the volunteer;*
- *of the volunteer's own free will and without coercion;*
- *for no financial payment; and*
- *in designated volunteer positions only.*

This definition captures many of the elements of Cnaan et al.'s pure conceptualization of volunteering but a weakness is its restriction to volunteering in not-for-profit organizations. While the not-for-profit (or voluntary) sector involves many volunteers, people also volunteer through public sector organizations (e.g. in a national museum, a council-run event, or at a regional government nature reserve), and, to a lesser extent, private sector organizations (e.g. a commercial event, privately owned historic house or through a commercial volunteer tourism provider).

There are also important cultural differences in the conceptualization of volunteering and the concept of volunteering takes on different meanings in different settings (Handy et al., 2000; Merrill, 2006; Tuan, 2005). Differences occur both internationally and within communities and can make the understanding, measurement and comparison of volunteering difficult. For example, in New Zealand, Māori and Pacific Islanders make contributions to their communities through fulfillment of their cultural obligations; while the government recognize this as volunteering, these activities may not be conceptualized as volunteering by the participants (OCVS, 2007).

In defining volunteering we also take on board the perspectives of volunteers and the organizations that involve them; if an organization or individual refers to a participant as a volunteer then we acknowledge them as volunteers. This does mean that this book includes examples of tourism volunteering which reflect some of Cnaan et al.'s broader categories, such as students who are obliged to volunteer to gain academic credit.

THE LANGUAGE OF TOURISM VOLUNTEERING: A NOTE ON TERMINOLOGY

There is a limited vocabulary for describing volunteering which has led to some deliberate decisions about the language used in this book. The terms volunteer 'workers' and volunteer 'work' are widely used in the literature, but in this book we use these more sparingly. We make the point (see Chapter 4) that for most tourism volunteers, their volunteering is a form of leisure. We therefore reserve the use of volunteer 'work' to refer to those who perceive their volunteering as a work-like activity. Typically these are full-time volunteers, often students undertaking internships or those on long-term gap year volunteer tourism projects for whom the activity is akin to work rather than leisure.

Many organizations and some volunteer management texts talk about 'using' volunteers but this is a contentious term as it suggests volunteering is a one way, and potentially exploitative, relationship. Volunteering should be a reciprocal and mutually beneficial relationship and as such we avoid the word 'use' in relation to involving volunteers.

There has also been dispute over whether volunteers are, or should be, 'managed'. At the heart of this debate is that management is an import from paid employment and can 'be at odds with the culture and values of volunteering' (Davis Smith, 1996, p. 187). Critics have concerns that formalization of volunteer management may act as a deterrent and alienation to some volunteers at a time when much is being done to open up volunteering to a wider section of society. As we will set out in the introduction to Part B, this book takes an organizational and management perspective on volunteering. We believe that in order to acknowledge and properly support volunteers' efforts, there needs to be a structured and organized approach to managing their involvement. Managing volunteers is not the same as managing paid employees and this needs to be recognized, but voluntary activities do need to be organized effectively and we will use the language of management to refer to organizing and involving volunteers.

We use the terms 'tourism volunteer' and 'tourism volunteering' to mean any or all volunteers who are involved in tourism settings (see Chapter 2). 'Volunteer tourism' and 'volunteer tourist' refer only to volunteering with a significant travel component, and there is a range of different terms used to refer to these experiences including VolunTourism, volunteer vacation and gap year volunteering (see p. 10 and Chapter 2). Some tourism volunteers are also referred to by terms other than 'volunteer', which partly reflects the broadness of volunteering definitions. For example, students who volunteer are often called 'interns', and in North America volunteer (and sometimes paid) guides involved at attractions such as museums, galleries and zoos are called 'docents'.

GLOBAL PARTICIPATION IN VOLUNTEERING

Volunteering is seen as an indicator of civic engagement and social capital (see Chapter 2) and an activity that should be encouraged. Measuring involvement requires data and throughout this book we will make reference to selected national surveys to identify trends in volunteering and volunteer management. Some countries include questions on unpaid work in their census (e.g. New Zealand) but we primarily draw on national surveys of volunteering (often in tandem with charitable giving behavior). The most comprehensive English-language examples we use here are from Australia (ABS, 2007), Canada (Hall et al., 2006) and the United Kingdom (Low et al., 2007). We will make some comparisons between these surveys to illustrate international variations and trends but stress that these should be treated with some caution due to differing definitions of what constitutes volunteering and varying methods, populations, and socio-cultural and political contexts.

To obtain comparative international data on volunteering, we need to look at a global study such as the World Values Survey (WVS) (http://www.worldvaluessurvey.org). Questions on unpaid work were asked in the fourth wave of the WVS (1999–2004) which gathered data in 67 countries. The proportion of a population volunteering is called the participation rate and the WVS data (Figure 1.1) shows considerable variation in participation rates across the world. China, where volunteering is mandatory, has the highest participation rate followed by the United States and South Africa. Other Western, English-speaking countries including Canada and Great Britain also have high rates of volunteer participation, which explains the level of academic interest in volunteerism within these countries. This is also the case in Australia; it was not included in the WVS fourth wave, but data from the Australian Bureau of Statistics national survey on volunteering in 2006 (ABS, 2007) shows 34% of the Australian population volunteering. Of course, while this data shows volunteer participation, there is no measure of intensity or regularity of volunteering activities.

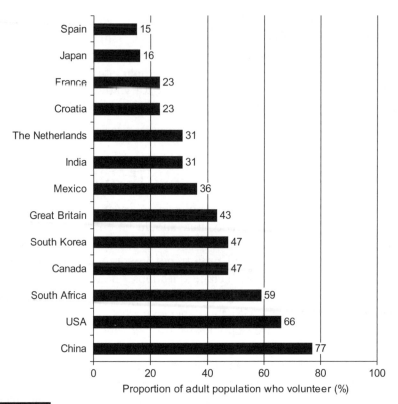

Volunteering rates also differ within a population, and government volunteering initiatives are often targeted at those groups seen as under-represented as volunteers. Research has identified factors which increase the likelihood that someone will volunteer, known as the propensity to volunteer. Table 1.1 summarizes factors identified in Australian and UK research.

Most notably, there is a clear lifestage effect to volunteering. The proportion of a population volunteering generally increases with age, and those in the middle-age groups are most likely to volunteer. These people are often in employment and might be expected to have the least time to volunteer, but volunteers are often busy people and volunteering is particularly linked to child-rearing responsibilities. Retirement and a desire to remain busy and socially active can lead to a surge in volunteering, but voluntary activity starts to drop off as people age and are more restricted by health and mobility issues. Young people typically have a lower volunteering propensity, but their voluntary work is often linked to educational requirements and the

Table 1.1	Factors Influencing Participation in Volunteering
	Higher volunteering participation rates associated with
Age/lifestage	Being of working age or recently retired
Gender	Being female
Family and household structure	Being partnered/married
	Having dependent children
Labor market status	Being in paid employment (full or part time)
Socio-economic status	Higher level of educational attainment
	Higher status occupation
	Higher income level
Disability or long-term illness	Absence of a disability or long-term illness
Ethnicity	Member of the dominant ethnic group
Geographical location and length of residence	Living in a rural rather than urban area
	Being a longer-term resident
Migration	Being born in the country (rather than an immigrant born overseas)
Religion	Being actively involved in formal religious activities
Civic and social participation	Being involved with voluntary associations
	Having a higher level of civic participation

Source: Zappalà and Burrell (2001), Finlay and Murray (2005), Low et al. (2007).

desire to gain experience and enhance their career prospects. Demographics are therefore a key influencing factor and one we will return to when discussing different types of tourism volunteering (Chapter 2). As we will see, tourism volunteering can attract parts of the population with a lower propensity to volunteer, particularly younger (e.g. as volunteer tourists or volunteers at events) and older age groups (e.g. as volunteers at heritage attractions).

Other factors are closely linked to demographics and are also inter-related. For example, in general, surveys have found that women are more likely than men to volunteer and this can be linked to women's employment status, their family role, and the allocation of leisure time. In countries such as Australia, the United Kingdom, Canada and the United States, people from ethnic minorities have lower participation rates but this is likely to be the result of other factors (e.g. lower socio-economic status) rather than as a result of any intrinsic cultural characteristics.

Research has identified various barriers to becoming a volunteer, staying a volunteer and becoming more involved as a volunteer. These can be practical or psychological (IVR, 2004) and factors include time pressures from employment, family and other leisure activities; financial barriers; mobility issues around getting to volunteering activities; health limitations; and personal interest and attitudes toward volunteering. Constraints also include a lack of knowledge about volunteering opportunities, not being asked, lack of confidence and barriers arising from how organizations involve volunteers (e.g. recruitment procedures). Barriers vary for different groups. For example, young people have to fit volunteering around their education or work timetables, anticipate future changes in their circumstances, and often have financial limitations and travel problems (Gaskin, 2003a). There can also be negative perceptions about volunteering and what it involves: 'it's just not cool' (Volunteering England, 2008). Travel and finance are also barriers for older people, along with physical health, mobility and fitness, and external commitments, particularly to their families but also leisure and holidays (Gaskin, 2003a). Overall, lack of time is the most frequently given reason for not volunteering or not doing more volunteering (Hall et al., 2006; Low et al., 2007), and these time pressures have been a driver in the emergence of different types of volunteering.

TRENDS IN VOLUNTEERING

Traditionally volunteering was seen as an ongoing (or sustained) and a regular contribution to a volunteering role and organization. National surveys of volunteering show that many volunteers still make this kind of commitment to an organization. For example, in 2006, 40% of Australian volunteers were involved on a weekly basis, with another 28.5% volunteering at least once a fortnight or month (ABS, 2007). This regularity means that some volunteers contribute large amounts of time each year; 8% of volunteers had contributed over 400 hours in the previous 12 months. Some Australian volunteers remain committed to an organization, or at least a sector, with 25.6% of volunteers having been with an organization for more than 10 years.

At the same time, national surveys also show a clear trend for shorter duration and less frequent volunteering. In the Australian survey, 31.3% had been involved in their organization or sector for less than 1 year. In terms of frequency, 17.2% volunteered several times a year and 14.7% volunteered less regularly. A total of 46% of Australian volunteers had contributed less than 50 hours in the previous 12 months. Although international data comparisons are complicated by different methodologies and reporting, evidence from the United Kingdom's *Helping Out* survey of voluntary activity (Hutin, 2008) also supports a distinction between regular and occasional volunteers, the latter defined as those who had volunteered for their main organization less than once a month or on only one occasion. Although there were similarities in the profile of these two groups of volunteers, 25–44 year olds were more likely to be occasional rather than regular volunteers.

The global development of volunteering is influenced by a wide range of social, economic and political factors. British consultants nfpSynergy (2005) identify seven key trends currently impacting on volunteering: the ageing population, unprecedented affluence, changing family and household arrangements, escalating education and delays in financial independence, mushrooming choice, the Information and Communications Technology (ICT) revolution, and raised aspirations. These are similar to those identified by other commentators (Brudney, 2005; Merrill, 2006). We will return to these trends in Chapter 10 when we consider how they might drive the development of tourism volunteering in the future.

As a result of these trends, people are becoming more selective in their choice of volunteering activities (nfpSynergy, 2005) and are looking for new ways of volunteering (Hall, McKechnie, Davidman, & Leslie, 2001). While regular volunteering is still important, there has been increasing development and promotion of other forms of volunteering that better fit the interests and lifestyles of volunteers and potential volunteers (Brudney, 2005; Volunteering Australia, 2006c). We will now consider six forms of volunteering that have emerged as particularly important in recent years, although most have a longer history:

1. International, transnational or cross-national volunteering
2. Volunteer tourism
3. Episodic volunteering
4. Virtual, online or cyber-volunteering
5. Family and intergenerational volunteering
6. Corporate, workplace, employee or employer-supported volunteering

International, transnational or cross-national volunteering

This form of volunteering involves the movement of volunteers from one country to another, and volunteering activities include emergency relief work, development projects, education and conservation work. There is a long history of international volunteering through organizations such as the Peace Corps, Voluntary Service Overseas (VSO) and the United Nations Volunteers, and recent years have seen an unprecedented expansion of international volunteering (Rochester, 2006; Sherraden, Lough, & Moore McBride, 2008). Davis Smith, Ellis, and Brewis (2005) argue that the form of international volunteering is changing and is no longer a 'gift relationship', whereby relatively unskilled young people from the North (developed countries) volunteer in the South (the developing world). Rather, there is recognition of a more reciprocal 'exchange relationship' which brings mutual benefits to the volunteer and host community. This can be North–North volunteering, but there has also been a growth in people from the South volunteering either in other developing countries or in the more developed North. Advocates of international volunteering highlight the role it can play in developing cross-cultural awareness and understanding, promoting global peace, and enabling people to get involved in international affairs and make meaningful contributions (Sherraden et al., 2008). Critics feel such contributions are ineffective or even damaging, reinforcing existing inequalities and tend toward imperialism (Sherraden et al., 2008). We revisit these debates when considering the outcomes of tourism volunteering in Chapter 3.

Transnational volunteering necessitates international travel, and cross-national volunteering is therefore linked to volunteer tourism, the second of our emergent forms of volunteering.

Volunteer tourism

Volunteer tourism combines volunteering and travel and is a phenomenon which in recent years has grown in scale and scope. It has also been an area of increasing interest for tourism researchers. One of the first academic publications on volunteer tourism was Stephen Wearing's 2001 book *Volunteer Tourism: Experiences That Make a Difference*. Although there is ambiguity and debate around the term volunteer tourism (Lyons, 2003; Uriely, Reichel, & Ron, 2003), many researchers adopt Wearing's definition of volunteer tourists:

> *tourists, who for various reasons, volunteer in an organised way*
> *to undertake holidays that might involve aiding or alleviating the*
> *material poverty of some groups in society, the restoration of certain*
> *environments, or research into aspects of society or environment*
> *(2001, p. 1).*

Volunteer tourism research has been grounded in the tourism rather than the volunteering literature. Participants are regarded as travelers who volunteer and a body of research has developed which sees this as a niche type of tourism. As such volunteer tourism has been linked to, amongst others, the concepts of alternative tourism, ecotourism, sustainable tourism and sustainable development (Callanan & Thomas, 2005; Lyons & Wearing, 2008b; Wearing, 2001, 2004). Volunteer tourism is a growth area and seen as part of a movement toward more authentic experiences and ethical consumption (Yeoman, 2008). Within volunteering studies, not much has been written about volunteer tourism with participants generally seen as volunteers who travel (international volunteers), rather than travelers who volunteer (volunteer tourists). From both perspectives, there is some reluctance from participants and some organizations to call themselves tourists (Raymond, 2008; Wearing, 2001).

Volunteer tourism is a broad and multi-dimensional concept and encompasses a wide range of activities, volunteering contributions and types of project. Based on the nature of the volunteering contribution and activities, we identify three main forms of volunteer tourism which we will expand upon in the next chapter: VolunTourism, volunteer vacations and gap year volunteering.

VolunTourism

Sometimes used as a synonym for volunteer tourism, here we use VolunTourism to refer to cases where only a small part of a trip is devoted to volunteering. This is in line with the United Nations' use of 'VolunTourism' where 'the traveller dedicates a portion of time to rendering voluntary service to a destination – its residents, environment, or infrastructure – in an effort to create a positive impact upon the destination' (Hawkins, Lamoureux, & Clemmons, 2005, p. 13). For example, on a 2-week VolunTourism trip, sightseeing is combined with a few days helping a local cause (Courne, 2009) (see Box 1.1: Tsunami Volun Tourism) and Brown and Lehto (2005) refer to these volunteers as being on a 'vacation-minded' holiday. This type of holiday where volunteer service and travel are both emphasized (VolunTourism. org, 2009) is increasingly popular but has been less well researched than other forms of volunteer tourism.

BOX 1.1 TSUNAMI VOLUNTOURISM, THAILAND

Since 2005 UK tour operator Go Differently has run a Tsunami Volunteering – VolunTourism Tour to Thailand. Working with local partners, this two-week trip includes time in Bangkok, adventure activities in Khao Sok National Park, relaxing on the island of Koh Kho Khao, and five days volunteering with a tsunami relief project. Based in a village homestay, volunteering activities have moved on from post-disaster reconstruction and now include teaching English, gardening, handicraft and youth projects.

http://www.godifferently.com

Volunteer vacations

This is where most of or the entire trip is devoted to volunteering. Brown and Lehto (2005) refer to these volunteers being on a 'volunteer-minded' mission. They are also called service trips in North America, and working holidays and conservation holidays in the United Kingdom and Europe. The volunteer element is the primary motivation for travel and the main activity undertaken at the destination. Trips typically range from a week to 3 months. Most volunteer tourism researchers have focused on this type of volunteer tourism experience, including Earthwatch research expeditions (see Web Resource 3.2, McGehee, 2002; Weiler & Richins, 1995), sea turtle projects in Costa Rica through Caribbean Conservation Corporation (Campbell & Smith, 2006) and Asociaci'on ANAI (Gray & Campbell, 2007), Habitat for Humanity construction projects (Stoddart & Rogerson, 2004), and projects with Māori communities in New Zealand (McIntosh & Zahra, 2007). While many volunteer vacations involve international travel, and so fit with the transnational volunteering trend, travel can occur on a domestic basis, although this has been less well researched. Chapters 18 and 19 are case studies of BTCV and Greenforce volunteer vacations, the latter demonstrating the overlap with gap year volunteering.

Gap year volunteering

A gap year, year out or bridge year is a period of between 3 and 24 months where participants combine travel, paid work, volunteering and/or study (Jones, 2004). 'Gap year' is a British term which refers to a break either before or after university study, so participants are typically in their late teens or early twenties (18–24 years old). While the term gap year is not necessarily used, this phenomenon has equivalents elsewhere: it is a growing trend in the United States, and Australians and New Zealanders often take an Overseas Experience or OE. Increasingly, older people are also taking a gap year, and there are two main segments for 'adult gap years': career breakers (mid-20s to 40s) who are looking for a change in lifestyle, and 'new life gappers', the 50+ Baby Boomers (Mintel, 2008). The whole gap year could be a single long-term volunteer placement or include one or more shorter volunteer vacations, often alongside other travel and paid employment. In recent years there has been a burgeoning of a dedicated gap year industry (Tourism Research and Marketing, 2008); this will be discussed in more detail in Chapters 2 and 19.

Volunteer tourism is a growing form of volunteering but one that has also been criticized, particularly from a development perspective (see dev-zone,

2008). Davis Smith et al. (2005) propose that the commercialization of international volunteering through its packaging and mass marketing to volunteer tourists (rather than volunteers who travel) has undermined some of the more positive changes within cross-cultural volunteering and has 'threatened to reinforce some of the power imbalances of the past' (p. 72). Much of the criticism has been leveled at gap year volunteering; for example, Simpson (2004) questions the gap year tourism industry's oversimplification of the concept of development. VolunTourism, where the emphasis is on travel rather than a meaningful volunteer contribution, has also seen criticism, particularly whether VolunTourists can make a difference given the limited time spent on volunteering. Courne (2009) also highlights the criticism that VolunTourism is just a way to make tourists feel good about themselves. There are more general concerns over how much of the volunteer tourists' fees end up with the project they are supposedly benefiting; this is discussed further in Chapter 2.

VolunTourism and volunteer vacations are short term and even longer volunteering projects within a gap year are often one-off experiences; this fits with the growth of episodic volunteering, our third emerging form of volunteering.

Episodic volunteering

The growth of more flexible volunteering contributions is well acknowledged (Brudney, 2005; Bryen & Madden, 2006; Gaskin, 2003a; Lockstone, Smith, & Baum, 2007; Merrill, 2006). Demographic trends, increased leisure choices and work-life balance issues are affecting the time people can commit to volunteering (Gaskin, 2003a; Merrill, 2006; nfpSynergy, 2005) and 'lack of time' is a key barrier to increased voluntary activity for both current and nonvolunteers (Kitchen, Michaelson, Wood, & John, 2006). Macduff (1991) first used the term 'episodic volunteering' to refer to volunteering assignments which offer a flexible relationship with an organization. Hustinx and Lammertyn (2004, p. 552) refer to this as a reflexive style of volunteering for people who 'demand a high level of mobility and flexibility in their involvement, and they are primarily functionally orientated'.

Volunteering at events typifies this type of volunteering and will be discussed in Chapter 2. but episodic volunteering can take place in any organization or setting. Just as regular volunteers will make different contributions to their organization (e.g. some volunteer full time, others on a weekly, fortnightly or monthly basis), the contributions of episodic volunteers also differ. Macduff (2005) has classified episodic volunteering along a time continuum: temporary (volunteering only for a short time); interim (volunteering on a regular basis but for a defined period, for example on a project) and occasional (those volunteering for short periods of service at regular intervals). This latter group of occasional volunteers return to an organization in a series of episodic engagements, a pattern called 'bounce-back' by Bryen and Madden (2006); they might therefore display a long-term commitment to their volunteering organization, even if each individual period of volunteering is short.

Flexibility is also a factor in our fourth volunteering growth area – virtual volunteering.

Virtual, online or cyber-volunteering

ICT has been a strong driver of changing volunteering patterns and practices. ICT has a role to play in how volunteers are recruited and managed, but virtual volunteering goes beyond this and the volunteering itself is done online. This remote form of volunteering can often be done 'any time, any place' and minimizes the barriers of time availability, geographical boundaries and physical limitations (Merrill, 2006). It is particularly attractive to those used to operating in a virtual world, particularly young people, and those with a disability which restricts their mobility (Rochester, 2006).

For those with caring responsibilities, a lack of time to volunteer can also be addressed through our fifth emergent form of volunteering: family or intergenerational volunteering which places the emphasis on volunteering as a social group.

Family and intergenerational volunteering

Volunteering as a family can be a fun and worthwhile activity that makes the most of the increasingly limited time families have together (The Commission on the Future of Volunteering, 2008). This can be parents volunteering alongside their children or grandparents spending time with grandchildren. While family connections are often a motivator or route into volunteering (e.g. a parent volunteering with their child's sports club), in family volunteering all members of the group participate as volunteers. This means roles and activities have to reflect the diversity of ages, skills and interests that a family group entails. Family volunteering can be a strategy for engaging volunteers who may not otherwise be able to give time due to caring responsibilities, although there may be obstacles to involving children as volunteers (such as liability, supervision and obtaining insurance coverage) (Bowen, 2002; Hegel & McKechnie, 2003; Volunteering Australia, 2006c).

Our final emergent form of volunteering can also involve volunteering as part of a group, this time with work colleagues.

BOX 1.2 MARRIOTT INTERNATIONAL'S SUPPORT FOR EMPLOYEE VOLUNTEERING

Marriott International has over 3,000 lodging properties in the United States and globally. 'Spirit to Serve' is the company's core philosophy. This includes a community and social responsibility program and the 'Associate Involvement' scheme supports Marriott employees (associates) to volunteer both on an ongoing basis and through the annual Spirit To Serve Our Communities Day. In 2007 Marriott employees volunteered almost 295,000 hours during company-sponsored events, with an equivalent value of US$5.7 million (Marriott, n.d.). These activities have benefits for the individual staff member and the company:

> Volunteer activities give our associates opportunities to grow, learn new skills, and take pride in their contribution, both on the job and away from work (http://www.marriott.com/corporateinfo/culture/communityInvolvement).

The company and employees also assist in disaster relief, especially in-kind donations and volunteer service from local hotels in an affected area. Since the mid-1990s Marriott have been involved with the charity Habitat for Humanity International, making individual and corporate donations and with employee volunteers building thousands of homes in fifteen countries. In the United States, Marriott's Fairfield Inn brand has made Habitat for Humanity International its signature community service activity and has included volunteering homebuilds as part of its internal corporate events, such as general manager and owner and franchisee conferences.

http://www.marriott.com/corporateinfo/culture/communityInvolvement.mi

Marriot (n.d.) *Social Responsibility Report*, http://www.marriott.com/socialresponsibility

Habitat for Humanity International: http://www.habitat.org

Corporate, workplace, employee or employer-supported volunteering

This form of volunteering involves employees being encouraged to volunteer by their employer. Initiatives range from companies supporting employees to volunteer in their own time (e.g. through flexi-time arrangements), giving staff unpaid or paid time off to volunteer, through to the employer organizing volunteering activities (see Box 1.2: Marriott International). Employees can be encouraged to volunteer individually, or groups of employees can volunteer as a team, mostly on an occasional or one-off basis. Employers can also support staff who undertake longer-term contributions as board members of not-for-profit groups (Rochester, 2006). The growth in adult gap years as a career break has also been influenced by employers' policies toward sabbaticals: an unpaid, partly or fully paid break (which may include volunteering) where the employee is expected to return to their place of employment after the time off (Mintel, 2008).

Employer-supported volunteering initiatives are often part of corporate social responsibility programs, and are currently most evident in larger companies and the public sector (Low et al., 2007). Benefits to the employer include building relationships with their local communities, increased staff job satisfaction and morale, company image enhancement, and the outcomes for the organization receiving the volunteers (nfpSynergy, 2005). Australian research found that the majority of companies with employee volunteering schemes reported positive effects on retention, job satisfaction and/or productivity, although there is a lack of empirical data to support these outcomes (Volunteering Australia, 2007b).

CONCLUSION

Volunteering is a complex concept over which there is debate and variation in meaning. Those who volunteer are also diverse, but there are a variety of socio-cultural factors that influence the likelihood that someone will participate in volunteering. As we will see in Chapter 2, volunteering in tourism settings is interesting because in age terms it attracts those that generally have a lower propensity to volunteer: younger and older people. Although ongoing and regular volunteering contributions are important, we have discussed six emerging types of volunteering that reflect changes in society and which fit the demand for more flexible and collective volunteering opportunities. In Chapter 2 we examine the different settings in which tourism volunteering takes place. One of these is tourists volunteering at a tourism destination as part of the trend toward volunteer tourism, and related to this, international volunteering. The emergence of episodic volunteering is typified by those volunteering in an events setting.

The other three emergent forms of volunteering discussed in this chapter also have implications for tourism settings, although they form less of a focus in the subsequent discussions. Tourism businesses can support employee volunteering (see Box 1.2: Marriott International) and tourism can also provide the setting for other sectors' corporate volunteering activities. The interest in intergenerational volunteering has also been recognized by some tourism organizations, particularly those where families are a key visitor market, such as museums and some volunteer tourism operators. As we will see in Chapter 2, many tourism volunteers are involved in roles where they are in face-to-face contact with visitors, and for volunteer tourists the travel is an integral part of the experience. For these reasons, virtual volunteering is not as evident as in some other volunteering settings.

DISCUSSION QUESTIONS

Q1.1 Volunteering is a broad concept and there is a lack of agreement over what it means. What are the implications of this for those research-ing and managing tourism volunteers?

Q1.2 What factors influence the range of participation rates across differ-ent countries?

Q1.3 Choose one of the following emergent volunteering trends and sug-gest how tourism organizations can respond to this trend and develop tourism volunteering opportunities:

- International volunteering
- Virtual volunteering
- Family volunteering
- Corporate or employee volunteering

RESOURCES

Volunteer management resources sites

Energize, resources for volunteer managers. http://www.energizeinc.com

OzVMP (Australasian Volunteer Program Management). http://www.ozvpm.com

Peak national volunteering bodies

Volunteering in America. http://www.volunteeringinamerica.gov

Volunteering Australia. http://www.volunteeringaustralia.org

Volunteer Canada. volunteer.ca

Volunteering England. http://www.volunteering.org.uk

Volunteering New Zealand. http://www.volunteeringnz.org.nz

Other international and national volunteering bodies can be found at http://www.energizeinc.com/prof.html

International volunteering

World Volunteer Web by The United Nations Volunteers. http://www.worldvolun-teerweb.org

Volunteer tourism

Comprehensive resource for volunteer tourism. http://www.voluntourism.org/

Episodic volunteering

Volunteering Australia's Subject Guide to Event Volunteering – Take a Closer Look. http://www.volunteeringaustralia.org

Virtual volunteering

The United Nations Online Volunteering Service. http://www.onlinevolunteering.org/

Family volunteering

Volunteer Canada resources. http://volunteer.ca/en/volcan/family/family

Volunteering Australia's Subject Guide Volunteering: An opportunity for the whole family. http://www.volunteeringaustralia.org

Corporate or employee volunteering

Do-It.org resources. http://www.do-it.org.uk/wanttovolunteer/evsvolunteering

Volunteer Canada resources. http://www.volunteer.ca/en/volcan/employ-support/resources

CHAPTER 2

Volunteers in Tourism

INTRODUCTION

Having explored the breath of volunteering activity in Chapter 1, this chapter focuses on volunteers in tourism. In the section 'Tourism volunteers as hosts and guests', p. 22, we argue that previous research on tourism volunteering has been piecemeal and examined only one type of volunteering (e.g. volunteer tourists, museum volunteers or event volunteering). This ignores some important commonalities between these forms of volunteering, not least that they all take place in tourism settings. We therefore take a more inclusive approach to tourism volunteering and consider tourism volunteers as hosts (those volunteering in tourism organizations within their own community) and guests (those traveling to volunteer as tourists at a destination). Each chapter in Part B of the book considers the management of volunteers across four tourism settings, which we will introduce in the section 'Tourism volunteer settings', p. 26:

- host volunteers in attractions;
- host volunteers in destination service organizations;
- host volunteers in events; and
- guests, or volunteer tourists, volunteering at the destination.

We also compare between different volunteering contributions or time commitments (see p. 40):

- ongoing;
- seasonal; and
- episodic.

The section 'Model of tourism volunteer engagements', p. 41 brings together the settings and contributions and presents a model of tourism

CONTENTS

Managing Volunteers in Tourism
Copyright © 2009 Elsevier Ltd. All rights reserved.

volunteer engagements (Table 2.1) and suggests where different examples of tourism volunteering fit (Table 2.2). Finally in this chapter, the section 'Researching tourism volunteering', p. 43 is a brief overview of the state of tourism volunteering research and the dominant research themes and approaches.

TOURISM VOLUNTEERS AS HOSTS AND GUESTS

The book is about volunteers in tourism. The tourism context enables us to bring together types of volunteering that from a research perspective have been considered quite separately but, we argue, have much in common.

Uriely et al. (2003) offer a broad conceptualization of tourism volunteering that encompasses volunteers as both guest (the volunteer as tourist) and host (the volunteer as part of their community's tourism services). We take a similar approach and use the commonality of tourism as the context for voluntary endeavors. Hosts and guests can both be volunteers in tourism: guests (the tourist) as a consumer of volunteer tourism experiences and products, and hosts (the local community) as a producer of tourism through their participation in the tourism workforce. We see parallels between volunteering hosts and guests which blur some of the distinctions between the two groups. As Holmes, Lockstone, Smith, & Baum (2007) set out, both groups give time and contribute to tourism organizations and destinations; they have similar motivations (Uriely et al., 2003); and there are parallels between volunteers and visitors (Holmes & Edwards, 2008), see Chapter 4.

In their book *Journeys of Discovery in Volunteer Tourism* (Lyons & Wearing, 2008b), the editors explore the overlaps and ambiguities of volunteer tourism and examine three types of experience that 'challenge conventional views and approaches to volunteer tourism' (Lyons & Wearing, 2008a, p. 152). These are service learning programs (which involve an element of mandated or coerced volunteering from students), cultural exchange programs (where paid and voluntary work can overlap and role ambiguity exists) and fund-raising adventure holidays (where the volunteering element, the fund-raising, may be separated both temporally and spatially from the travel element). While their chapter and some others in their book (e.g. Raymond, 2008) importantly recognize the blurred boundaries of the volunteer tourism phenomenon, they tend to focus on the overlap between volunteer tourism and other forms of tourism (e.g. cultural, indigenous and ecotourism), rather than the overlaps between volunteer tourism and other forms of volunteering. Thus, with the exception of Holmes and

Edwards (2008), they do not recognize how volunteers can contribute to tourism as participants in its production rather, or as well as, consumers of tourism experiences.

In taking a more inclusive approach to tourism volunteering, we draw together bodies of literature that have previously been considered largely in isolation. Reference will be made to research and examples from, among others, volunteer tourism, museum and heritage volunteering, conservation volunteering and event volunteering, all of which have tended to be researched and considered as separate forms of volunteering. There has been little attempt to draw these areas together and make comparisons (see Holmes et al., 2007).

Tourism volunteering is therefore volunteering that takes place in a tourism setting. We focus on formal volunteering (see Chapter 1) and divide tourism volunteers into host and guest roles. Hosts, those volunteering in tourism organizations within their own community, are involved in three tourism settings: attractions, destination service organizations and events. Guests are those traveling to volunteer as tourists in a destination setting. We acknowledge there are some overlaps between these roles and settings (see p. 41) but this host/guest and setting distinction allows us to explore systematically the range of different forms of tourism volunteering.

While this is a more integrated conceptualisation of tourism volunteering, we have had to impose some limitations on what we consider as a tourism setting. Volunteer tourists are guests who travel to undertake their volunteering. However, it is worth noting that volunteer tourists may not perceive themselves as such and both tourists and organizations may avoid using 'tourist' or 'tourism' to delimit and detach themselves from what they perceive as negative aspects of commercial tourism operators and the adverse impacts of mass tourism (Raymond, 2008; Wearing, 2001). For host volunteers, we have focused on those settings where serving tourists or visitors is the main objective of the organization. Volunteers will often be in roles directly interacting with visitors or in behind-the-scenes roles that support the provision of the visitor experience. More recreation- and leisure-based roles, which do not have a visitor or tourism component, have been excluded. So, for example, volunteering at sports clubs is excluded but volunteering at major sports events is included as they serve a large audience of spectators. Environmental and conservation volunteering is included at sites that are promoted to tourists or involve volunteer tourists in conservation work, but more local level environmental initiatives focused on improving a community's neighborhood are excluded.

The examples in Box 2.1 illustrate that volunteers contribute across the tourism sector. Volunteers are in highly visible 'front-of-house' roles where they are in direct contact with visitors, and in more hidden 'behind-the-scenes' positions supporting the work of various organizations. We will return to these examples in the section 'Model of tourism volunteer engagements', p. 41. While most of these roles, and almost all of the research, focus on volunteers in operational roles, volunteers can also take management, organizing and supervision roles within tourism organizations. Volunteers are also involved in governance roles, for example, as trustees of a not-for-profit organization running an event or attraction. These governance roles have received little attention in the tourism volunteering literature and we

BOX 2.1 EXAMPLES OF TOURISM VOLUNTEERS

All these volunteers are tourism volunteers:

- Once a month, Anna is a volunteer guide at a National Museum where she is also a member of the Museum's Friends Group.

- Ben is a volunteer weekend ticket seller at a local Historic Garden which opens to the public each spring and summer. He also maintains the attraction's website.

- As part of her Bachelor of Tourism degree, Chloe is volunteering for one-month as an intern at a Regional Zoo and is involved on a short-term project to set up a new interpretative trail for school groups.

- Daphne volunteers two days a month at a busy downtown Visitor Information Center. She is usually based in the back office answering telephone and email enquiries.

- Every Friday during the summer season Eddie staffs the information booth at a National Park Visitor Center.

- Fiona is part of her local council's Meet-and-Greet program to welcome cruise line passengers at the docks. She only volunteers when a cruise liner is berthed.

- Gita loves folk music and is heavily involved in a local folk club, and as a Board Member she volunteers throughout the year to organize their annual Folk Music Festival.

- When the Olympic Games were held in Bejing, Hongyan volunteered behind-the-scenes assisting international journalists in the Media Accreditation Center.

- Every year, Ivan volunteers with his work colleagues to steward the car parking and admissions gate at the Regional Show.

- Johanna is a recent university graduate and is taking a gap year. She has backpacked around South East Asia for 6 months and is now volunteering for three months at a school in Thailand.

- Ken and Lorna retired last year, he was a civil engineer and she was a teacher. They are traveling round Australia in a campervan (RV) for a year and when they stop in a community for a few weeks they try to find a local volunteering project to help with.

- As part of a two week organized trekking holiday in Central America, Miguel and his fellow travelers spent one day volunteering at an orphanage and another day building a boardwalk on a National Park trail.

make some reference to them in this book, including the case study of the St. John River Society in Canada (Chapter 13).

TOURISM VOLUNTEERING SETTINGS

This chapter and those in Part B are structured using the host/guest framework. First, we examine host volunteering at attractions, destination service organizations and events. Although there is minimal research on destination service volunteers, for example, those at visitor information centers, we identify them as an important component of tourism volunteering where host volunteers promote and facilitate the visitor's experience. We then consider guest roles, the tourist traveling to volunteer at the destination (see p. 33). Excluding the paucity of research on destination services, these are the main areas on which tourism volunteering research has focused (see p. 43). Commonalities and differences between the settings and volunteers, including the profile of participants, will be highlighted. As we take a management approach to tourism volunteering (see Introduction to Part B), the nature of tourism organizations typically involving volunteers in each setting will also be discussed.

Host volunteers: attractions

Tourist attractions are described by Boniface and Cooper (2005, p. 40) as the 'raison d'etre for tourism: they generate the visit, give rise to the excursion circuits and create an industry of their own' in terms of ancillary and support services such as transport, souvenirs, refreshments and accommodation. Attractions can be built or natural and Swarbrooke (2002) classifies attractions into four categories based on their permanence and original purpose. In this book, we use 'attractions' to refer to Swarbrooke's three types of permanent attractions; his fourth, temporary special events, is considered separately (see p. 30). Volunteers can be involved in the management and operation of all types of attraction.

Natural attractions

Attractions based on natural features include beaches, mountains, waterfalls and national parks. Volunteering at natural attractions is often referred to as environmental volunteering, although not all environmental volunteering takes place in the outdoors or at natural attractions, and there can also be overlaps with heritage volunteering (Ockenden, 2007). Natural attractions provide the setting for many volunteering activities, either organized by the managers of the natural attraction (e.g. Web Resource 2.1: Zealandia – The Karori Sanctuary Experience) or as the location for other organizations' volunteering activities (e.g. an environmental volunteering organization such as BTCV (see Chapter 18) whose volunteering programs take place at a range of natural attractions, none of which they own or directly manage). There are a number of large-scale government volunteering schemes in natural environments. For example, the United States National Parks Service calculates that in 2005, 137,000 volunteers donated 5.2 million hours through their Volunteers-In-Parks Program (www.nps.gov/gettinginvolved/volunteer/index.htm).

Human-made attractions

Swarbrooke (2002) has two categories of human-made attractions depending on their original purpose. First, sites that were not originally designed for tourists but have become attractions; these include heritage attractions such as monuments, castles and palaces, temples and archeological sites. Swarbrooke points out that at many of these attractions, the emphasis is on visitor management to deal with the, often negative, impacts of tourism. Volunteers can be involved in both front-of-house service delivery roles where they interact with visitors, as well as operational behind-the-scenes roles, management positions and governance roles as trustees. For example, the Mary Valley Heritage Railway in Queensland, Australia, involves volunteers at all levels of operation. Volunteers are train drivers, guards, train managers and carriage attendants and also assist with the administration of the railway and its museum (www.thevalleyrattler.com).

Second, sites purpose-built to attract and cater for visitors; examples include theme parks, museums, aquaria and zoos. Again, volunteers can be involved in a diverse range of roles. For example, the National Palace Museum in Taiwan operates a particularly popular volunteer guide program, with 300 current guides and a waiting list of 200. The team of volunteer guides provide between 10 and 20 tours each day for visitors (www.npm.gov.tw).

Involvement of volunteers at attractions

Attractions in the not-for-profit and public sectors are significantly more likely to involve volunteers than those in the commercial sector. There are often more volunteers than paid staff in places of worship, steam and heritage railways, historic houses and castles, museums and art galleries and gardens (VisitBritain, 2007). Extant research on volunteer programs at attractions has focused primarily on these attractions, particularly museums and cultural heritage attractions. In this book, these are represented by in-depth case studies of volunteer programs at three Australian museums (Chapter 11), two heritage attractions operated by the National Trusts in Japan and England (Chapter 12). The St. John River Society (Chapter 13) provides a natural attraction example.

The most common roles undertaken by volunteers at attractions are front-of-house; these are labor-intensive roles and involve direct interaction with visitors, for example, admissions or tour guides. Older volunteers dominate at cultural attractions (Edwards, 2004; Holmes, 2003; Howlett, Machin, & Malmersjo, 2005) and are particularly relied upon to provide the volunteer workforce during an attraction's weekday opening hours when younger people are more likely to be in paid employment. Older volunteers are also evident in the profile of environmental volunteer, although Ockenden (2007) notes that there is considerable variation between organizations and some, for example BTCV (see Chapter 18), are able to attract younger volunteers. Internships are also used by attractions to involve younger volunteers seeking professional experience in the attractions sector (Holmes, 2006). Obtaining paid employment in the competitive areas of conservation and heritage management typically requires applicants to demonstrate their commitment through volunteering. Attractions in Canada and the United States often have internship programs specifically designed for those seeking paid work, while in the United Kingdom, this tends to be more ad hoc. The requirement for aspiring professionals to (effectively) fund their own training has received particularly criticism in the United Kingdom (see Holmes, 2006) but is likely to remain the case as these career paths retain their popularity.

While many attractions volunteers are involved on a regular ongoing basis, most will contribute their services on a weekly, fortnightly or even monthly basis. Therefore, a large number of volunteers will be required to provide the equivalent of one full-time permanent paid position. Some attractions, mostly smaller, not-for-profit attractions, are entirely volunteer-run, with no paid staff. Attractions that operate seasonal opening often only involve front-of-house volunteers during the season but behind-the-scenes roles may be all year round. Attractions can also involve volunteers on short-term projects or at events. Volunteers may also be involved in management roles as trustees of attractions, as at the St. John River Society (Chapter 13). Research has shown that there is variation in attraction volunteers by socio-demographic factors such as gender and educational attainment of volunteers according to the subject of the attraction (Holmes, 1999). For example, art galleries attract more women as volunteers, and transport attractions are more popular with men.

Host volunteers: destination service organizations

Destination service organizations are those promoting and facilitating tourism in a destination. Volunteering in this setting includes those in:

- visitor information centers (also called tourist information centers, visitor centers or visitor bureaux);

- meet-and-greeters based at transport hubs such as airports, major train stations and ports;

- accommodation hosting roles such as campground hosts; and

- rescue services in tourism destinations, such as surf life-saving and mountain rescue teams.

This latter group, rescue services, may not perceive themselves to be tourism volunteers but we include them here as while these services are provided to ensure the safety of anyone in trouble, visitors to a destination are often the beneficiaries.

There are parallels between destination services and attractions in terms of the involvement of volunteers and the type of roles they undertake. Information-based roles usually require the volunteer to build up a detailed knowledge of a local area, its geography and tourism sector, so volunteers tend to be local residents who volunteer on an ongoing or seasonal basis. Local knowledge is also invaluable in rescue service roles and these volunteers have to be highly trained and skilled. There is a dearth of published research and data on destination service volunteers, but from our own ongoing research, it appears that in terms of demographic profile, these volunteers are similar to the attraction setting with a predominance of older volunteers in information delivery roles such as visitor centers and meet-and-greet programs, but younger volunteers involved in rescue services.

Visitor information centers have multiple tourism functions including 'promotion of the area, orientation to and enhancement of the area's attractions, control and filtering of visitor flows and substitution for on-site visits' (Pearce, 2004, p. 9). In addition, visitor centers have important community roles, including involving local people through volunteering. There is no single model for the provision and funding of visitor information services. Although most have at least some public sector funding, they are often a joint initiative between tourist businesses, conservation organizations and state, regional and local governments, or can be privately run (Fallon & Kriwoken 2002). Centers are often related to Destination Marketing Organizations (DMOs, also known as convention and visitor bureaux or tourism boards) and can also be run by national conservation bodies such

BOX 2.2 THE BIG APPLE GREETER PROGRAM, THE UNITED STATES

Since 1992, the Big Apple Greeter program has welcomed over 75,000 visitors to 'See New York through the eyes of a New Yorker'. This not-for-profit organization involves over 300 volunteers who are matched with visitors based on language and interest preferences. Volunteers show visitors around the different neighborhoods in New York, offering a personal tour based on shared interests. Thirty volunteers also work behind-the-scenes in the Big Apple Greeter's office. In 2008, they introduced a corporate volunteering program: 'Greeter for a Day' in which business, community, and government leaders join with a regular Greeter to share their favorite New York locations with visitors.

www.bigapplegreeter.org

as the United States' National Park Service. The Destination Marketing Association International (2007) found that 20% of staff in DMO-operated visitor centers were volunteers.

Meet-and-greet volunteer programs at transport hubs are often operated by the commercially run airport or port, or are linked to a visitor information center or a DMO. They can also be run by an independent organization, such as the Big Apple Greeter Program in New York (Box 2.2). Rescue services are usually not-for-profit organizations although they may receive some government funding. Destination service organizations can operate all year round or open for only the tourism season. While a meet-and-greet program at an airport or train station may operate on a continuous basis, a cruise port scheme will only operate when a vessel is berthed, which for less visited ports may be on a seasonal or occasional basis. Some rescue volunteers may only actively volunteer when there is an emergency situation but they are still involved with the organization on an ongoing basis due to the high training and skills requirements.

Host volunteers: events

Swarbrooke (2002) classifies events as a type of temporary attraction but we and other volunteerism researchers consider them separately as the involvement of volunteers is distinct when compared to permanent attractions. As we will discuss in the section 'The volunteer contribution', p. 40 event volunteers are typically involved on an episodic (short-term or occasional) basis. Special events encompass a wide variety of activities and experiences and volunteers are involved in all scales of leisure event, from the large and high-profile volunteering programs at the Olympic Games, through to volunteer-run local fairs and festivals. Volunteers can also be involved at business events such as expos and conventions; this is yet to be a topic for research although Pazanski and Pennington-Gray (2008) discuss the potential to incorporate VolunTourism (see p. 36) as part of convention delegates' organized leisure time.

At many events, a distinction can be made between core and noncore event volunteers (see Web Resource 2.2: Sydney Olympic and Paralympic Games). Core volunteers make greater time contributions, typically over a longer period, and often in organizational, managerial or governance roles within the event organization. In contrast, noncore, or what (Saleh & Wood, 1998) refer to as 'rank-and-file' volunteers, largely fill the operational roles only during the delivery of the event. These volunteers contribute fewer total hours although their involvement will be intense during the event.

This book focuses on leisure events that are of a scale to attract at least some visitors from outside the immediate area. Using a combination of Getz's (2005) hierarchy of tourism events and Gratton, Dobson, & Shibli (2000) economic impact-based typology, we consider the role of volunteers at four scales of events: mega, major, regional and local.

Mega events

These are the largest scale events and have an international reputation and appeal. Many are sporting events such as the Olympic Games (see Web Resource 2.2: Sydney 2000) and Commonwealth Games (see Chapter 16: Melbourne 2006). They are either one-off events or move locations after a highly competitive bidding process and their scale means they actually feel like a 'one-time event for a particular place' (Getz, 2008, p. 408). In addition to a substantial paid workforce, mega events typically involve large numbers of volunteers and require sophisticated volunteer management systems and procedures. Volunteering at a mega event is typically a one-off and a 'once-in-a-lifetime' experience, although some volunteers may be involved over an extended period as these events have a long lead-in time.

Major events

These large-scale events can attract tourists and produce significant benefits for the host community. They include major international and national sporting events and large-scale cultural festivals. These event organizations usually have a paid workforce that is supported by large numbers of volunteers to deliver the event. Events can also be categorised on the basis of their frequency (one-off or periodic) and for periodically recurring events, their location (roaming or fixed); these have implications for the involvement of volunteers.

- One-off major events have to build a volunteer team from scratch, although their profile and novelty can often be an attraction for volunteers.

- Roaming periodic events move between locations sometimes on a regular cycle or as the result of the host location winning an event-bidding process. In terms of volunteering, periodic roaming events are similar to one-time events as a location's volunteer workforce will be involved in a single hosting of the event.

- Fixed periodic events, which are always held in the same location, can develop strong relationships within their community and build up a pool of loyal volunteers who return, or bounce-back, to the event each time it is held. While most volunteer only at the event, some core volunteers may be involved all year round on a regular behind-the-scenes basis (see Web Resource 2.3: The Roskilde Festival). When the event becomes so identified with the location that the two are intractably linked they are known as hallmark events (Getz, 2005) and here the prestige of the event can help attract volunteers. Chapters 14 (Vancouver International Children's Festival) and 15 (Kongsberg Jazz Festival) illustrate the challenges of involving volunteers in these types of event.

Regional events

These events still have the ability to attract some tourists but are smaller in scale than major events. They can also be one-off or periodic, usually reoccurring in the same location. Whilst there may be a smaller number of volunteers, these events rely heavily on a volunteer workforce, and may even be managed by a volunteer committee. Like their major counterparts, periodic regional events can build up ongoing relationships with their local community and draw on repeat volunteers. Pride in the local community is often an important part of hosting and volunteering at these events.

Local or minor events

These are the smallest scale events and while they can be important for tourists already visiting in a particular destination, their tourism potential is more limited (Getz, 2008). These local events are often completely run by volunteers and many local community festivals would fall under this category. While volunteers are crucial to their operations and existence, they are not a focus of this book because of their focus on community participation rather than tourism.

Involvement of volunteers at events

Research shows that different events attract a different profile of volunteers (Treuren & Monga, 2002); however, not surprisingly, many volunteers have a link to and interest in the theme of the event. For example, 70%

of volunteers surveyed at the 1997 World Ice Hockey Championships in Norway were members of an ice hockey club or had family members who were (Solberg, 2003). This concurs with Green and Chalip's work (1998) on sport volunteering where volunteering is a means of attaining status as a 'insider' within a particular subculture. Volunteers tend to reflect the profile of the participants, spectators or members of the associated sport, art form or community. However, mega events have the ability to attract the widest range of volunteers: 'the larger and more unique the event, the broader the volunteer profiles' (Downward, Lumsdon, & Ralston, 2005, p. 223).

Event organizations are different from more traditional organizations as they require a large workforce for a short period of time. There is a period of rapid hiring before the event, a labor-intensive workload during the event, and dismissal after the event (Yufang, 2005). For a one-off event, such as many mega events, the organization is time-limited and the workforce, including volunteers, is employed only once (although there may be a central governing body that oversees the operation of an event that moves between locations). For periodic events which recur on a regular basis, these organizations can be described as 'pulsating' organizations as they hugely expand their structure and personnel numbers for the event before quickly contracting back to their original size (Hanlon & Jago, 2004). In many cases, it is volunteers who provide much of the increase in staff during the event. Pulsating event organizations are therefore similar to seasonal attractions, although the active period for a seasonal attraction may be months, compared with a few days or weeks for an event.

The size of event influences how volunteers are involved and managed. Broadly speaking, mega and major events have complex organizational structures and a formalised and structured approach to volunteer management. In smaller-scale event organizations volunteer management is usually informal, ad hoc, and often insufficiently resourced. The type of event organization is also important. Not-for-profit organizations commonly run many smaller-scale events and are also involved in larger-scale events, especially in the cultural sector. They will involve volunteers in governance roles as a board of trustees and may be completely volunteer based with no paid staff. Volunteers are also involved with events, which are run on a profit-making basis (e.g. many sporting events), and although this can cause tensions and raise ethical considerations, these are rarely discussed (Ferdinand, 2008; Nogawa, 2004); we will consider these issues as part of program design and planning (Chapter 4).

Guests: volunteer tourism

We view volunteer tourists as guests traveling to volunteer in a destination setting, and volunteer tourism has been the focus of much recent research.

As discussed in Chapter 1 volunteer tourism covers a diversity of travel and volunteering combinations. Travel is often international but can be domestic, although this is less well studied. Volunteering can be the main part of the trip or only a small portion. The volunteering contribution can range from as little as one day of a VolunTourism holiday, to an extended period of months in the case of a gap year. There is a trend towards shorter duration volunteer tourism placements, typified by volunteer vacations with many programs lasting between a couple of weeks and three months (Callanan & Thomas, 2005; Cousins, 2007). Driven by job security concerns and related employer policies (Mintel, 2008), a shorter 'mini' gap year is also popular, particularly for career breakers. A gap year can consist of more than one volunteering episode as well as other elements, and so can overlap with volunteer vacation programs as a number of these may make up a longer gap year.

Volunteer tourism has been dominated by young people, typically 18–24 year olds in education or taking a gap year or other break (Callanan & Thomas, 2005; Power, 2007). Older participants are also an important segment, particularly those taking an adult gap year. Tourism operators specialising in the senior market are also responding to the demand for volunteer tourism; for example, over-50s British tour operator Saga has developed four-week volunteer travel projects to South Africa and Nepal (see Box 2.3). Those providers offering shorter duration holidays attract more mature participants (Cousins, 2007). Females dominate both the gap year and volunteer vacation markets (Cousins, 2007; Jones, 2004; Mintel, 2008).

The size of the volunteer tourism market is hard to calculate because of the diversity of providers, projects and volunteering positions, and the lack of published data, especially from smaller-scale organizations (Tourism Research and Marketing, 2008). To get an idea of the scope of the sector, The Lonely Planet Guidebook: *Volunteer: A Traveller's Guide to Making a Difference Around the World* (Hindle, 2007) lists almost 200 organizations offering a diverse range of volunteering placements around the globe. Research published in 2005 by Callanan and Thomas analyzed the GoAbroad.com online database and identified 289 organizations offering 698 volunteer tourism projects (and 1222 different project activities) across 156 countries.

While this book focuses on volunteering undertaken formally through an organization, like other voluntary activities, volunteer tourism can also be done informally. The picture is blurred further by those arranging their volunteer travel independently even though the actual volunteering at the destination is done through an organization. The Lonely Planet Guidebook (Hindle, 2007) calls these 'Do-It-Yourself' (DIY) volunteer placements and Courne

(2009) recommends this as a way of countering the negative criticisms of some volunteer tourism, particularly regarding who gets the participant's fees (see later in this section).

What is clear is that this is a sizeable and growing form of both tourism and volunteering; Callanan and Thomas (2005) call it a 'mainstream tourism niche'. Since the mid-1990s, there has been a burgeoning of a dedicated volunteer tourism industry. Prior to this, volunteer tourism was dominated by not-for-profit and nongovernmental organizations (NGOs) who were usually set up as development or conservation organizations but had moved into tourism volunteering (Cousins, 2007). Religious and faith-based organizations also have a long involvement in volunteer tourism through overseas missions. They are still important providers of volunteer tourism opportunities today, for example, Israeli Kibbutzim (Uriely & Reichel, 2000) and Habitat for Humanity, a nondenominational Christian housing charity (Stoddart & Rogerson, 2004), although McGehee and Andereck (2008) argue that the role of religion in volunteer tourism is both under-researched and under-recognised. In recent years, new for-profit operators have entered the market or expanded their programs and the volunteer tourism sector has become increasingly commercialized and complex.

There are multiple layers of organizations involved in volunteer tourism (Raymond, 2007; Sherraden et al., 2008; Tourism Research and Marketing, 2008), and three key players are sending, servicing, and hosting organizations. Host organizations are those that the tourists undertake their voluntary activities with in the destination. They can be charities, not-for-profit organizations, NGOs, government, religious organizations or private businesses. Sending organizations are providers who develop and organize volunteer tourism programs (Raymond, 2007). They can also be public, private or not-for-profit/NGOs and are often based in the main traveler-generating regions rather than the destination.

There are a number of possible relationships between sending and hosting organizations. Sending and hosting roles can be undertaken by the same provider, where a single organization both develops and markets programs as well as hosting the volunteers on the project in the destination. In other cases, a sending organization will work in partnership with one or more host organizations to develop volunteer tourism projects. BTCV (Chapter 18) is an example of a sending organization also running the project in the destination but in partnerships with local NGOs. Volunteers can also arrange their volunteering independently, connecting directly with the host organization from home or when they are already in the destination. WWOOF (Chapter 20) is an example of a semi-DIY arrangement where the WWOOF organization is a network listing volunteering opportunities for members but the volunteer independently contacts the individual placement host.

Servicing organizations can be a third element, acting as a broker or intermediary and linking the other organizations and volunteers. Websites (e.g. www.goabroad.com and www.charityguide.org/volunteer/vacations.htm) and umbrella organizations (e.g. the UK's Year Out Group: www.yearout-group.org and the International Volunteer Programs Association: www.volunteerinternational.org) can act as portals for tourism volunteering opportunities and link potential volunteers and sending organizations. Servicing organizations can also act as the link between volunteers and host organizations, marketing and selling volunteer tourism opportunities, which will be provided by a range of different host organizations. Many of the commercial volunteer tourism operators work on this model (for example see Web Resource 2.4: i-to-i), and gap year providers often offer a range of products, not just volunteer placements. With the growth of VolunTourism, commercial travel companies selling travel packages which include (minimal) volunteering are also acting as a link between the tourist and the host organization (see Box 1.1: Go Differently's Tsunami VolunTourism trip to Thailand).

The volunteer tourism sector is currently fragmented but Mintel (2008) predict that, in the gap year market at least, there will be a consolidation of providers as recent purchases of smaller for-profit players by larger travel companies will continue, and be matched by not-for-profits and NGOs also working more collaboratively to attract and refer volunteer tourists. Chapter 19 on Greenforce discusses some of the debates around the structure and evolution of the gap year industry, and some of the tensions arising from the commercialization of international volunteer tourism.

Different providers have very different motivations for being involved in the volunteer tourism market, and this is often reflected in the nature of the volunteering projects on offer and the operation of the business or organization (see Chapter 4). The three types of tourism volunteering introduced in 'Tourism volunteering settings': VolunTourism, volunteer vacations and gap year volunteering have some overlap with Callanan and Thomas' conceptual framework for volunteer tourism (2005). They identify shallow, intermediate and deep volunteer tourists and projects. Although they are presented separately, each category of tourist and project has clear overlaps, with shallow volunteer tourists likely to choose shallow projects, while those wanting a deeper experience will look for deeper projects.

Shallow VolunTourism and short-term volunteer vacations

Shallow volunteer tourism projects tend to be short duration, require no specific skills or qualifications, offer little or no pre-project training and promote the experience and the destination with the actual volunteering project a secondary factor. While Callanan and Thomas (2005) state these projects are at least two weeks in duration, their shallow label can equally apply to VolunTourism as well as shorter volunteer vacations. Their shallow volunteer tourist is focused on self-development and self-interest (including gaining academic credit, enhancing their CV and ego enhancement). The lack of specific skills and the limited duration of the project mean volunteers make little direct contribution to the local environment or community. Tourism Research and Marketing (2008, p. 17) describe these volunteer vacations as an 'intensive high impact strategy' with 'direct action projects' that are highly structured. Volunteers are often sent as a group, although they may sign up individually. Callanan and Thomas' analysis of the GoAbroad.com portal (2005) found that community welfare, building activities and environmental regeneration were the main types of short duration projects on offer, because of the lack of skills required from participants, and the ability to start and finish a project (e.g. a construction task) in a short period of time.

Deep gap year volunteering

At the other extreme, Callanan and Thomas present deep volunteer tourism projects as longer-duration contributions (at least six months), which require volunteers with specific skills and qualifications. Although the destination is a factor, the project and its value to the local community/environment are most dominant in promotion and there will be extensive pre-departure information and training. Tourism Research and Marketing (2008) notes that longer projects such as this are usually undertaken by individual volunteers and are less structured, with scope for volunteers to direct and shape the project once they arrive in the destination. These projects are typified by gap-year volunteering and are likely attract deep volunteer tourists who have skills they want to use and a desire to commit to a longer stay and make a direct contribution to the location community or environment (Callanan & Thomas, 2005). For these volunteers, altruistic motives are more important than self-interest (see Chapter 5). Medical and teaching placements are common deep volunteer tourism projects as they require both time and skills to make a meaningful contribution.

Intermediate tourism volunteering – volunteer vacations

Between the two ends of the spectrum are intermediate volunteer tourism projects, which promote the value of both project and travel elements. These volunteer vacations require some skills and experience. They attract those who want to contribute a reasonable length of time (two to four months), who have both altruistic and self-interest motives, and want to directly contribute to the project and local community while also having some 'holiday time'.

A provider can offer a portfolio of products to cater for different parts of the volunteer tourism market. For example, i-to-i has trips ranging from shorter and 'shallower' i-to-i Meaningful Tours to longer and 'deeper' i-to-i Life-changing Travel (see Web Resource 2.4).

Paying to volunteer as a tourist

We will examine the costs of volunteering in more depth in Chapter 3, but it is important to recognize a key distinction between volunteer tourism and other forms of volunteering: payment. While there is a range of remuneration evident in Cnaan et al.'s (1996) volunteering definition spectrum (see Chapter 1), volunteer tourists are distinct as they normally pay to volunteer. Other tourism volunteers may be out of pocket due to local travel and other expenses (see Chapter 3), but the volunteer tourists typically pay significant fees to the sending or servicing organization. In fact the cost of a volunteer vacation is often higher than that of a 'normal' holiday to a similar destination (Wearing, 2002).

Those operating volunteer tourism projects have associated costs. There are project expenses relating to logistics and hosting, including training, food, accommodation, local transport and destination-based staff to manage the volunteers and project. International travel is usually organized or costed separately. Costs for the sending and servicing organizations include organizing, marketing and managing the program (including staff costs and administrative overheads). By charging a fee, the volunteers rather than the host organization are bearing the costs (Tourism Research and Marketing, 2008). In addition, the sending or servicing organization may make a donation or payment direct to the host organization.

There is some controversy around these payments, including the transparency of fee structures and the amount of fees that reach the host organization or project as opposed to sending or servicing organization or another intermediary (Courne, 2009; Power, 2007). The type of organization (not-for-profit/NGO, public, private) influences funding models (Sherraden et al., 2008), and the proportion of the fee reaching the destination in Cousins's analysis (2007) of UK conservation volunteer tourism operators ranged from 35% to 80%. Some providers, including commercial operators, are more explicit about the costs and beneficiaries of the volunteer tourist's money. Saga Volunteer Travel (Box 2.3) is an example of an operator being transparent about the costs of volunteer tourism and who the beneficiaries

BOX 2.3 SAGA VOLUNTEER TRAVEL: WHERE THE MONEY GOES

The Saga Group have been involved in holidays for the UK 50+ market for over fifty years. The Saga Holiday product range has expanded significantly in the last ten years; part of this expansion has been Saga Volunteer Travel developed in partnership with responsible volunteering organization People and Places (www.travel-peopleandplaces.co.uk).

The intentions of Saga Volunteer Travel are:

- To ensure a good match between volunteer and project
- To provide a challenging and rewarding experience for volunteers and communities alike
- To ensure that the vast majority of the volunteer funds benefit the local economy (www.saga.co.uk/)

To demonstrate this last point, Saga takes a transparent approach to detailing where the cost of the volunteer vacation goes.

Saga's South African Schools Support trip involves volunteering at primary schools in the townships of Port Elizabeth. Saga volunteers are often experienced or retired teachers and they not only engage with pupils but importantly support and train the teachers. Other volunteers have brought professional and practical skills in areas such as health and IT. Saga offers support through the Saga Charitable Trust, which has funded physical improvements and equipment purchases, and a school visit is often part of Saga's mainstream package tours.

Expenses	Details	Where the money is spent	2009 figures
Direct expenses whilst on the project	Daily transport, refreshments, orientation, regular briefing meetings	Host country	£215
Project management fee	Project support and development work and supervision of volunteers (including operational cost of staff and emergency support)	Host country	£285
Project contribution	Goes directly to the needs of the specific project	Host country	£195
Placement fee	Covers the time involved in the matching and preparation process between projects and volunteers	Origin country (UK)	£200
Travel costs	International flights, hotel accommodation, some meals, services of a resident Saga representative	Host and origin country	From £1704
Total			From £2599

The four-week Schools Support volunteer vacation costs from £2599 and Saga's website clearly details how this money is used and where.

Saga involves both volunteer and the school (host organization) in deciding how the project contribution will be used. Examples have included the purchase of IT and other equipment and the funding of teacher training programs.

www.saga.co.uk/travel/General3/volunteer_intro.asp

of the volunteer's holiday fee are. The costs and beneficiaries of tourism volunteering will be discussed further in Chapter 3.

The reverse situation also sets volunteer tourism apart as Tourism Research and Marketing (2008) point out that those on longer-term placements may get paid to volunteer through provision of a stipend. This is particularly for deep tourism volunteering projects where volunteers have to be highly skilled or qualified and so will normally be taking a career break gap year or be supported by their employer. These are exemplified by VSO or VSA (Voluntary Service Overseas or Abroad) and Peace Corps. These programs are highly selective and long term; for example, the U.S. Peace Corps has a three-month training program before a two-year overseas placement (www.peacecorps.gov). These long-term placements include a living allowance or stipend and there are some similarities with internships in the attractions sector (see, p. 26) although those are often aimed at volunteers looking to gain their first work experience rather than experienced professionals sharing their knowledge and skills.

THE VOLUNTEER CONTRIBUTION

Across these tourism settings, volunteers can be divided by the nature of their time contribution. While recognizing that both ongoing and episodic volunteering cover a diverse range of contributions, we will use these broad terms to demonstrate some of the similarities and differences between volunteers in different tourism settings.

Ongoing volunteers are those who volunteer with an organization on a regular and sustained basis.

Episodic volunteers are those with flexible volunteering patterns who volunteer with an organization on an infrequent, occasional, or short-term basis.

This distinction between ongoing (or regular) and episodic (or occasional) volunteers is commonly made; however, the tourism context has led us to add a third category of volunteers: seasonal. This reflects the situation where volunteers are involved only during the tourism season. For example, those in visitor service roles in attractions only open for part of the year. They display elements of both episodic and ongoing volunteering: episodic because they volunteer for a set time (the season) but ongoing because during the season they will typically volunteer on a regular basis. Like the episodic bounce-back volunteers (see p. 30 for example event volunteers who are involved with an annual festival each year), many seasonal volunteers will return to an organization each opening season.

Seasonal volunteers are those who volunteer with an organization on an ongoing and regular basis during the tourist season.

MODEL OF TOURISM VOLUNTEER ENGAGEMENTS

A model of tourism volunteer engagements can be created by combining the type of volunteer (host, guest), the volunteering setting (attraction, destination service, event, tourist destination) and the nature of the volunteer contribution (ongoing, seasonal, episodic). Table 2.1 illustrates how most volunteers in the different tourism settings fit into the model. Table 2.2 illustrates these categories using the earlier examples of tourism volunteers (Box 2.1).

Attractions and destination service organizations can involve volunteers on an ongoing, seasonal or episodic basis depending on their requirements. For example, where attractions operate all year round they need a regular contingent of volunteers, however, many attractions only operate on a seasonal basis and rely on volunteers returning at the start of each season. Attractions can also involve volunteers in special events or projects, which require an episodic contribution. Although one form of volunteering contribution can dominate within a single organization, an attraction or destination service organization can operate a variety of volunteer programs at one site. For example, San Francisco Botanical Gardens has over 600 volunteers involved across 13 different areas (www.sfbotanicalgarden.org). These include ongoing roles such as garden guides and garden greeters

Table 2.1	Model of Tourism Volunteer Engagements		
	Ongoing	**Seasonal**	**Episodic**
Host			
Attractions	Many tourist attraction volunteers	Most volunteers at seasonal tourist attractions	Some project-based tourist attraction volunteers
Destination services	Many destination services volunteers	Most volunteers at seasonal destination services	Some occasional destination service volunteers
Events	Some core volunteers at periodic events		Most event volunteers
Guest			
Tourist destinations	Some longer-term volunteer tourists		Most volunteer tourists

Table 2.2	Examples of Tourism Volunteer Engagements*		
	Ongoing	**Seasonal**	**Episodic**
Host			
Attractions	Volunteer Museum Guide (Anna)	Seasonal Volunteer Ticket Seller (Ben)	Zoo Student Intern (Chloe)
Destination services	Visitor Information Centre volunteer (Daphne)	Seasonal Visitor Information volunteer (Eddie)	Cruiseship Meet-and-Greeter (Fiona)
Events	Music Festival volunteer and Board Member who volunteers all year round (Gita)		Olympic Games volunteer (Hongyan) Employee-volunteer at a Regional Show (Ivan)
Guest			
Tourist destinations			International gap year volunteer (Johanna) Domestic volunteer tourists (Ken and Laura) VolunTourist (Miguel)

*see Box 2.1 for named examples

and episodic opportunities such as assisting at the annual plant sale or selling memberships at special events. Roles in the Children's Garden are more seasonal as this area is open September through May. Volunteers at Zealandia: The Karori Sanctuary Experience (Web Resource 2.1) similarly contribute in different ways.

Event organizations and those involving volunteer tourists are dominated by episodic volunteering, although in both cases volunteers can be involved on a more continuous basis. For example, an event may have a small core of ongoing volunteers involved all year round and a larger number contributing only during the event itself (see Web Resource 2.3: The Roskilde Festival). With volunteer tourism, the deeper volunteer programs where volunteer tourists spend a considerable amount of time at the destination may begin to feel like an ongoing contribution where the volunteer lives at rather than simply visits the destination, although as a time-limited duration there is still the notion of an episodic commitment. On a volunteer tourism program there may well be volunteers who are involved for different lengths of time and have a different relationship with the host or sending organization. For example, on the Caribbean Conservation Corporation (www.cccturtle.org) sea turtle conservation program in Costa Rica, there are both Research Assistants (approximately 20 per year who are involved for three to four months and receive room and board in return for their volunteering), and Participant Researchers (approximately 50 per year who are involved for between one and three weeks on a volunteer vacation where they pay a fee which includes tours at the destination). The Research Assistants have more responsibilities and are assisted by the Participant Researchers (Campbell & Smith, 2006).

As explained in the section 'Tourism volunteers as hosts and guests', p. 22 we use host and guest to distinguish whether someone is volunteering within their own community (host) or traveling to volunteer at the tourist destination (guest). Nevertheless, we also accept that this distinction can be fuzzy and there are examples where the boundary between these two forms of tourism volunteering blurs. This is particularly the case where a guest travels to volunteer but undertakes volunteering roles at the destination that are more akin to the host settings. Volunteer tourists may be based at a tourist attraction or destination service within a destination. For example, Sepilok Orang-Utan Sanctuary in Sabah, Borneo involves international volunteer tourists in a range of behind-the-scenes activities, which contribute to both the conservation of the endangered orangutans and the operation of one of Sabah's foremost tourist attractions (www.orangutan-appeal.org.uk/sepilok-rehabilitation-centre). Campground hosts (see Chapters 6 and 7) are in a hosting role in a destination service organization but the participants may be traveling as volunteer tourists. On a similar basis, some event volunteers are willing to travel great distances, including overseas, to volunteer at an event they see as prestigious. They can be classified as both volunteer tourists and event volunteers, for example, Australians who volunteered at the 2000 Sydney Olympics then traveling to volunteer at Athens in 2004 (see Fairley, Kellett, & Green, 2007). The boundaries can also be blurred when hosts and guests volunteer on the same project or undertake similar tasks; for example, a heritage railway attraction involving both local volunteers and volunteer vacationers (see Wallace, 2006).

Overall, the tourism volunteer engagements model enables the dimensions of tourism volunteering to be explored systematically, while recognizing the overlaps that can occur. The three host (attractions, destination services, events) and one guest (volunteer tourism) settings will form the structure for considering the management of tourism volunteers in the chapters in Part B. Variations in terms of volunteering contributions will be highlighted within this framework to explore both differences and similarities across tourism volunteering.

RESEARCHING TOURISM VOLUNTEERING

Before we move on to the management of tourism volunteers, this section gives a brief overview on the state of tourism volunteering research.

Dominant themes and methodologies can be identified, at least in English-language research publications.

Of the different types of tourism volunteering discussed, volunteer tourism is the most researched and has seen a burgeoning of studies in the last decade. Volunteer tourism researchers have focused on international volunteering and developed world volunteers traveling to developing world projects. There is some research on projects in the developed world and domestic volunteer tourism, but little evidence of research on the South–South volunteering trend highlighted in Chapter 1.

Those researching tourist attractions have focused on museums and to a lesser extent other cultural and heritage attractions, with limited research on zoos, parks and gardens, although environmental volunteering (which may include natural attractions) is a related research area. In terms of destination services, there is limited research on visitor information center volunteering, but other roles such as meet-and-greet programs have been ignored. Sport events and particularly mega events and roaming major events are most dominant in the event volunteering research. There is less research on cultural events; this has focused more on major and minor scale festivals, many of which are repeat events that remain in a fixed location.

In all tourism volunteering settings, most research has been carried out with volunteers themselves. Most research focuses on operational volunteers in both front-of-house and behind-the-scenes roles with attractions, destination services and events, with longer-term or core event volunteers less acknowledged. In all three host volunteering settings, the role of volunteers in governance roles as board members of voluntary societies and organizations has largely been ignored. Volunteer tourism research has tended to focus on those taking volunteer vacations and gap years, with less research on VolunTourism. This focus on the volunteer is evident in the main themes of tourism volunteering research: the motivations, experiences and value of tourism volunteering to the individual (see Chapter 3).

With the exception of research within museums and heritage attractions, there is little on the views of the managers of volunteers or other paid staff working alongside tourism volunteers. In volunteer tourism, there is some acknowledgment of the host community's perspective, but the views on volunteers of attraction, event and destination service visitors, spectators or tourists are largely absent. Other perspectives are also rare; for example, Lockstone and Baum (2009) highlight the paucity of research on the image of event volunteers in the media, and this also applies to other tourism volunteering settings.

Across tourism volunteering research, the case study approach dominates, whether it is volunteering at a single attraction, event, volunteer tourism organization or project. Most of this focuses on a single case study but there is some cross-case analysis comparing volunteering at a number of organizations in the same sector, for example, museums or events. As we have noted, with the exception of Uriely et al. (2003), Lyons and Wearing (2008a) and our own research (Holmes et al., 2007), there has been little attempt to conceptualize tourism volunteering more widely and compare across volunteering in different settings.

Most research projects focus on a single point in time and there is limited multi-stage or longitudinal research. In events, where the volunteering is time-limited, research usually takes place at or immediately after the event. In host settings, particularly attractions and events, research is usually quantitative (surveys) or multi-method (surveys with interviews or focus groups), with limited qualitative studies. This contrasts with volunteer tourism research where qualitative methodologies are much more prevalent.

CONCLUSION

Volunteers are involved across tourism but our understanding of their contributions has been limited by consideration of the different types of tourism volunteering in isolation. In bringing together the different forms, settings and contributions of tourism volunteering, we believe there is much to be gained from looking across the tourism sector and transferring knowledge and research approaches.

Tourism volunteering takes place in destinations and involves tourists or residents of those destinations. We describe programs which involve residents as 'host volunteer programs' and those which involve tourists as 'guest volunteer programs'. There are three main settings for host volunteer programs: attractions, destination service organizations and events. Guest volunteer programs are encapsulated within the term volunteer tourism. There are of course overlaps between these settings, as host programs attract guest volunteers and volunteer tourists assist with tourist attractions, events and services at the destination where they are volunteering. Our typology of four settings, however, facilitates examination of the similarities and differences between different volunteer programs.

The Model of Tourism Volunteer Engagements combines the four tourism volunteer settings (hosts: attractions, destination services, events; and guests: volunteer tourism) and three volunteering contributions (ongoing, seasonal and episodic). These settings will act as a framework for considering the management of tourism volunteers in Part B. Chapter 3 first provides a context for understanding this management by evaluating the outcomes of tourism volunteering for the volunteers themselves, the organizations involved, visitors who benefit from their services, communities and wider society.

DISCUSSION QUESTIONS

Q2.1 Using an online volunteering opportunities database, search for examples of volunteering roles that fit into each of the categories of the Model of Tourism Volunteer Engagements (Table 2.1). You may need to be creative about how you search. Are there any categories where you can't find volunteer roles using these databases? How else could you find out about these roles?

Examples of online volunteering opportunities databases are:

www.volunteermatch.org
www.timebank.org.uk
www.do-it.org.uk
www.volunteer.com.au
www.volunteernow.org.nz

Q2.2 For an attraction, destination service or event that you are familiar with, identify the roles of volunteers in the organization and divide them into ongoing, seasonal and episodic contributions. How do the types of volunteers differ in terms of their time contribution and the activities they undertake?

Q2.3 From the Year Out Group website (www.yearoutgroup.org), select one volunteer tourism organization and identify the activities and locations where they run projects. Using the shallow, intermediate, deep volunteering categories, classify their projects and if possible identify examples of each. How do they differ in terms of length of time in the destination, balance of volunteering and other activities, and the skills required?

FURTHER EXAMPLES

Web Resource 2.1: Volunteering at Zealandia: The Karori Sanctuary Experience, New Zealand

RESOURCES

The American Association for Museum Volunteers. www.aamv.org

International Life Saving Federation. www.ilsf.org

Volunteering Australia's Subject Guide to Event Volunteering – Take a Closer Look. www.volunteeringaustralia.org

Voluntourism – resources for all types of volunteer tourism. www.voluntourism.org

Volunteering in America VolunTourism resources. www.nationalserviceresources.org/via2008

CHAPTER 3

The Outcomes of Tourism Volunteering

INTRODUCTION

Volunteering has multiple outcomes for all those involved: volunteers, organizations, communities and the wider society. Valuing the contributions of volunteers and assessing their impacts is challenging. Some outcomes are more obvious and quantifiable; others are less tangible and harder to qualify. There are different ways of measuring the impacts of volunteers with a focus on assigning an economic value to voluntary activities, assessing the community and social value of volunteering or reporting the benefits to the volunteer, linked to their motivations and rewards. Most information is known about the positive outcomes or benefits of volunteering. Ideally, volunteering should be mutually beneficial but we need to recognize that as well as generating benefits volunteering also involves costs or more neutral or negative outcomes.

The recipients of volunteering contributions are manifold; for example, in relation to international volunteering Sherraden, Lough, and Moore McBride (2008) identify outcomes for the volunteer, host community and sending community, and Jones (2004) discusses the benefits of gap year volunteering to participants, employers and society. This chapter will cover the outcomes of tourism volunteering at four levels, moving from the micro- to macro-scale and discussing the benefits and costs to

- the volunteers themselves;

- the organizations hosting and/or sending tourism volunteers;

- the clients or recipients of the tourism volunteering contributions, namely visitors and communities; and overlapping with this,

- society and the contributions tourism volunteering can make on a wider and global scale.

Managing Volunteers in Tourism
Copyright © 2009 Elsevier Ltd. All rights reserved.

OUTCOMES FOR THE VOLUNTEER

Much of the research on volunteering focuses on the benefits to the individual volunteer. This is linked to the motivations they seek and the rewards they receive; both of which will be explored further in Chapters 5 and 8. The volunteer is said to gain most of the benefits of volunteering. When asked about benefits, both volunteer tourists (Power, 2007) and host volunteers (Holmes, 2009) talk about the personal outcomes for themselves and recognize they are the primary beneficiary. As will be discussed in Chapter 5, volunteers are often motivated by self-interest and volunteering is 'mostly about me' (Edwards, 2005a). This bias toward the volunteer benefits rather than positive outcomes for other parties, particularly destination communities, is at the heart of criticisms of some international volunteer tourism (Davis Smith, Ellis, & Brewis, 2005).

Benefits for tourism volunteers in host and guest settings are similar and may include personal development; education and learning; skills and work experience; increased confidence; spending time doing something for oneself (as opposed to work and family obligations); and potentially increased employability (Broad, 2003; Davis Smith et al., 2005; Holmes, 2009; Kemp, 2002; Sherraden et al., 2008). Personal development, establishing identity and exploring the self are dominant themes in the work of Wearing (2001, 2002) and other volunteer tourism researchers (e.g. Harlow & Pomfret, 2007). The self is less of a feature of research on host volunteers but seeking an identity through volunteering is still important. Green and Chalip (2004) discuss how event volunteering can give entry to a subculture (e.g. a sport) and make the volunteer feel like an insider, and the personal identification with an attraction, its collection or cause is also evident in other tourism settings (Smith, 2003). Stebbins (1996) has also cited the benefits of deeper or longer-term forms of volunteering in his analysis of volunteering as a form of serious leisure (see Introduction to Part B). These benefits include personal development, a sense of achievement and belonging and the creation of a social world for participants.

This focus on the benefits for the volunteer is perhaps not surprising when we realize that the decision to volunteer often follows a significant life change, for example, completing education, desiring a career change, migration, retirement, or family changes such as divorce, death of a spouse or children leaving home. As we will discuss in later chapters, volunteers are motivated by the expectation of certain benefits and are rewarded when these or other benefits are realized.

Volunteering itself also has the potential to be a transformational experience. Volunteer tourism is described as a rite of passage and volunteering can change the way people view their lives and the world (Broad, 2003; Sherraden et al., 2008; Wearing, 2001). This is clearly evident for longer-term and gap year volunteering (e.g. Broad, 2003; McGehee & Santos, 2005) but research on shorter 10- to 14-day Earthwatch volunteer vacations shows that this intense period of volunteering can also precipitate life and behavioral changes (McGehee, 2002; McGehee & Norman, 2002). Volunteer tourism experiences can have an immediate affect on behavior and values but can also have long-lasting, cathartic and life-changing impacts (Zahra & McIntosh, 2007).

The international setting of most volunteer tourism can bring additional benefits including international knowledge; increased cultural awareness and mutual understanding; intercultural competence; and language skills (Davis Smith et al., 2005; Sherraden et al., 2008). Being a volunteer tourist can lead to a deeper experience of the destination and culture (Broad, 2003). There is a suggestion that VolunTourists get more from their vacations than traditional travelers (Brown & Morrison, 2003) and volunteering leads to increased satisfaction with the holiday trip (Brown & Lehto, 2005). The more enduring benefits are the development of the self and others and the enhancement of social relationships (Brown & Lehto, 2005). This recognizes that while the focus of volunteer tourism research has been on the 'self', the social networks and friendships enhanced and created during volunteering continue after the trip, and impact on the volunteers' lives and existing social networks at home (McGehee & Santos, 2005). Social interactions can enhance relationships with family members who are also travelling (Brown & Lehto, 2005) and volunteer tourists develop friendships with other members of the travel group who are likely to share similar interests and values (Broad, 2003; Brown & Lehto, 2005). The social benefits are also crucial to host volunteers, particularly for volunteers in visitor-oriented roles (Holmes, 2003; Smith, 2002), with one museum manager complaining in Osborne's study (1999) that their museum hosted a social club for retirees, rather than a volunteer program.

For young people, there is some evidence that a gap year can enhance subsequent educational performance, and both young people and career-breakers can benefit from improved employability and general life skills (including interpersonal and communication skills, independence, problem-solving and leadership) (Jones, 2004). These benefits are also evident for younger volunteers in other tourism settings; in her study of visitor attractions, Smith (2002) calls these volunteers 'experience-seekers' who are focused on the benefits that will enable them to move on to paid employment or further education.

The drawbacks of volunteering to the participants are discussed more rarely but include the costs to the volunteer in terms of time, resources and emotional investment. The various time contributions have been discussed in Chapter 2, and while some volunteers are motivated to volunteer because they have spare time, others deliberately find time to volunteer within an already busy schedule (Edwards, 2005a). For many volunteers in tourism, volunteering is a leisure activity undertaken during leisure or vacation time. The opportunity cost of volunteering is therefore other leisure activities rather than the loss of productive paid employment. Those choosing to take a career break, delay entry to the job market, or who are fitting volunteering alongside paid employment may be making a deliberate choice of volunteering over earning income. Although episodic volunteering can fit in with other responsibilities (see Chapter 1), the intensive and short-term nature of events means that during the event volunteers may have little choice over volunteer shifts. Nevertheless, Lockstone and Smith (2009) found that episodic volunteers are generally accepting of the constraints on workload and scheduling that the event setting presents. Ralston, Downward, and Lumsdon (2004) also found that volunteers understand that there may be day-to-day problems during an event and they were willing to accept minor downsides (or costs) if the overall volunteering experience (or benefits) is positive.

Beyond the time contribution, volunteers will experience financial costs, which may act as a barrier to participation. For volunteer tourists, the substantial fees are a clear financial payment (see Chapter 2 and Box 2.3: Saga Volunteer Travel) and there are also the costs of travel to and within the destination. The cost of a program influences the ability to volunteer and the length of stay (Broad & Jenkins, 2008). In some instances, notably in the United States, volunteer tourism trips run by not-for-profit organizations may be tax deductible.

Ongoing and other episodic volunteers will also experience a range of financial costs. There could be one-off costs on joining a program or occasional payments such as for training and qualification fees, uniform or equipment purchases, membership dues to a volunteer organization, or a police check as part of the screening process (see Chapter 6). Box 7.1 (Denver Zoo) illustrates the potential costs for roles such as docent guides where specialist or extensive training is required. Ongoing expenses include travel, parking, refreshments, and for some episodic volunteers, accommodation. In many cases the host organization will cover some or all of these costs, but most volunteers will have at least some out-of-pocket expenses that are not reimbursed (Volunteering Australia, 2007c). There is also an established link between giving time and giving money and volunteers may also make financial donations to the organization with which they are volunteering (Handy & Srinivasan, 2004). Some tourism volunteer roles will include fund-raising, for example those volunteering through a membership or Friends group are likely to also raise and donate funds to the organization as part of the Friends' role. The Friends of Kings Park in Perth, Australia, volunteer to grow plants, which are sold at fund-raising events, which the Friends also organize and host (www.bgpa.wa.gov.au). Box 3.1 illustrates how Airline Ambassador volunteers contribute both time and money.

Costs not only act as a barrier to recruiting new volunteers, they also have implications for retaining existing volunteers. In Chapter 8, we will discuss that as volunteering is a discretionary activity dissatisfied volunteers will tend withdraw. A survey by Volunteering Australia (2007c) found 1 in 10 volunteers had stopped or reduced their volunteering involvement in the past year due to the costs of participating, with increased petrol prices a key factor. While most tourism volunteering is an enjoyable leisure activity, volunteers who overcommit, have too heavy a workload, or are over-relied upon may suffer burnout (Getz, 2002). Windsor, Anstey, and Rodgers (2008) found that older adults who volunteered at least 15 hours a week or more reported lower levels of personal well-being than other volunteers. There can therefore also be an emotional cost to volunteering. For volunteer tourists, this could be the mental, and physical, challenge of adapting to different living conditions, but also more profound consequences from encountering suffering and recognizing personal limitations and shortcomings (Zahra & McIntosh, 2007). Chapter 13 discusses absenteeism and burnout of those volunteering as trustees in a voluntary organization.

There are other potential downsides, which may only become evident after a period of episodic volunteering has ceased. Jones (2004) found mixed evidence about whether a gap year improves employability, with many employers being unable or unwilling to recognize or utilize the skills and experience developed. For longer periods of volunteering, there is the opportunity cost in terms of time and money, depending on what the individual would otherwise be doing (e.g. studying or working). The costs of a gap year can mean a young person is in debt even before their higher education, and there is some evidence that time out can lead to demotivation to continue study or difficulties returning to formal education. For those returning from an extended period of volunteering, there can be reverse cultural shock and reassimilation challenges (see Chapters 7 and 8).

A volunteer will balance the benefits and costs they receive or expect when they are judging whether to start or continue volunteering. These themes will be taken up in Chapters 5 and 8. While the impacts on tourism volunteers have gained most attention, there are also costs and benefits at other levels.

BOX 3.1 AIRLINE AMBASSADORS, UNITED STATES

Airline Ambassadors is a U.S.-based not-for-profit organization that began as a way for flight attendants to use flight privileges to provide humanitarian aid to children. Its membership has now expanded to include non-airline members and all pay at least US$50 in annual membership dues. In 2007, the 6000 Airline Ambassador members spent US$550,000 of personal income in the course of 93,000 hours of volunteering. In addition, 70% of Airline Ambassador volunteers are airline staff who use their flight privileges to support the organization, for example travelling to volunteer on humanitarian aid and education placements and escorting children requiring overseas medical care.

www.airlineamb.org

OUTCOMES FOR THE ORGANIZATION

In this section, we will focus on the benefits and costs for the tourism organization sending or hosting the volunteers, which includes attraction, event, destination service and volunteer tourism organizations. These organizations operate within a community and these wider benefits and those for the organization's clients (e.g. visitors) will be covered in the following section.

There are multiple reasons why organizations decide to involve volunteers in tourism settings, and Chapter 4 discusses the need for an organization to clearly determine the rationale for involving volunteers as part of volunteer program design. Many tourism organizations are highly dependent on volunteers and in some cases the whole organization is volunteer-driven and would not otherwise exist. In other cases, an organization would operate on a reduced scale without the assistance of volunteers. For example, an information center would open for fewer hours, an attraction might reduce the areas on display or an event may take place on a smaller scale over a shorter time period. In terms of volunteer tourism, the activities of a host organization may be less extensive without the input of volunteer tourists.

Volunteers can make sense economically by cutting the operational costs of hosting an event, operating an attraction or running a project (Gray & Campbell, 2007; Strigas & Jackson, 2003). Smith's (2003) interviews at visitor attractions found that although 'need' was a dominant reason why volunteers were involved (both in terms of enabling the site to operate and in requiring particular skills), managers preferred to focus on more positive rationales, namely the enthusiasm of volunteers and encouraging access and community involvement. Enthusiasm and interest can be directed at multiple sources; for some volunteers it is an enthusiasm for the volunteering task (e.g. conservation, guiding, marshalling). For others, enthusiasm is focused elsewhere: on the event, attraction or project itself; the type of event, attraction (or its collection) or project (e.g. a steam railway or a particular sport); the host or sending organization; or the community or destination.

The benefits of involving volunteers can change over time and Ferdinand's case study (2008) of a small music event business involving students as volunteers demonstrates some of the potential positive outcomes for event organizations. Benefits in the shortterm include cost reduction and an expanded workforce; in the medium term, enhanced levels of customer service; and in the long term, there could be competitive advantage through enhancement of existing events and creation of new event opportunities. Other benefits for tourism organizations include the role volunteers can play in recruiting additional volunteers through word-of-mouth recommendations (see Chapter 6) and their promotion of the organization to new visitors (see p. 55). Within an organization, volunteers can enable paid staff to concentrate on core tasks or undertake additional projects that would not otherwise be possible.

These benefits to the organization can be hard to quantify but increasingly there are attempts to use economic approaches to assign a numerical value to the contributions volunteers make (Volunteering Australia, 2008). Attaching a value to volunteers' contributions in this way can be important politically, both justifying and valuing a volunteer program within an organization and recognizing the contributions of volunteers externally, for example, to visitors, funders, policy-makers and communities.

The simplest measures are a count of volunteers and the number of volunteering hours. For example, at the 2008 three-day Dublin Irish Festival in Ohio, United States, 1070 volunteers contributed 11,970 hours of service (www.dublinirishfestival.org). Hours can be converted into a monetary value (see Box 3.2: Mount Rainer National Park) or a full-time (paid) staff equivalent. For example, the hours volunteered at Florida Park Service's 160 state parks are equivalent to having 505 additional full-time positions (www.floridastateparks.org/volunteers). More complex methodologies include calculating the replacement cost of volunteer labor, or asking volunteers to assign a value to their activity; see Web Resource 3.1 for calculations of the value of volunteers at the World Ice Hockey Championship.

Another approach measures the tangible outcomes that volunteers make to an organization's work, whether this is research data collected, wildlife protected, trails restored, artifacts displayed, visitors assisted, refreshments served or sport matches held. For a destination service organization such as Surf Life-Saving Western Australia, whose volunteers patrol many

BOX 3.2 VALUE OF VOLUNTEERS AT MOUNT RAINER NATIONAL PARK, UNITED STATES

At Mount Rainer National Park in Washington State, volunteers contributed 70,130 hours in the 2007–08 fiscal year, volunteering on long- and short-term projects including trail maintenance, tour guiding, conservation research, visitor information, and as campground hosts. Using data from the Independent Sector organization (www.independentsector.org) based on average hourly earnings, the National Parks Service (NPS) calculates the value of volunteer contributions at US$1,368,000. To obtain this, the NPS invests around US$200,000, which includes the Volunteer Program Manager's salary and benefits, some supervision time from other staff members, a $16,000 volunteer program budget and $3500 living allowance payments for each summer student internship. This creates a net benefit of $1,168,000 from the volunteer program.

www.nps.gov/mora/supportyourpark/volunteer.htm; rainiervolunteers.blogspot.com/2008/11/2008-volunteer-value-137-million.html

popular beaches, the outcomes are measured in terms of people rescued (413 rescues in 2003–04) and preventative actions (2409 in the same period) and the 60,000 hours of active patrol service are valued at AU$2.1 million (www.mybeach.com.au). This valuation has the advantage of providing an explicit statement of the difference volunteers have made. Web Resource 3.2 illustrates the many outcomes of Earthwatch volunteer tourists. These approaches vary in complexity but all require accurate records to be kept of volunteer activities as part of evaluating a volunteer program (see Chapter 4).

The Mount Rainer National Park (Box 3.2) and Saga Volunteer Travel (Box 2.3) examples importantly acknowledge that there are also costs to an organization from involving volunteers. These investments in the volunteer program include the costs of staffing (for those coordinating and supervising volunteers), recruitment, training, recognition, administration, equipment (including clothing and badges), food, accommodation, insurance, overheads and volunteers' out-of-pocket expenses (Gaskin, 2003b). Within volunteer tourism, concerns have been raised over the level of these organizational overheads and the transparency of where the volunteer tourists' fees are spent (see Chapter 2).

By calculating the costs of recruiting, training and rewarding paid staff and volunteers at two Australian visitor information centres, Jago and Deery (2002) found that even accounting for employing a volunteer manager and other supervision costs, volunteers are a cost-effective means of providing a quality visitor information service. Managers interviewed in Smith's study of visitor attractions (2002) were overwhelmingly positive about volunteers but also identified downsides to their involvement including the time taken to organize and manage them, problems with individual volunteers' overcommitment and disillusionment, and a potential lack of professionalism when compared to paid staff. Ferdinand's (2008) event case study also identified unintended consequences of involving volunteers including some loss of reputation and a questioning of whether it is ethical for a for-profit business to involve volunteers. We will return to the ethics of involving volunteers in Chapters 4 and 10.

As with volunteers' personal outcomes, what is important is for the benefits of volunteers to the organization to outweigh the costs. Tools such as a Volunteer Investment and Value Audit can help organizations calculate the balance of volunteer costs and value (see Gaskin, 2003b), but this can be difficult to undertake if comprehensive data is not collected or the costs and benefits are less tangible and measurable.

OUTCOMES FOR CLIENTS: VISITORS AND COMMUNITIES

We use 'clients' to refer to the recipients of volunteers' contributions through tourism organizations. First, we discuss visitors (we use visitors rather than tourists to avoid confusion with volunteer tourists); for example, visitors at a volunteer-supported attraction, travelers assisted by visitor information center volunteers, spectators at an event run by volunteers or those visiting a destination or site conserved or developed through the efforts of volunteers. Second, we focus on local people in the community hosting the tourism volunteering program. In both cases, we discuss the benefits but also the potential downsides for clients of volunteers' involvement. In addition, there is some overlap with the organizational outcomes discussed above where other people benefit from the voluntary activity (e.g. artists or athletes participating in an event) and the benefits to wildlife, environments and buildings and artifacts that are the recipients of volunteers' endeavors.

Visitors and spectators

With volunteers enabling attractions, destination services and events to operate, visitors benefit by being able to participate in an experience which might otherwise not have occurred. Many volunteers are involved in service delivery roles and so have a direct impact on the visitor experience. Their enthusiasm, passion and desire for interaction and learning can all be transmitted to visitors. In the case of host settings such as destination service meet-and-greeters or surf life-savers, visitors benefit directly from the volunteer's efforts, and front-of-house roles are a growing area of volunteer involvement at museums and heritage attractions (BAFM, 1998). Visitors also benefit, sometimes in more subtle ways, even when the volunteers are involved in behind-the-scenes roles, such as developing a new exhibit or supporting the event participants.

Researchers have found similarities between volunteers and visitors at museums and heritage attractions (Holmes, 2003; Holmes & Edwards, 2008) and have argued that volunteers are as much a part of an attraction's audience as visitors (see Chapter 5). Volunteers therefore may assist the organization's clients but the volunteers are also clients and being involved at an attraction as a volunteer enables visitors to get to know one attraction in depth rather than several at a more shallow level. Volunteer tourists are also clients of the host organizations as they are their customers.

Despite the importance of the front-of-house or service delivery role, surprisingly few studies have examined the impact volunteers have on the visitor experience. Researching at a regional visitor information center, Jago and Deery (2002) found that visitors were highly satisfied by the level of service they received regardless of whether they had been assisted by a volunteer or a paid member of staff. Volunteers and paid staff did have 'quite different views about what constituted quality service, with volunteers emphasising "passion" and paid staff emphasising "professional"' (p. 235). The volunteers and paid staff worked alongside each other, both providing information to visitors; however, there were some tensions between the two groups and their respective roles and selling merchandise distinguished paid staff from volunteers with the latter believing that their role was not a commercial one.

Smith (2003) found that interaction with visitors was a positive aspect of the volunteer experience at heritage attractions and a key motive and source of rewards. Learning was a two-way experience, with volunteers sharing their knowledge with visitors but also learning from them. The personal qualities, enthusiasm and skills that volunteers bring are important and where volunteers are in service delivery roles these contribute to visitor satisfaction. Holmes' PhD thesis (2002) also examined the relationship between visitors and volunteers in front-of-house roles at heritage attractions. Visitors reported that they valued being welcomed to the attraction by friendly volunteers and looked to information stewards for more informal information about the attraction, such as 'historical gossip', which may not be included in the guide books or other forms of interpretation. There is also some evidence that volunteers have the potential to positively affect the behavior of visitors, their conservation values and environmental awareness (Christensen, Rowe, & Needham, 2007; Hendricks, Ramthun, & Chavez, 2001).

In Smith's study (2002) volunteers did identify isolated negative incidents with visitors as a downside of volunteering, but there are potential costs for the visitor too. An unprofessional volunteer can negatively impact on a visitor's enjoyment and satisfaction. Lack of knowledge, skills or training can mean incorrect information is given to visitors. This is of concern when it leads to misinterpretation, but has even more serious consequences when volunteers are in safety roles such as rescue destination service volunteers or crowd control at an event. Many volunteers also have to be prepared to act in an emergency, for example the evacuation of an attraction or event venue.

Communities

Tourism volunteering can be a force for change within communities. The literature discusses most of these benefits in the context of host communities (we will subsequently call these destination communities to avoid confusion with host volunteers) where tourists volunteer (see Davis Smith et al., 2005; Sherraden et al., 2008; Wearing, 2001). However, these positive outcomes can also apply to the communities where hosts volunteer in attractions, destinations services and events at home, and the sending communities where volunteer tourists originate. Positive outcomes for all these communities can include:

- tangible results and provision of services that would not otherwise be funded or supplied (such as new infrastructure, conservation of historic sites and artifacts);

- environmental benefits (for both flora and fauna, including conservation of species and habitats, scientific research, increased environmental stewardship);

- social development outcomes (e.g. improvements in education and health through volunteer tourist projects);

- political outcomes (such as community empowerment, increased awareness and understanding and perhaps funding of local resources and culture);

- development of human capital through the acquisition of skills and practice;

- civic pride and recognition of local culture and environment (such as the celebration of a community's culture through hosting an event); and

- increased voluntary activity within the community, which is discussed further in the section 'Outcomes for society', p. 60.

The outcomes of volunteers' efforts can result in improved quality of life for both individual residents and the community as a whole. The travel element of volunteer tourism brings additional economic benefits as many volunteer tourists undertake additional travel at the destination (Broad, 2003). Those travelling to volunteer at an event can have a similar impact but their spending is rarely measured in event evaluations, despite the strong tradition of event impact assessments (Baum & Lockstone, 2007). McGehee and Andereck (2008, p. 22) point out that through 'direct injections of resources into communities and less leakage' volunteers tourists may make more positive economic impacts on destination communities than mass tourists. Cross-cultural interaction and understanding can also forge ongoing links between individuals and countries, and can challenge the perceptions volunteers and destination communities hold of each other (Davis Smith et al., 2005; Sherraden et al., 2008).

Despite these potential benefits, there can also be more negative outcomes for communities. Although good practice states that volunteers should never replace paid staff (see Chapter 4), there is this possibility, thus reducing the employment opportunities in a community. Tourism volunteer settings may attract volunteers away from less 'fun' but more essential community services, particularly welfare services. Finally, volunteers may not direct their efforts toward the best outcome for the organization. For example, steam railway volunteers are often keen to rebuild the railway as big as possible, without considering the viability of operating costs.

Volunteer tourism has received most criticism for its potential negative impacts on destination communities. International volunteer tourism can do more harm that good (Davis Smith et al., 2005) and be 'ineffective and even contribute to existing or new inequalities' (Sherraden et al., 2008, p. 407). The dominant 'North delivering development to the South' relationship can reinforce dependency between receiving and giving nations even when volunteer tourists and organizations are trying to challenge this (Davis Smith et al., 2005; Simpson, 2004). The human capacity of the destination community can actually be reduced as volunteers carry out tasks and bring skills that would otherwise be undertaken and developed by residents. An environment of dependency can develop where a community or individuals come to rely on the contributions (both economic and in terms of volunteering activities) that volunteer tourists bring (McGehee & Andereck, 2008; Sherraden et al., 2008; Simpson, 2004). This can make them vulnerable if these contributions are withdrawn and the location of projects may create or reinforce rivalries between and within local communities (Davis Smith et al., 2005; McGehee & Andereck, 2008). Volunteers and their activities may actually impact negatively on the environment, they may use resources that would otherwise go to the local community and an imbalance between the conditions for volunteers and locals (e.g. accommodation) can create tensions (McGehee & Andereck, 2008; Sherraden et al., 2008).

The nature of the local–volunteer interaction is central to the outcomes of volunteer tourism with most research focusing on the volunteer's perspective rather than the destination community's. For the volunteers, the importance of social relationships with other volunteers as a personal benefit has been highlighted earlier (see p. 48). Interactions with the community can also bring potential benefits such as promoting mutual understanding, appreciation and friendships (Brown & Lehto, 2005). However, in their interactions with the community, volunteer tourists can, usually unwittingly, offend local residents and undermine their dignity (McGehee & Andereck, 2008).

McGehee and Andereck (2008) explore the complex relationships between two communities (one in the United States, the other in Mexico) and the volunteer tourists who visit them (domestic and international volunteer tourists respectively). Alongside the positive contributions that volunteer tourists can make in a community, they highlight some of the more negative aspects of the volunteer–local relationship. This includes the potential for well-intentioned but misguided actions by volunteers, which can offend the dignity of local residents and create dependency issues. The cultural and geographical distances and differences (and this includes volunteers from the same country) can lead to 'othering' of community members by the volunteer tourists. McGehee and Andereck detail some of the coping strategies that host organizations and destination communities have adopted, including having tourists volunteer alongside locals to create a more equal relationship, or, conversely, separating volunteer tourists from the local beneficiaries to reduce the expectation of gratitude and obligation. The dependency issue can be addressed by policies seeking to prevent hand-outs, although they note that these are often circumvented once personal relationships between the volunteer tourists and locals develop. They also point to the need to control and track volunteer activities to maximize the benefits for the destination community and minimize the negative outcomes, alongside better matching of volunteers' skills and interests with those of local communities.

The success of the volunteer–local relationship is determined by a range of factors. McIntosh and Campbell's research (2001) with WWOOF hosts (see Chapter 20) stresses the need for the placement host and guest (volunteer tourist) to have shared values, expectations and motivations in order to ensure a degree of compatibility and maximize the volunteer's contributions.

OUTCOMES FOR SOCIETY

Related to community outcomes are the potential benefits for society more broadly. These outcomes are less tangible and harder to capture and rather than identifying costs for society, the focus is on how far the benefits are realized. We will focus on three themes: the contribution of volunteering to the development of social capital; the development of volunteering capacity and active citizenship; and changes in social and environmental values as a result of volunteering.

Volunteering has in recent years been cited as both a source and an indicator of social capital (Onyx & Leonard, 2000; Putnam, 2000). While there is disagreement as to what social capital actually is and how it can be measured, governments have typically adopted Putnam's approach, viewing social capital as a public good. Social capital is about the networks created between individuals and the resources these networks generate. There are three types of social capital reflecting the constitution of these networks: bonding (between people with similar backgrounds); bridging (between people with different backgrounds); and linking (between people and organizations at different levels, e.g. local and national). Bridging and linking capital offer more community benefits than bonding. Although there is minimal research on social capital in a tourism volunteering setting, studies in other contexts have shown that bonding capital is more common within volunteer programs, which attract similar people, as is the case in tourism. Recruitment methods are partly the cause of this and these issues are considered further in Chapters 6 and 9.

With many tourism volunteers contributing on an episodic basis there is potential to encourage these participants to continue volunteering and build volunteer capacity and activities more generally. Reviewing the legacy of the 1988 Calgary Winter Olympics, Ritchie (2000) identified the feeling of civic pride and social cohesion derived from the success of volunteerism as the most profound legacy for the city. A large-scale and high-profile event can attract those who have never volunteered before and continued volunteer service can be a significant legacy of an event. Karkatsoulis, Michalopoulos, and Moustakatou (2005, p. 588) suggest that the 2004 Athens Olympic Volunteer Program 'helped strengthen a sense of community service in Greek society that is left to be exploited by the state and other public bodies'. However, without the creation and promotion of further opportunities to volunteer, intention and motivation may not lead to action (Solberg, 2003). A legacy strategy for active citizenship is increasingly being built into mega-event volunteering programs (e.g. see Chapters 16

[Melbourne Commonwealth Games] and 17 [Newham Volunteers]). Without longitudinal research tracking these volunteers and evaluating programs, it is unclear how significant this impact is or how long this legacy will last (Ralston, Lumsdon, & Downward, 2005). Volunteer tourism experiences can also lead to starting or increasing volunteering activities at home (Broad, 2003) but again there is an absence of tracking data.

Many of the personal benefits to the volunteer discussed earlier can also benefit society. The potential for volunteering to change an individual's outlook and values can have wider impacts on society. For example, the social relationships established on a volunteer vacation and the challenges overcome during participation can also have a significant effect on social movement activities and have the potential to raise volunteer's consciousness and perceptions about society and global issues (McGehee, 2002; McGehee & Norman, 2002). This can enhance the volunteer tourists' role as agents of change after returning home (McGehee & Santos, 2005). Of course, it is important to remember that many volunteers will already have high levels of awareness and activism before volunteering and it is these values that have at least partly motivated them to choose a volunteer vacation, participate in an event or volunteer at a local attraction.

CONCLUSION

In discussing these outcomes of volunteering, it is evident that different outcomes are derived from different forms of volunteering in different tourism settings. Certain outcomes, such as the benefits to the volunteers, have been more researched than others, particularly the benefits to the clients. The outcomes obtained will vary depending on the volunteer, program and organization. Different factors will influence the outcomes of volunteer programs and this model has wider application (see Sherraden et al., 2008). Outcomes are thus influenced by:

- the volunteer's attributes and individual capacity (socio-demographic characteristics of volunteers, their knowledge, skills, prior experience, motivations, and time constraints);

- the volunteer program and organization (the type of organization, goals, size, costs and funding model and recruitment policies) and

- the organization's institutional capacity (resources, access, financial and other incentives, training, support, supervision, accountability and organizational networks)

Factors that are particularly relevant for tourism volunteering are duration and location of volunteering and whether volunteering is in a group or if volunteers are placed individually. Volunteer placements of different durations are likely to accomplish different objectives (Sherraden et al., 2008). Ongoing volunteering gives continuity of service and volunteers can be integrated into the organization and the costs and benefits spread out over time. As such, the outcomes for volunteers are also likely to be ongoing, although there may be a frontloading of costs relating to training and membership requirements. Episodic volunteering generates shorter-term benefits and concentrates the costs of the program.

Host volunteers are contributing within their own community and the outcomes for the community can be a significant motivation for volunteering and reward obtained by individuals. Research on gapyear volunteering (Jones, 2004) points to evidence suggesting that home-based volunteering is likely to yield greater benefits for the society as a whole because of more effective support for participants. Shorter-term and international gap year volunteers may be able to make more limited contributions because of the duration and the lack of relevant skills and experience of young volunteers.

In volunteer tourism, structured group projects are likely to have greater benefits for destination communities and organizations than volunteers placed in small groups or individually (Jones, 2004). This is because of the greater level of support from the sending organization and the mutual support that volunteers can offer each other. Across tourism volunteering, groups of volunteers can achieve more in a shorter time frame (e.g. a group of employee volunteers) but individual volunteers may stay for longer or volunteer on a more ongoing basis, which can lead to longer-term benefits.

Finally, it is important to realize that there are also barriers to gaining the full positive impacts of volunteer contributions. For example, cultural and language barriers during a volunteer tourism placement will limit the benefits a volunteer can gain and involving a homogenous group of volunteers limits the social capital which the program may contribute to. Organizations need to be proactive in their recruitment and use interventions in order to ensure a widely accessible volunteer program (see Chapter 9, Managing Diversity).

It is important to consider both the benefits and costs of tourism volunteering as it cannot be assumed that potential benefits of volunteering will necessarily occur; the positive impacts of volunteering are often the result of carefully planned and managed volunteer programs (Raymond, 2007). Part B takes an organizational approach to involving tourism volunteers in order to maximize the positive outcomes for all while acknowledging and addressing the potential costs.

DISCUSSION QUESTIONS

Q3.1 Who are the main beneficiaries of tourism volunteering? Who do you think benefits the most?

Q3.2 What are the different ways in which organizations can calculate the economic value of their volunteers?

Q3.3 Using a tourism volunteer program you know or one of the case studies in this book, what are the costs to the volunteer? What are the likely costs of running the volunteer program for the organization?

FURTHER EXAMPLES

Web Resource 3.1: Value of Volunteers at the 1999 World Ice Hockey Championship, Norway

Web Resource 3.2: The Value of Earthwatch Volunteers

RESOURCES

The Independent Sector produce an annual estimated US dollar value of volunteer's time. www.independentsector.org/programs/research/gv01main.html

Imagine Canada's online volunteer value calculator. nonprofitscan.imaginecanada. ca/en/vvc_toolkit

The Institute of Volunteering Research has a number of tools for valuing volunteers including Impact Assessment Toolkit and Viva-the Volunteer Investment and Value Audit. www.ivr.org.uk

Managing Tourism Volunteers

INTRODUCTION

Part B examines a range of management procedures and issues, which enable a manager (voluntary or paid) to design and manage an effective volunteer program. In this book, we take an organizational approach to examining the phenomenon of volunteering within tourism settings. As noted in Chapter 2, most studies examine the volunteers' perspective and overlook management issues and concerns. While the volunteer is clearly central to any volunteer program, it is imperative that the volunteer's contribution is organized properly. Indeed, surveys report that one of the most common drawbacks of their volunteering is that the volunteer program could be better organized (Low et al., 2007). People's time is precious, with donations of time considered of higher value than money (Low et al., 2007). Effective organization of the volunteer's activities is therefore essential to creating a satisfying experience for both volunteers and the other beneficiaries of the volunteering.

Overlooking the organizational aspects of volunteerism within tourism settings has also meant that volunteers involved in management and governance roles have hitherto been excluded from the extant literature. Where the term 'manager' is used in this book it is as likely to refer to a paid staff member as a volunteer. In the not-for-profit sector, paid staff can also find themselves in a 'volunteer sandwich', being accountable to a Board of (volunteer) Trustees and themselves managing a group of volunteers.

In particularly complex cases, these can actually be the same individuals, although this is not recommended practice.

Both the academic and practitioner literature on volunteer management advocates a human resource management (HRM) approach to organizing volunteers (Cunningham, 1999; McCurley and Lynch, 1998). As noted above, volunteers' activities do need to be organized effectively. This is particularly important in specific tourism settings, such as large-scale events involving thousands of volunteers for an intense period of time or rescue services in a destination, where volunteers need to be trained to provide life-saving assistance. Often, however, volunteer programs are organized in an ad hoc way, with few standardized procedures. This can be appropriate for small, all-volunteer organizations, but even these will benefit from making the best use of everyone's time.

Applying an HRM approach to volunteers is however contentious, as these are not paid individuals and their motivations are different. In the chapters of this book, we adapt the HRM approach but are mindful that for many volunteers (and especially volunteer tourists), this is a leisure, rather than work-like activity. The conceptualization of volunteering as leisure dates back to the 1980s (Henderson, 1984) and has been explored in a number of settings. Most influential has been Stebbins' concepts of casual, serious, and project-based leisure (1992, 1997, 2005). Serious leisure involves activities, including volunteering, which demand considerable effort on the part of the participant. Stebbins (1996) notes that serious leisure volunteering is inspired by self-interest, rather than altruism and he contends that serious leisure volunteering is career volunteering, rather than a one-off act or a series of sporadic acts of voluntary activity. Indeed it is the participant's commitment and the development of a career, which helps to distinguish serious leisure from casual leisure. Project-based leisure is 'a short term, reasonably complicated, one-off, or occasional, though infrequent, creative undertaking carried out in free time' (Stebbins, 2005, p. 2), which can be aligned to episodic volunteering. We consider the implications of leisure volunteering for managing volunteers in Chapter 4.

Part B covers:

- Designing a volunteer program (Chapter 4)
- Motivating volunteers (Chapter 5)
- Recruiting and selecting volunteers (Chapter 6)
- Training and developing volunteers (Chapter 7)
- Rewarding and retaining volunteers (Chapter 8)
- Managing diversity (Chapter 9)

The chapters are presented in this order as this mirrors the process in which a manager is likely to consider these issues. The exceptions to this are motivating volunteers (Chapter 5) and managing diversity (Chapter 9). Both motivation and diversity concerns need to be considered across all areas of a volunteer program. We believe that motivation is so central to designing satisfying volunteer roles, recruiting and selecting volunteers who will want to do these, and in training and rewarding these volunteers that this chapter needs to precede these topics. While diversity management is equally applicable across all aspects of volunteer management, we have placed this following the other management chapters so the reader can reflect on how current management practice largely fails to address this concern.

A well-planned program, with appropriate and efficient recruitment and selection procedures, will mean that volunteers will be matched with roles which meet their and the organization's needs and reduces the risk of dissatisfaction for either party. Volunteers need appropriate training in order to complete their activities satisfactorily for themselves, the organization and its clients, and volunteers also need appropriate rewards and recognition of their activities. All of these chapters are designed to create the best possible volunteer experience for the volunteers, organizations, and their clients. While many of the chapters echo the practitioner literature's personnel approach to volunteer management, this is not a 'how to' guide and we do not include detailed discussion on all volunteer management policies and procedures (see Resources below for general volunteer management texts). These processes will also be governed by different legislative frameworks and national lead bodies for volunteering, such as Volunteering England and Volunteering Australia (see Resources in Chapter 1) are excellent sources of information on procedural aspects of volunteer management.

Each chapter is structured with an introduction to both current and good practice in volunteer management within that topic. We then examine current practice and issues within each of the host and guest tourism settings in turn. Next we reflect on current practice and consider issues of concern and finally we present key principles for good volunteer management practice. Examples illustrate current good practice within the different tourism settings and provide ideas for managers and researchers. Chapters conclude with discussion questions for students and further resources.

RESOURCES

Australian Sports Commission. (2000). Volunteer Management Program: Managing Event Volunteers. Australian Sports Commission.

Bowgett, K., Dickie, K., & Restall, M. (2002). The Good Practice Guide: For Everyone Who Works with Volunteers. Volunteering England.

Fryar, A., Jackson, R., & Dyer, F. (Eds.), (2004). Turn Your Organisation into a Volunteer Magnet. OzVMP. Available: http://www.ozvpm.com

McCurley, S., & Lynch, R. (1998). Essential Volunteer Management. Directory of Social Change.

Energize Inc.; http://www.energizeinc.com

OzVMP (Australasian Volunteer Program Management); http://www.ozvpm.com

Volunteering England Good Practice Bank: http://www.volunteering.org. uk/Resources/goodpracticebank

CHAPTER 4

Designing a Volunteer Program

INTRODUCTION

A well-designed and organized program will mean that the volunteer's efforts will be managed in the most effective way and this should bring positive outcomes for the volunteer, the organization and other beneficiaries (see Chapter 3). This chapter will discuss what goes into establishing a new program but it is also important to periodically review and evaluate an existing volunteer program.

Tourism volunteering researchers have tended to overlook the program design aspects of volunteer management in favor of stages where the volunteer is directly involved: the recruitment, training, rewards, retention and framing all these, motivation. In contrast, there are a number of practitioner guides (e.g. Bowgett, Dickie, & Restall, 2002; McCurley and Lynch, 1998; also see Introduction to Part B: Resources) to setting up and managing volunteer programs in general. As explained in the preface, the aim of this book is to not replicate these excellent 'how to' resources, but rather to highlight the key management issues and relate them to research in the tourism volunteering context. This chapter begins by highlighting key program design considerations: the rationale behind the program, how the program relates to the wider organization, role specification, scheduling and evaluation. While these issues cross the four tourism volunteering settings, we use each setting to highlight extant research on different program design elements: organization (attractions), scheduling (destination service organizations and events), role specification (events), program design and the role of the volunteer coordinator (volunteer tourism).

Managing Volunteers in Tourism
Copyright © 2009 Elsevier Ltd. All rights reserved.

Rationale: why have a volunteer program?

There are multiple reasons for involving volunteers in an organization (see Chapter 3), including economic factors, the need for specific skills, the enthusiasm of volunteers and increasing access and community participation. Many organizations, especially in the not-for-profit sector, are first established as a volunteer-run organization so designing the volunteer program is entwined with setting up and operating the organization more generally. In other cases, changes within an existing organization will promote the decision to start a volunteer program for the first time, expand an existing program or develop a new type of volunteer program within the organization (e.g. a new area of activity, or a new form of volunteering, such as corporate volunteers). Societal changes and the volunteering trends discussed in Chapter 1 may lead to an organization reassessing its volunteer program, either driven by a decline in its traditional pool of volunteers, or as a more proactive effort to attract a new profile or type of volunteer.

McCurley and Lynch (1998) recommend that a new volunteer program be aligned with the organization's mission; that the organization develops a rationale for involving volunteers; and that paid staff are involved and consulted. It is also important to have input from other stakeholders; this can include host organizations and destination communities. If volunteers are already involved in the organization, their views on new program developments are also valuable.

The involvement of volunteers in the not-for-profit and public sector is widespread and largely accepted as long as volunteers complement rather than replace paid employees. A commercial organization looking to involve volunteers will need to consider the ethics of involving volunteers where there is a likely financial gain (profit) for the organization (Ferdinand, 2008; Nogawa, 2004). There are also debates whether volunteer tourists are the best, or even an appropriate, means of addressing some of the problems experienced by destination communities (dev-zone, 2008. Also see Chapter 1).

Organization: how does the volunteer program relate to the wider organization?

There are various models for how a volunteer program operates in relation to the organization which benefits from their efforts (i.e. the attraction, destination service, event or volunteer tourism organization). While many tourism organizations run their programs internally, external groups can also organize volunteers. The sending–(servicing)–host organization model of volunteer tourism (see Chapter 2) is an example of this. Volunteer tourists involved in a project at a destination are often volunteering through a sending organization that either directly manages them in the field, or may work in partnership with a host or other local partner to deliver and manage the volunteer program on the ground. In attractions, the volunteers may be members of a 'Friends' group who donate their time to the attraction (see Chapter 2). External groups can be a source of volunteers for events (see Chapter 6) and in some cases the external partner (e.g. community organizations, educational institutions and businesses) may also manage the volunteers during the event.

The nature of the organization will partly determine the style of volunteer management, particularly its level of formality. As we have discussed in the introduction to Part B, volunteer management ranges from highly formalized through to a very ad hoc approach. While a highly structured and formalized approach is not appropriate in all cases, particularly for very small organizations, we also make the case that some formalization is required for all organizations that value the input of volunteers. It is very important in establishing a new volunteer program to recognize that volunteers are unpaid but not free and any well-organized program must be resourced properly. Subsequent chapters will detail the costs in terms of recruitment, training and reward, but time and funds are also needed to design and plan a successful program. A volunteer program can be managed by either paid employees or volunteers although if the organization has a paid staff, then the volunteer manager or coordinator should ideally be paid as well. Frequently, paid staff are expected to manage a volunteer program along with several other responsibilities. If this is a volunteer program of any size, then this expectation is unrealistic and suggests that senior management do not value the volunteers' contributions.

An organization should have clear policies and procedures on volunteer involvement and their management. Volunteering Australia's 2008 *National Survey of Volunteering Issues* found that most volunteer-involving organizations who responded have volunteer management processes in place including health and safety standards, a designated contact person, an orientation process, insurance for volunteers and opportunities for volunteers to give feedback. While Volunteering Australia notes that many organizations are striving for best practice in volunteer management, more than half said that they face barriers to involving volunteers. Most notably, these include a lack of capacity and resources, in terms of both funding and time, to effectively recruit, manage, train, develop and support volunteers. Diversity management should also be considered early in the design of a volunteer program (see Chapter 9).

Concern for the lack of volunteer commitment has led some organizations to introduce volunteer contracts or agreements. These are similar to a contract of employment, although their legal status varies from country to country. In some cultures it is considered normal for a volunteer to be asked to sign a contract but in others this formality is often replaced with a volunteer agreement, which requires no signature, particularly as regular volunteers usually show a high level of commitment to their organization (Holmes, 2003). Volunteer agreements can be useful if problems emerge between the volunteer and the organization as it reminds both parties of their rights, responsibilities and obligations. Web Resource 4.1 discusses a pro forma written agreement produced by the British Association of Friends of Museums in their *Handbook for Heritage Volunteer Managers and Administrators* (1999).

Role specification: what will volunteers do?

As part of designing a volunteer program it is important to develop appropriate roles and tasks to be undertaken by volunteers. This will then indicate the demands on resources that volunteers will make. McCurley and Lynch (1998) identify four components of a motivating volunteer role: ownership; the authority to think; responsibility for results or outcomes; and the ability to 'keep score', that is, the role involves an element of performance measurement. A volunteering role needs to be motivating; volunteers should not be recruited simply to do all the boring, repetitive and unpleasant tasks that paid staff do not want to do. Nor should a volunteer replace a member of paid staff, which would be illegal, or at least unethical, in many countries. Ideally, volunteers should offer something in addition to paid staff, perhaps complementing their services or offering something entirely new which paid staff do not have the time for in their busy schedules.

Good practice recommends setting out the requirements of a role in a job description and person specification (Wilson and Pimm, 1996), similar to those used in paid employment. Data suggests take up is variable (Low et al., 2007; Volunteering Australia, 2008) although they are more common for regular volunteers than occasional volunteers (Low et al., 2007). When current volunteers were asked if receiving a role description for their volunteering activity would be 'a good thing', two-thirds disagreed (Low et al., 2007). This suggests that volunteers do not necessarily support the formalization of volunteer management.

In the introduction to Part B we note that many volunteers see their volunteering as leisure rather than a work-like activity and this may lead to ambivalence toward management tools, such as job descriptions, which originate in the management of paid employment. Nevertheless, there is a clear need to design meaningful roles and the scope and expectations of the role need to be communicated to volunteers so that they can indicate a preference for the role(s) that most interest them and/or directly relate to their motivations and skills. Potential volunteers also need to understand what the role itself will involve, including details of the time commitment required. While a written job description can be a detailed document, this information can be delivered more succinctly, particularly when the role is short-term and relatively self-explanatory (see Box 4.1: Oxfam Trailwalker). Multimedia can also be used. For example, Real Gap provides online information packs that detail the volunteering role, project, destination and reviews by past volunteers. In addition, Real Gap has online videos of their most popular volunteer projects 'in order to give you a better idea of what

BOX 4.1 VOLUNTEER ROLES AT OXFAM TRAILWALKER, NEW ZEALAND

Trailwalker is a fund-raising event for international development charity Oxfam where teams are challenged to walk or run 100 km in 36 hours. The New Zealand Oxfam Trailwalker in Taupo involves up to 500 teams, each raising at least NZ$2,000. While each team brings its own support crew, Oxfam New Zealand involves almost 400 volunteers. Volunteers are needed onsite over four days: from Thursday afternoon setup, through Friday team registration, the 36 hours of the event (including all night on the Saturday), finishing on the Sunday shutdown. Shift lengths vary but do not exceed eight hours. Many volunteers come from the local area, which is important as volunteers have to arrange their own transport and accommodation. Others get involved because they want to support the event and Oxfam, and some have friends doing the trailwalk.

Organizers have divided volunteering roles into three categories: individual, specialist and group. Individual roles include registration, driver/runner and equipment crew. Specialist roles require professional expertise and include IT support, massage/physiotherapist and podiatrist. Group roles enable an established team (such as a community group or corporate team) to take on responsibility for a whole area of the event, for example, by adopting a checkpoint or being a trail team (marking, marshaling and checking a portion of the trail).

Oxfam clearly set out the rights and responsibilities of their volunteers. Rights are Oxfam's recognition that to work effectively a volunteer needs certain support; responsibilities detail the expectations Oxfam has of its volunteers. Roles are set out on the Trailwalker Web site, including the dates and times of shifts, in addition to the approximate number of volunteers required. Role descriptions are kept short but nevertheless clearly state what is involved and required. For example:

Equipment Crew – An eye for detail is essential and a love of checklists desirable. We won't lie – you might get grubby and there will be lifting involved.

Various shifts, Thursday to Sunday. Approximately 16 volunteers required.

www.oxfam.org.nz/oxfam_trailwalker/

life is like as a Real Gap volunteer' (www.realgap.co.uk). Another volunteer tourism provider, i-to-i (see Web Resource 2.4), hosts Campfire, an online community of gap year and volunteer travelers, which includes both company postings and user-generated content (www.i-to-i.com).

Scheduling: when will volunteers be required?

In tandem with role specifications, an organization will need to work out when it needs volunteers and how many. This can include which times of the year, week, and day. For roles involving contact with visitors, opening hours will be a key determinant; for other roles, the capacity to supervise and provide a physical workspace can determine how many volunteers can be involved at any one time. From the volunteer's perspective, lack of time has been identified as a key barrier to volunteering (Low et al., 2007) and a factor in the growth of more flexible forms of volunteering (see Chapter 1). The number of hours, the total length of commitment, and the working hour requirements may all be taken into account when a volunteer chooses a volunteering role and organization (Volunteering Australia, 2008).

The scheduling of volunteering is therefore important for both organization and volunteer and can be a logistical challenge. If at any point the organization has too few volunteers, they may unwittingly overwork available volunteers, have to close facilities, or cancel a volunteer vacation (Holmes, 2008). Conversely, too many volunteers at one time can mean the organization will not have the capacity to deal with them all and the volunteers may feel unneeded or underutilized. Scheduling for regular and seasonal volunteering is discussed further in relation to destination service organizations, (p. 76) and contrasting with scheduling event volunteers (p. 76).

Review: how will the program be evaluated?

It is important to build in evaluation at the program design stage. The program needs to be regularly reviewed to determine if it is meeting its objectives. The importance of measuring the outcomes of a volunteer program has been discussed in Chapter 3, and as with program design, evaluation should involve a range of stakeholders, not least the volunteers themselves. Judging whether the volunteers are satisfied is a key element of evaluation. To measure the value of volunteers to the organization using the techniques discussed in Chapter 3 requires accurate records to be kept of volunteer activities. Program design therefore needs to set up systems for recording data such as volunteer hours.

HOST VOLUNTEERS: ATTRACTIONS

Attractions illustrate the complex managerial relationships than can exist between an organization and its volunteers, particularly when a membership organization, such as a Friends or supporter group exists and is involved in the volunteer program. In some volunteer-run organizations the membership group and the attraction organization are the same entity; it is members who run the organization and volunteer to operate the attraction. As a volunteer-run organization grows it is important to distinguish between managing the attraction and managing the volunteer program. Having a distinction between contributing as a trustee and as an operational volunteer is important for clarifying roles and responsibilities, ensuring clear lines of control and preventing volunteer burnout through overcommitment.

Where the Friends group is separate from the organization managing the attraction, there are a number of different relationships that can exist (Kuyper, 1993). The Friends group may actually manage the volunteer program with membership being a requirement for volunteering. This can be linked to legal obligations, for example at the Severn Valley Railway, UK, all volunteers need to be members of the Friends association in order to comply with insurance requirements (www.svr.co.uk). While this arrangement can relieve paid staff from much of the operational management tasks, there needs to be clear communication between attraction managers and Friends group so that the program achieves both their, and the volunteers', goals. In other cases, the Friends or other membership group can be the main or sole source for recruitment but the volunteer program is run internally within the organization. Individuals are therefore donating money as a Friend and time as a volunteer but these are separate roles. This membership development model enables the organization to effectively target those who have already demonstrated an interest through their donations (see Chapter 6), but the organization has direct control of the volunteering activities. Finally, an attraction can have both a Friends group and volunteer program but they operate as separate schemes, supporting the attraction in different ways.

HOST VOLUNTEERS: DESTINATION SERVICE ORGANIZATIONS

Destination service organizations are typical of those having to schedule volunteers who make different time contributions: ongoing, seasonal and episodic. If volunteers are involved on a regular basis, say once a fortnight or month, then to cover one fulltime equivalent position will require a large number of individual volunteers. Many volunteers will choose a regular day to volunteer but they will also suffer from illness, want to take holidays and have other commitments that prevent them from volunteering on occasion. The volunteering shift may not always take priority and as volunteers are not paid they are not compelled to attend on a regular basis in the way paid staff might be. All of this can make organizing the roster for the volunteer program the biggest job for a volunteer manager. This task can become even greater when volunteers are needed at times when they are more likely to have other commitments, such as weekends, public holidays and during the school breaks. These are the precise times when clients (the visitors) most need their services, and this is a downside of the 'volunteering as leisure' model. In addition, destination service organizations also need volunteers at unsociable times, for example aeroplanes arrive at night and emergencies happen early in the morning, which requires flexible scheduling in order to meet the tourists' needs.

HOST VOLUNTEERS: EVENTS

Episodic volunteering brings different scheduling challenges to ongoing volunteering but planning is no less complex and time consuming for organizers due to the short-term nature of events and the intensity of event roles. Volunteers who are dissatisfied with their roster schedule may withdraw their services (Gordon and Erkut, 2004). There are suggestions that the oversupply of applicants wanting to volunteer at mega events means organizers can select those who are willing to be flexible and work long and late hours (Downward et al., 2005). Nevertheless, Lockstone and Smith (2009) found that episodic volunteers are generally accepting of the operational pressures and lack of flexibility necessitated by the event context. Chapter 16 discusses some of these rostering issues in relation to the Melbourne Commonwealth Games. It is important when presenting available volunteering roles at an event to also state the times when volunteers will be required (see Box 4.1: Oxfam Trailwalker); given the short time period of most event volunteering, this could determine if someone is able to volunteer or not.

GUESTS: VOLUNTEER TOURISM

As part of the focus on the volunteer, volunteer tourism researchers have concentrated on the running of individual projects rather than examining the whole organization, which is the level where program design takes place. Volunteer tourism programs present more complex planning issues when the program is being coordinated from one country but volunteering actually takes place elsewhere. The mutual benefits of volunteer tourism cannot be assumed to occur automatically (Raymond, 2007), rather they are the result of the sending organization developing a carefully planned and managed program.

In a report for New Zealand's Ministry of Tourism, Raymond (2007) presents a model of good practice for volunteer tourism sending organizations, divided into four stages: developing the program, preprogram, program and postprogram. These are in line with the code of conduct and operational guidelines for members of the UK-based Year Out Group (www.yearoutgroup.org) who set standards for their members in planning the placement, monitoring and measuring satisfaction/refining the process.

Developing a program involves first considering the type of volunteer tourism program that the sending organization wishes to develop and the volunteers they will be targeting. This includes deciding on:

■ whether volunteers are traveling as individuals or groups;

■ the duration of trips, and if a program will operate all year round or only at certain times;

■ if volunteers require specific skills or not; and

■ the amount and nature of tourism activities.

In relation to this last point, in VolunTourism tour companies incorporate volunteering as part of their product planning (Brown and Lehto, 2005) but the volunteer activities are more of an optional excursion rather than the focus. In contrast, organizations developing volunteer vacations and gap year products will need to focus on the volunteering but incorporate an appropriate amount of tourism opportunities within or around the program. For example, for gap year programs involving travel to a different culture, an intensive phase of language tuition is often undertaken prior to volunteering and a travel-orientated expedition may also be included (Söderman and Snead, 2008).

Raymond (2007, p. 4) emphasises the importance of matching the needs of volunteers and destination (host) community to ensure 'that the program developed is worthwhile for all those involved'. Sherraden et al. (2008) use the example of a program where the objectives include increasing cross-cultural contact and immersion; to achieve this, sending individuals rather than groups of volunteer tourists is more appropriate. This program can also be designed so volunteer tourists are paired with local volunteers or workers, their accommodation can be in local homestays, and if a group of volunteers is sent, it should be multinational.

Once the type of program has been established, appropriate volunteering tasks must be found; these need to be meaningful for the volunteers, but an important ethical consideration is making sure that it is not work that local people can be employed to do. Raymond (2007) suggests focusing on projects and tasks where there is a lack of funds for locals to carry out the work, or there are not enough local people with the required skills.

Developing and maintaining relationships between host organizations and destination communities is essential. This includes the sending organization visiting and assessing potential partners and maintaining regular communication, visits and program evaluations (Raymond, 2007). Power's study (2007, p. 5) on the UK international volunteering sector attempted to assess whether it is 'an organisation's commercial considerations and desire to give the volunteer attractive options or the assessing of actual needs of the host community' that are more important in program planning. Although the data was inconclusive, it appears that sending organizations do try to consult destination communities in designing volunteer projects. Several respondents stressed that host organizations/communities actually approach the sending organization with volunteer tourism project ideas.

The Grey Nomads project (Box 4.2) demonstrates how a feasibility study can identify potential success factors at the program design stage, which can lead to the development of more appropriate and effective volunteer tourism programs. Raymond (2008) questioned volunteers, sending and host organizations and identified three program success factors. First, the sending organization develops a strong relationship with host organizations, based on mutual respect and trust. Second, education is included alongside the volunteering experience in order to develop experiential learning and encourage volunteer reflection. Third, that sending organizations approach the program as 'a process rather than an isolated experience' (p. 58) so program design needs to include 'volunteer selection, pre-departure preparation, orientation and debriefing [as] important components of this process'.

On a volunteer tourism project, the volunteer coordinator manages the project in the destination through motivating, rewarding and recognizing the volunteers, being involved in their training (although others may deliver this), offering them support and encouraging volunteers to reflect on their experience, maintaining safety standards and managing the relationships between volunteers, host and sending organizations (Raymond, 2007). The volunteer coordinator needs to be in the destination with the volunteers but they

BOX 4.2 INVESTIGATING THE FEASIBILITY OF A NEW VOLUNTEER PROGRAM: THE GREY NOMADS PROJECT, AUSTRALIA

Grey Nomads are an Australian phenomenon, similar to Snowbirds in North America. A popular activity among retirees is to travel around Australia for an extended period of time, staying in campsites or driving motor homes (RVs). These grey nomads often travel through remote destinations, communities who are experiencing a decline in population, skills and volunteers. Volunteering Australia in partnership with Professors Jenny Onyx and Rosemary Leonard has investigated the feasibility of developing volunteer programs for grey nomads. The research involved individual interviews and town meetings in selected remote communities. The concept of developing volunteer programs for grey nomads was well-received by residents and Leonard, Onyx, & Maher (2006) highlight a number of factors needed for a program to be effective. These include:

- low-cost campsites and facilities for tourists, which will attract grey nomads and encourage them to stay longer;

- a central and accessible location within the region;

- interesting natural and historical attractions, which would attract grey nomads;

- friendly people, accepting of outsiders; and

- a supportive shire council, who can coordinate the program.

Leonard, R., Onyx, J., & Maher, A. (2006). Constructing short-term episodic volunteering experiences: matching Grey Nomads and the needs of small country towns. Paper presented at the 8th ANSTR biennial conference, University of South Australia, Adelaide.

Further information under Research at: www.volunteeringaustralia.org

can be based within the host organization or be a representative of the sending organization; in both cases they can be paid or be voluntary. For example, BTCV sends volunteer leaders to run their international conservation holidays (see Chapter 18). Coghlan's research (2008) on conservation volunteer tourism highlights the central role that the expedition leader plays in making the program a success. However, these expedition leaders are typically scientific research staff and not necessarily selected or trained in the volunteering, or tourism, aspects of their role. There is a need to prepare expedition leaders to understand the needs of volunteers (see Chapter 7, and Chapters 18: [BTCV] and 19: Greenforce).

REFLECTIONS ON VOLUNTEER PROGRAM DESIGN

Design and planning are essential in the development of a volunteer program. While many tourism volunteer programs have long histories and have developed organically, in this chapter we identified the key factors involved in the design of a new program. The nature of many volunteer programs means that there can be complex relationships to manage between, for example, an attraction and their Friends association or volunteer tourism sending and host organizations. In these instances, it is essential that there is clear and regular communication between these different organizations and that responsibilities are clearly established to avoid confusion for the volunteers.

Ideally, an organization would conduct a brief feasibility study involving management, current paid staff and volunteers and potential volunteers. This would help identify any resourcing issues (such as budgeting for expenses and allocating a space for refreshment breaks) and also help to design meaningful volunteer roles. A volunteer role needs to meet the needs of a range of stakeholders, including the organization, clients and the volunteers themselves. Unlike paid work, remuneration cannot substitute for an unattractive volunteer role.

Clear policies and procedures for the volunteer program need to be established at the start, and communicated not only to volunteers but also paid staff and managers within the organization. Scheduling is one of the most complex and time-consuming volunteer management tasks. The roster needs to meet the program's objectives by matching the organization's and the volunteers' needs. This may not always be possible and the organization will need to decide what level of time contributions can be realistically expected from the volunteers.

The program also needs to be evaluated to ensure it is meeting the needs of all the stakeholders: organization, clients, paid staff and volunteers. Evaluation should take place regularly so that potential problems can be identified and addressed before they manifest. In the case of episodic programs, such as events or volunteer tourism, evaluation should take place after each event or holiday so that any changes can be incorporated next time.

This chapter has raised a number of ethical questions around involving volunteers. Firstly, volunteers should not replace paid staff, nor should they be given the unpleasant tasks that paid staff are not willing to do. Secondly, the volunteer program needs to be properly resourced in terms of staff time, facilities and out-of-pocket expenses. Thirdly, there are concerns around the involvement of volunteers in commercial organizations, which may benefit financially from the volunteer labor. We will look further into these ethical issues in Chapter 10.

PRINCIPLES FOR GOOD PRACTICE

- An organization needs to have a clear and positive rationale for involving volunteers.

- A volunteer program needs to be properly resourced with both staff time and financial requirements.

- An organization needs to set out clearly the rights and responsibilities (or expectations) of both volunteers and the organization.

- Volunteers should be provided with a role specification, detailing the requirements for the role.

- There needs to be clear and regular communication between the various bodies involved in the volunteer program.

- The volunteer program needs to be evaluated regularly to ensure it is meeting everyone's needs.

DISCUSSION QUESTIONS

Q4.1 What should be included in a volunteer role specification?

Q4.2 What are the challenges involved in managing a volunteer program for an attraction where the program is operated by a separate Friends association?

Q4.3 Why is scheduling such a complex part of managing a volunteer program?

FURTHER EXAMPLE

Web Resource 4.1: Volunteer Agreements: British Association of Friends of Museums (BAFM), UK.

RESOURCES

Energize Inc. www.energizeinc.com/art/subj/workdes.html

OzVMP. www.ozvpm.com/resourcebank/resource_volmgtpractices.php

Raymond, E. (2007). *Volunteer Tourism in New Zealand: the role of sending organisations in ensuring that volunteer tourism programs 'make a difference'*. New Zealand Ministry of Tourism. Available: www.tourismresearch.govt.nz

Volunteering Australia. (2006). *Tips for Involving Volunteers*. Volunteering Australia. Available: www.volunteeringaustralia.org

Volunteer Canada. (2001). *A Matter of Design: job design theory and application to the voluntary sector*. Volunteer Canada. Available: volunteer.ca

CHAPTER 5

Motivating Volunteers

INTRODUCTION

Understanding motivation, the reasons why people choose to volunteer, is essential in order to design successful recruitment campaigns, effectively allocate roles, devise an appropriate reward strategy to ensure volunteer satisfaction and also retain the services of a volunteer over time. An individual's motivation also influences the style of management they may prefer. Motivation is the defining difference between managing paid staff and volunteers. Not surprisingly, volunteer motivation is the most researched aspect of volunteerism and most studies conclude that motivation is complex and personal. In Chapter 3, we discussed how motivation is related to the positive outcomes of volunteering: the anticipated benefits for the volunteer personally and for other beneficiaries (the organization, clients and society). How these motivations can be met and rewarded will be explored in Chapter 8.

Volunteers may be motivated for more altruistic reasons (although they are rarely entirely altruistic) or for more instrumental reasons. There are a range of approaches to measuring volunteer motivation and a number of motivational scales have been developed. At a basic level, current volunteers can be asked why they volunteer. The Australian Bureau of Statistics (ABS, 2007) found the main reasons were: help others/community, personal satisfaction, personal/family involvement, to do something worthwhile and social contact. A more complex and widely adopted approach is The Volunteer Functions Inventory (VFI) (Clary et al., 1998; Snyder, Clary, & Stukas, 2000), which divides all motives for volunteering into six groups:

- Values (e.g. reinforcement or expression of personal values);
- Enhancement (e.g. learning);
- Social (e.g. be part of a group);
- Career (e.g. work skills and contacts);

CONTENTS

Managing Volunteers in Tourism
Copyright © 2009 Elsevier Ltd. All rights reserved.

- Protective (e.g. increasing confidence); and
- Understanding (e.g. personal growth).

The VFI uses a questionnaire instrument to assess a volunteer's motivations across these dimensions to try and match the volunteer to a role which meets their needs. These and other approaches highlight the multifaceted and complex nature of volunteer motivation and reward. Understanding is further complicated as volunteers may find it hard to articulate their reasons for volunteering, or, as Jago and Deery (2001) suggest, they may not admit their true motivations when questioned by recruiters, managers or researchers. They may prefer to give more socially acceptable altruistic reasons rather than more instrumental reasons where they themselves are the main beneficiary.

HOST VOLUNTEERS: ATTRACTIONS

In the attractions sector volunteer management practice often mirrors that of paid workers, yet it is this sector that has received the most attention from leisure researchers, particularly the motives of museum and heritage attraction volunteers. Edwards' study (2005a) of museum volunteers in Australia found that motivation has eight underlying dimensions: (1) personal needs, (2) relationship network, (3) self-expression, (4) available time, (5) social needs, (6) purposive needs, (7) free time and (8) personal interest. Of these, personal needs were found to be the strongest motivational dimension and reflects people's need to broaden their horizons, vary their regular activities and do something for themselves that they are interested in, in an organization they considered to be prestigious (Edwards, 2005b). This concurs with UK research (Holmes, 2003), which found that most heritage volunteers were initially motivated to volunteer in order to pursue an interest or hobby but they continued to volunteer because of the opportunities for social interaction with other volunteers and visitors, which volunteering enabled. Smith (2003) also found that the motivations of volunteers at literary heritage sites changed with length of service, with some volunteers developing a greater interest in the literary personality associated with the attraction than was initially held.

Lifestage seems to be a significant factor in understanding volunteers' motivations. Studies of volunteers at museums and heritage attractions have found that these individuals are mostly older, retired individuals (see Chapter 2). There is debate as to whether volunteering replaces the aspects of paid work lost in retirement or whether retired volunteers are seeking to pursue a leisure interest. Osborne's study (1999) of the motives of a predominantly retired group of museum volunteers reported that volunteers were more interested in meeting people and making friends than performing their tasks. While a smaller group numerically, museums also attract younger volunteers, often motivated by the desire to gain experience in the sector to move into further study and a paid professional career (Smith, 2002) (see Chapter 2).

In the light of these findings on the motivations, Holmes (2003) argued that heritage volunteers have more in common with visitors than paid staff, proposing that heritage volunteers are extremely frequent visitors, who choose to visit one attraction in depth rather than several on a more casual basis. This has been supported by Smith's study of literary enthusiast volunteers (2003) and this concept has been developed further by Holmes and Edwards (2008). They propose a continuum of visitors from the nonvisitor to the volunteer (Figure 5.1). Orr (2006) argues that with a decrease in the leisure day visits market, volunteering offers attractions a way of engaging visitors in longer-term relationships. Bruyere and Rappe's study (2007) of environmental volunteers in conservation and outdoor-based organizations supports this visitor/volunteer idea in a natural attraction context. Using the VFI, 'helping the environment' was by far the strongest motivation, but 'user' motives also emerged as important. People are motivated to volunteer in a natural area they use for recreation and enjoyment. Volunteering relates to both the past visiting but also future visiting. By undertaking volunteering activities (e.g. access improvements), their future recreational experience will be enhanced; for example, a mountain biker volunteering to improve a trail that they use for riding.

The idea of the volunteer as visitor also relates to Stebbins' concept of serious leisure (see Part B, Introduction). The motivation to volunteer in order to gain entry into and develop a career within a 'special social world' (Stebbins, 1992, p. 16) is evident in the context of attraction volunteers. This social world is clearly part of the motives of preserved steam railway volunteers (Wallace, 2006); wearing the railway uniform or overalls contributes to a sense of belonging to a team, pride in the railway and camaraderie. This camaraderie reinforces a sense of agreeable obligation to fellow volunteers to complete even demanding yet repetitive tasks such as cleaning locomotives.

FIGURE 5.1 *The Visitor – Volunteer Continuum.*
Source: Holmes and Edwards (2008, p. 161)

There have been few studies of the motivations of volunteers at other forms of visitor attractions. Holmes' study (2009) of volunteers in a variety of tourism settings, including a zoo and a science center, reported a range of benefits that motivate volunteers. These include social opportunities, ego-enhancement, personal development such as confidence and learning both skills and knowledge. Our ongoing research suggests that for zoo volunteers, unlike those at heritage attractions, their volunteering does not replace visiting as most of the volunteers had previously visited the zoo only infrequently. The volunteers can, however, be considered as leisure-seeking as the zoo was described as a place to escape from the demands of everyday life.

What should be clear from these various studies is that the motivation of attraction volunteers is complex and varied, there is no 'one-size-fits-all' model. This means that managers need to be proactive in finding out what drives their volunteers.

HOST VOLUNTEERS: DESTINATION SERVICE ORGANIZATIONS

Many of the roles undertaken by volunteers in destination service organizations involve face-to-face contact with visitors. For these individuals, the opportunity to meet people is a key motivator. Other motivations include being able to help people and pride in the destination, the volunteers' hometown. Using the VFI, Anderson and Cairncross (2005) found the 'understanding' function was the primary motive for volunteers in a visitor information center in regional Australia. This suggests volunteers want to use their existing skills and knowledge and are also seeking opportunities for new learning experiences.

In our ongoing research with Australian tourism volunteers including campground hosts and airport meet-and-greeters, the overwhelming motivation is the opportunity to meet a wide range of visitors and to assist in their holiday experience. These pro-social benefits should not overlook the other more instrumental motives and the motivation of doing something for oneself. As with attractions, major life changes can also play a role and most respondents were looking for something to fill their time due to retirement (enforced or voluntary), migration or children leaving home. The Australian Grey Nomad phenomenon (see Box 4.2) means travelers can be motivated to volunteer in destination services such as campground hosts in national parks and protected areas. Getting to the volunteering site, often in a remote location, gives traveling a sense of purpose.

The social club aspect of volunteering is also evident as a motivation within destination service organizations. In addition to altruism, social motivations are also an important part of emergency services such as surf life-savers where social interaction through the club system is central to the volunteering experience. The Fast Israeli Rescue and Search Team (Box 5.1) illustrates how complex volunteer motives can be, with volunteers frequently motivated by a variety of reasons. An element of altruism is usually combined with self-interest and volunteering typically involves some benefit for the individual volunteer as well as the organization and clients.

HOST VOLUNTEERS: EVENTS

Event volunteers are as likely to have complex and diverse motivations as volunteers in other settings. However, the episodic nature of the volunteering means event volunteers' motivations are distinct from those for other more traditional ongoing forms of volunteering. This has lead to the development of specific scales for measuring event volunteering, such as Farrell, Johnston, & Twynam's (1998) Special Event Volunteer Motivation Scale (SEVMS). Application of this model at different events (also see Johnston, Twynam, & Farrell, 1999/2000; Twynam, Farrell, & Johnston, 2002/2003) established that the most important motivation for volunteers was 'to help make the event a success'. Four motivational factors were identified. The first two are purposive (contribution to community and event; this is related to altruism) and solidary (social interaction and personal development). These are in line with the motives identified in ongoing volunteering, such as attractions and many destination services settings. Two additional motivational factors were identified from the event context: external traditions (external obligations linked to extrinsic motivations) and commitments (fulfilling obligations to the event or community); these last two were combined as material motives in Johnston et al.'s study (1999/2000) of volunteers at a scout jamboree.

The findings on event volunteers' motivation from the SEVMS are supported by other studies of event and festival volunteers, using other scale instruments or qualitative methods. Focus groups carried out by Ralston, Downward, & Lumsdon (2003, 2004) prior to the 2002 Commonwealth Games in Manchester found that the major reasons for volunteering at the event were altruism (wishing to give something back to society, sport or the city and community), involvement (wanting to feel useful, respected and be part of a team) and the uniqueness of the Games and being part of this.

BOX 5.1 MOTIVATIONS OF THE FAST ISRAELI RESCUE AND SEARCH TEAM (FIRST) VOLUNTEERS, ISRAEL

The Fast Israeli Rescue and Search Team (FIRST) is the national association for search and rescue in Israel. FIRST draws on the services of 550 volunteers and trains, co-ordinates and supports 11 regional units. FIRST provides a rescue and search service in Israel and overseas. This includes Israel's remote desert areas, which are increasingly popular with tourists for adventure activities, particularly hiking. In a study of FIRST members' motives, Uriely, Schwartz, Cohen, & Reichel (2002) found that while members stated that they were motivated by a responsibility for the hikers, they also mostly blamed the hikers for needing their services. This study also reported that volunteers were equally as likely to report as their motive the opportunity to participate in challenging hikes as helping to rescue hikers. Many FIRST volunteers have a background in army combat units and their experience of challenging activities such as hikes and abseiling may also motivate their participation. The FIRST volunteers are therefore motivated by a combination of leisure and altruistic reasons and participation as a FIRST volunteer enables individuals to pursue their interests while doing something worthwhile, that is assisting tourists.

Uriely, N., Schwartz, Z., Cohen, E., & Reichel, A. (2002). Rescuing hikers in Israel's deserts: Community altruism or an extension of adventure tourism? *Journal of Leisure Research*, 34, 25–36.

www.israaid.org.il/member_page.asp?id=6

Monga (2006) studied volunteers in five events of different types (including sport events, a community parade, a cultural festival and an agricultural show) and found that motivations were similar across all events. This suggests it is the episodic nature of event volunteering rather than the type of event which differentiates this type of volunteering from more traditional ongoing forms.

Mega-event volunteers have distinct motivations. The status and prestige of the highest profile events can motivate people to volunteer, driven by the opportunity for a 'once-in-a-lifetime' experience. When an event moves between locations, motivations are associated with community promotion and advancement (MacLean and Hamm, 2007), and mega-event volunteers are strongly motivated by pride in their country and culture (Kemp, 2002). This was a clear motivational factor at the 2004 Athens Olympic Games (see Web Resource 5.1). National or local pride means event volunteers, at least at larger events, play a similar role to volunteers in destination services in promoting a positive image of the destination, although in this case it may be as much to international television audiences as visitors.

As with attractions and destination services, there are differences in event volunteers' motivations based on lifestage and other factors. Kemp (2002) focused on younger volunteers at two Olympic Games and found they were motivated more by social factors and acquiring future employment skills, rather than national pride or self-worth issues. Young people's tendency to identify personal skills development as a motivation was also evident in Williams, Dossa, & Tompkins' investigation (1995) of volunteers at the Men's Whistler World Cup of Skiing. They further found that residents rated more highly building community image and spirit, and support for the national team motives; nonresidents' motives focused on the socializing activities. Tangible physical and economic rewards (e.g. lift tickets, job contacts, souvenirs) were the least important motivators for all groups of respondents (also see Chapter 15).

There are also differences in terms of the role volunteers take at an event and at periodic events whether they are first time or returning volunteers. For example, at a university sporting tournament, 'enjoyment' was the most important motive for all volunteers but first aid volunteers (mainly students and medical professionals) were strongly motivated by gaining skills whereas students volunteering in more general roles were motivated by the free uniform and social events (Andrew, 1996). In Coyne and Coyne's study (2001) of golf tournament, volunteers, 'love of golf' was the threshold motivation without which people did not volunteer, otherwise there were distinct variations between the other motivations of first time and returning volunteers (see Box 8.2: Honda Classic).

GUESTS: VOLUNTEER TOURISM

As with volunteers in other settings, researchers debate whether volunteer tourists are motivated by altruism or instrumental reasons. Personal development is the most researched aspect of volunteer tourism (see Chapter 3) and frequently presented as the primary motivator (Wearing, 2001), but motivation is actually much more complex. Volunteering as part of a leisure trip is influenced by both volunteering and tourism motivations. Using Plog's tourist typology, Brown and Lehto (2005) label volunteer vacationers as allocentrics: 'explorers and adventure seekers, who tend to choose remote and untouched (by tourists) destinations' (p. 493). We have already adopted Callanan and Thomas' continuum (2005) of volunteer tourists from shallow to deep (see Chapter 2), and Brown and Lehto's volunteer-minded and vacation-minded categorization (2005) (see Chapter 1). Motivations are integral to both models, and while different types of volunteer tourists may have similar motivations, their relative importance will differ.

The motives of 'shallower' VolunTourists are evident in Brown and Lehto's research (2005) with members of the Ambassador Travel Club in the United States. Those who had volunteered as part of a vacation were motivated by both travel and volunteer motivations. These include the desire for cultural immersion, wanting to give back or make a difference, seeking camaraderie, and seeking education and bonding opportunities for children. This last motivation highlights that as VolunTourism involves very short periods of volunteering and is done with other members of a travel group, there is the potential to build on the growing demand for intergenerational volunteering discussed in Chapter 1. This social motivation is less evident in Broad and Jenkins' study (2008) of volunteer tourists on deeper volunteer tourism experiences at the Gibbon Rehabilitation Project in Thailand. They identify four key motivations: altruism, travel, career development and personal interest/development. The primary motivation for volunteers on a ten-week Greenforce conservation expedition in Zambia (Harlow and Pomfret, 2007) was contributing to the environment and conservation; the same main motivation of ongoing volunteers in the natural attractions setting (Bruyere and Rappe. See p. 84). The Greenforce volunteers were also motivated by personal development through acquiring knowledge and the challenge of the expedition and destination. Their motivations were influenced by both previous experience and their environmental attitudes.

Volunteer tourists also have motivations for choosing a particular project. Broad and Jenkins (2008) found volunteer tourists were attracted to the Gibbon Rehabilitation wildlife conservation project by the opportunity to work for/with animals/wildlife, the cheap cost, and its location in Thailand, a popular low-cost destination for young travelers. Individuals may choose to become a volunteer tourist as a means of engaging with the destination, its culture and residents in a more meaningful and in-depth way. Some volunteer tourists are already traveling and motivation or choice is about being in the right place at the right time (Wearing, 2001). This is particularly evident for volunteer tourists arranging their placement direct with the host organization once in the destination and here their altruistic desire to volunteer sets them apart from other travelers (Mustonen, 2005).

Our interviews with domestic volunteer tourists in Australia reveal that individuals are likely to be traveling to these destinations anyway, but the chance to volunteer gives them an opportunity to engage with the community in a different way from that of the itinerant traveler. The volunteers, participants in Volunteering Western Australia's Visiting Volunteers program (www.volunteeringwa.org.au/About-Us/Our-programs/Visiting-Volunteers. aspx) are also able to save money as volunteering is largely cost-free compared to taking part in organized trips or other typical tourist activities. Indeed, domestic volunteer tourism in Australia can be considered as a form of budget travel for the largely older, retired Grey Nomad participants who volunteer as they travel around Australia (see Box 4.2).

As with the experience-seeking attraction volunteers discussed earlier (p. 84, volunteer tourist motivations can be based around gaining experience and developing skills. Young people and career breakers may be motivated to take a gap year to enhance their CV, demonstrate employability and further their career (Jones, 2004). Some volunteer tourism can be used to gain academic community service or study abroad credits, and some volunteer vacation programs may enable participants to undertake research as part of their studies (see Box 5.2: Operation Wallacea).

REFLECTIONS ON MOTIVATING VOLUNTEERS

The research reviewed in this chapter shows that tourism volunteers are largely self-motivated and seek out volunteer opportunities that they believe will meet their needs. It is the volunteer manager's role to uncover these motives at the recruitment stage; this can be difficult if a large number of volunteers are recruited at once (say at an attraction or for an event) (see Chapter 6). Asking volunteers directly their reasons for volunteering may

---

BOX 5.2 OPERATION WALLACEA AND THE MOTIVATIONS OF RESEARCH VOLUNTEER ECO-TOURISTS, INDONESIA

Operation Wallacea is a UK-based research ecotourism operator, which runs expeditions in seven countries: Indonesia, Honduras, Egypt, Cuba, South Africa, Mozambique and Peru. The expeditions are research-orientated and include a range of scientific surveys and some community-based conservation work. Operation Wallacea targets university students either as research assistant volunteers on surveys run by university academics in conjunction with local NGOs, or students wanting to undertake their own field research for a final year honors project or masters research.

Galley and Clifton (2004) studied the motivations of volunteers on Operation Wallacea expeditions in Indonesia. The majority of their respondents were female, single, aged between 20 and 22, and university students reading for a degree in science or an environmental subject. They identified three main motivations (p.76, 77):

- personal development (including 'to experience something completely new', 'to take part in a rare opportunity', and 'to seek challenging things to do')

- academic achievement (including 'to stand out on my CV as a valuable experience' and 'to take part in a rare opportunity'); and

- the experience factor (including to experience something new' and 'to seeking challenging things to do').

Galley and Clifton conclude that their findings are similar to the motivations of other research volunteer eco-tourists, such as Weiler and Richin's study (1995) of Earthwatch Australia participants.

---

www.opwall.com

Galley, G., & Clifton, J. (2004). The motivational and demographic characteristics of research ecotourists: Operation Wallacea volunteers in Southeast Sulawesi, Indonesia. *Journal of Ecotourism*, 3, 69–82.

Weiler, B., & Richins, H. (1995). Extreme, extravagant and elite: a profile of ecotourists on Earthwatch Expeditions. *Tourism Recreation Research*, 20, 29–36.

not uncover the whole picture. Major life changes (e.g. graduation, migration, children leaving home, retirement, separation or death of a partner) can act as a driver to begin volunteering but the resulting motivations can be very different. Volunteers may be looking to volunteering to replace something they have lost (e.g. social contact or a sense of being needed) or to do something different (e.g. develop a new interest).

It is also the manager's job to ensure that volunteers are matched with roles that will interest and stimulate them; this task is made easier if the volunteer roles are well designed (see Chapters 4 and 6). However, understanding motivation is not enough; there is also a need to explain how a volunteer program, project or role can meet volunteers' motives as this may not always be obvious, particularly to someone who does not know the organization, its location or its activities. For example, if the motivation of a volunteer is to contribute to the success of an event, then how their individual role achieves this needs to be made clear. This needs to be part of program design (Chapter 4) and incorporated into recruitment materials (Chapter 6). It also relates back to how volunteering is valued (Chapter 3) and we will explore this further when discussing rewards and retention (Chapter 8).

Despite commonalities, there does seem to be some significant differences in motivation between volunteers in different tourism settings. Volunteers at attractions, destination services and volunteer tourists are more motivated by personal interest and the receipt of personal benefits, such as enjoyment or personal development. Event volunteers are more motivated by participation in and the success of the event. The shorter-term nature of episodic volunteering therefore differentiates it from ongoing and seasonal volunteering. Volunteer tourists have both travel and volunteering motivations, and there is the need to understand how shallow or deep an experience is desired and thus the balance of volunteering and more typical tourist activities sought.

As well as the motivation for volunteering in a certain tourism setting, a volunteer will have reasons for choosing a particular organization, program and role. Learning the motivations for this volunteering can help in managing the volunteer and attracting future volunteers. For example, Smith (2003) found that while volunteers in literary heritage attractions were motivated by a range of reasons, the choice of a particular property could simply be its location.

Social motivations are most evident in ongoing volunteering such as in attractions and destination service organizations. The ongoing contribution means volunteers will become part of a team that will bring socializing opportunities both during volunteering and more generally. Social motives are not as dominant in episodic tourism volunteering; in particular, the intense event experience gives more limited opportunities for socializing. Nevertheless, although not an explicit motivation, social factors are an important part of the volunteering experience and rewards for event volunteers and volunteer tourists (Chapter 8), demonstrating that managers need to think beyond motivation when designing their volunteer program.

Managers also need to revisit their volunteers' motivations over time as the reasons for starting to volunteer with an organization may not be the same reasons that keep people volunteering, or in the case of episodic volunteers, keep them coming back. Retention will be discussed further in Chapter 8.

The tourism context has highlighted the important relationship between visiting and volunteering. A desire to meet visitors can be the reason for choosing to volunteer in a tourism setting. Visitors can be a source of new volunteers (see Chapter 6). Volunteering can be a replacement for visiting or attendance, giving the opportunity for deeper engagement, access to a particular subculture and the pursuit of serious leisure.

PRINCIPLES FOR GOOD PRACTICE

- Volunteer motivation is personal and often complex and it can change over time.

- Motivation can be linked to different age cohorts of volunteers, with younger people more likely to be motivated by skills development and work experience than older people.

- Volunteer managers must not expect volunteers to be primarily motivated to help the organization.

- Managers need to accept that they may have little control or influence over the motives of their volunteers.

- Motivation needs to be linked to the volunteer role and reward and recognition.

- Motivation is frequently linked to social opportunities and managers need to create ways in which social interaction between volunteers (and paid staff) can be facilitated.

- Managers need to revisit the motivation of their volunteers, whether they are ongoing, seasonal or bounce-back episodic volunteers.

DISCUSSION QUESTIONS

Q5.1 How can motivation to volunteer vary across the lifecourse?

Q5.2 For a tourism organization you are familiar with, what do you think might motivate people to volunteer with this organization?

Q5.3 How will the motives of a bounce-back volunteer at an annual festival held in the same (fixed) destination vary from those of a volunteer at a periodic roaming sporting event, which moves location each time?

FURTHER EXAMPLE

Web Resource 5.1: Motivations of Volunteers at the 2004 Athens Olympic Games, Greece.

RESOURCE

Motivation is often covered in conjunction with Recruitment (see Resources in chapter 6) and Retention (see chapter 8).

Recruiting and Selecting Volunteers

INTRODUCTION

The recruitment process is an opportunity to present the volunteer experience to potential applicants and Green and Chalip (1998) argue that recruiting volunteers is fundamentally a marketing problem. Recruitment should inspire, create realistic expectations of roles and commitment, communicate core values of the organization, and the support and benefits a volunteer can expect. A poorly conceived and executed recruitment process can fail to engage new volunteers or create dissatisfaction for those recruited, negatively influencing other expectations of the volunteering experience and may cause applicants to withdraw.

An active approach to recruitment involves an organization proactively seeking new volunteers through both ongoing activities and targeted recruitment drives for a specific purpose, project or shortage. In contrast, where initial contact is volunteer-initiated, the organization reacts to this offer of support.

There are several routes into volunteering but national surveys of volunteering repeatedly reveal that word-of-mouth recommendation to a potential new volunteer is the most common stimulus. Canada's *Giving and Volunteering Survey* reported 89% of all volunteers were asked by someone to volunteer (Hall et al., 2006). Of particular importance is that in most cases the person asking already had some link with the organization. This means that paid staff and volunteers at an organization actually do most of the recruiting. Related to word-of-mouth recommendation is that other existing links with an organization also form a route into volunteering, such as previously using the services of an organization (Low et al., 2007). This means customers, clients, suppliers and members can be important sources of voluntary labor. In tourism settings, this would

Managing Volunteers in Tourism
Copyright © 2009 Elsevier Ltd. All rights reserved.

include visitors to an attraction, event attendees and members of a Friends' association. These individuals have already stated their support or agreement with the aims or purpose of the organization; it is up to the organization to capitalize on this existing positive attachment through targeted recruitment and membership development (Wilson and Pimm, 1996).

In the Canadian survey, only 45% of volunteers approached the organization on their own initiative rather than waiting to be asked (Hall et al., 2006). To capture these potential volunteers, an organization needs to promote their volunteering opportunities in various ways. Advertising through leaflets or posters is most common, as well as newspapers, television and radio, with local media generating more success than national outlets (Low et al., 2007). Becoming involved via the Internet is growing, with an organization's own Web site a more important recruitment tool than general volunteering sites (Low et al., 2007). Organizations can also use volunteer centers or bureaux and online volunteering databases (see Q2.1) to list their vacancies and promote them to those interested in volunteering.

In summary, most people need to be personally asked to volunteer rather than responding to an advertisement or leaflet seeking volunteers. The reliance on personal contacts and existing links means that an organization's volunteers can become very homogenous in terms of their profile and the implications of this for diversity management are discussed in Chapter 9. It is also worth noting that the Canadian research found that those who approached the organization volunteered more hours than those who were asked to help out. The recruitment method may therefore be linked to motivation with those actively seeking out volunteering opportunities wanting to get more involved than those who respond to a request to volunteer.

We have looked at how volunteers get involved with an organization but we also need to consider selection of volunteers. This can be a contentious issue as there is an inherent dilemma in refusing the services of someone offering their time for free. Nevertheless, selection procedures are important as the consequences of inappropriate selection can mean an unsatisfactory experience for the volunteer and potential damage to the organization and its clients (such as a poor visitor experience). There are also the lost financial and time costs of recruiting and training a volunteer who then leaves or has to be dismissed (see Chapter 8). Rather than discussing selection and the acceptance or rejection of a candidate, it may be better to think of selection as screening. This involves making a judgment about the suitability of a candidate through screening and allocating them to the most appropriate role within an organization, which may not be the one for which they applied.

McCurley and Lynch (1998) recommend screening and interviewing all potential volunteers. This can involve various mechanisms including asking potential volunteers to:

- complete an application form;

- provide references;

- undergo a police or criminal record check if their role will involve contact with children or vulnerable adults, money or other valuable items (in some countries legislation may require this, e.g. Australian's Working with Children Checks); and

- attend an interview.

The complexity and formality of the screening process may depend on factors such as competition for volunteer posts, level of responsibility of the volunteer or prestige of the organization or volunteering role.

Practice does not necessarily follow these recommendations. For example, in the UK's *Helping Out* survey (Low et al., 2007) only 19% of volunteers reported that they had been asked to attend an interview or an informal chat before commencing their activities, although the practice is becoming more common. Other screening tools were used even less frequently. For all selection methods, levels of use were higher for regular volunteers than occasional volunteers. Of those who had been subject to these processes almost all said they did not mind being screened in this way, although there was less support for having written role descriptions (see Chapter 2).

HOST VOLUNTEERS: ATTRACTIONS

Most research on the recruitment of attraction volunteers comes from the cultural sector. Word-of-mouth is a key recruitment method, along with membership development (Davis Smith and Chambers, 1997; Howlett et al., 2005). Volunteers often approach a museum (Howlett et al., 2005) or know about a heritage organization's work and want to volunteer (BAFM, 1998). There is still a need to publicize and promote volunteering opportunities otherwise potential volunteers may not know about the different volunteer roles at an attraction or how to apply. Attractions can provide this information on their own Web sites and through posters and leaflets on display at the attraction. Effective places to put posters include the admissions desk, the restaurant and the toilets. Advertisements need to be honest about what the role will involve so that they set realistic expectations. For example, Perth Zoo docent program states on their recruitment leaflet 'If you are looking for voluntary work where you will have regular contact with animals, or can feed animals or clean enclosures, then becoming a Docent will not give you the job satisfaction you deserve'. Docents at the zoo are primarily involved in visitor services and only occasionally have direct contact with animals (www.perthzoo.wa.gov.au).

Some attractions have an annual intake of new volunteers and will organize an information session rather than interviewing each one individually, which would take too much time. This enables staff to meet and assess volunteers and potential volunteers can meet each other and existing volunteers. Other attractions with a stable number of volunteers may only recruit a small number each year and so choose to deal with each new recruit on an individual basis. Attractions also need volunteers for ongoing, seasonal or episodic roles, depending on their operations (see Chapter 2). Seasonal or past episodic volunteers will need to be recontacted each year or when they are needed; how these volunteers can be retained and reinvolved through ongoing communication and training are discussed in Chapters 7 and 8.

Where episodic volunteers are needed to assist with a specific project or a special event at the attraction, they can be recruited from the existing pool of ongoing volunteers. For a new attraction, one involving volunteers for the first time or needing a large number of extra volunteers due to new projects or developments, an active and targeted recruitment drive is the most effective approach. Web Resource 6.1 details a recruitment drive by the National Trust for Places of Historic Interest and Natural Beauty (National Trust) for their historic property Scotney Castle in southeast England. The appeal to National Trust members through their newsletter and a letter sent direct to members were the most effective methods, the letter acting as a personal invitation to volunteer. Special tours of the property enabled potential volunteers to gain an insight into what the role might involve.

Successful recruitment is often related to the profile of the attraction and large, popular attractions such as World Heritage Sites or national museums rarely struggle to recruit. Smaller, less well-known attractions may not have as much choice over their volunteers (Osborne, 1999). While they will rarely turn away a prospective volunteer, screening is still important, particularly given the role of many attraction volunteers in delivering a quality visitor experience.

HOST VOLUNTEERS: DESTINATION SERVICE ORGANIZATIONS

Destination service organizations usually involve volunteers on an ongoing or seasonal basis. There is a lack of research on destination service volunteers in general (see Chapter 2) but their recruitment patterns are similar to attractions. Most destination service organizations rely on word-of-mouth recruitment or their Web sites. Few actively recruit or advertise in other media. Large destination service volunteer programs may hold an annual intake, as at some large attractions. For example, Tourism Western Australia's airport meet-and-greet program recruits annually to coincide with their training program (www.tourism.wa.gov.au/Visitor_Servicing/West_Oz_Welcomers).

Our research suggests that due to the local knowledge and high skill and training requirements, many destination services primarily recruit from their local market. Some destination services are able to recruit through their clients and visitors to an area. For example, campground host programs often recruit travelers who have used their services in the past (see Box 6.1: Minnesota Campground Host Program). While knowledge and skills are useful prerequisites for destination service volunteering, for many programs, enthusiasm, interest and willingness to learn and commit to training are as important as selection criteria. Emergency service volunteers are normally recruited through individual branches or clubs. Surf life-saving clubs are popular and recruitment tends to be reactive with potential volunteers approaching the club. The club system is focused on skills development from the age of 5 years upward, so active recruitment is usually focused on junior members called 'nippers', who will be the surf life-savers of the future.

BOX 6.1 CAMPGROUND HOST PROGRAM, MINNESOTA, UNITED STATES

Minnesota Department of Natural Resources (DNR) runs the State Park and State Forest Campground Host program. Volunteers enroll for at least a four-week period in the summer season to assist campers, provide information on the campground, state park or forest and local facilities, perform light maintenance work and various other duties. A free campsite is provided and while volunteers must be familiar with state park and forest campground rules, they have no law enforcement responsibilities and report to the park or forest personnel.

Information and an application form can be downloaded from the DNR Web site. The application form includes personal details and names of accompanying family members, preferred campground(s) and previous camping experience, availability, outdoor interests/hobbies, special needs, which may limit volunteer roles, and two personal references. Potential hosts are then invited to be interviewed by the campground manager at their chosen park and to undergo a background check. All returning campground hosts must undergo a new background check each year. Both new and returning hosts must sign a volunteer agreement; the principal factor in this is to ensure their campsite is vacated in the event of the agreement being terminated by either party. While volunteers are encouraged to return, hosts may be limited to two consecutive years at the same campground, but can return the subsequent year.

www.dnr.state.mn.us/volunteering/stateparks/campgroundhost.html

HOST VOLUNTEERS: EVENTS

Recruitment for events varies depending on whether it is a new event, a one-off event or a regular periodic event. For periodic events that remain in the same location, recruitment overlaps with retention as many volunteers are returnees or veterans who have volunteered at the event before and 'bounce-back' (see Chapter 2). These events typically rely on local residents to volunteer, or have a loyal band of volunteers attached to the subject of the event and see volunteering as a way to experience the event (e.g. folk music aficionados who annually travel to volunteer at a folk festival). These reoccurring events face a similar challenge to attractions that have a closed season: the returnees mean the event (or attraction) builds up an experienced group of volunteers but they need to maintain contact with their pool of volunteers in the downtime between events (or seasons). This can be achieved through social events such as fund-raisers, or communication through newsletters. Box 6.2 (Marblehead Festival of the Arts) illustrates how an annual cycle of volunteering activities can combine recruitment and social activities, thereby facilitating the integration of new recruits, keeping existing volunteers involved throughout the year, and also playing a part in both reward and retention (see Chapter 8).

Depending on their retention rate and whether they require additional volunteers to accommodate growth in the event's activities, periodic events are also likely to recruit new volunteers. This recruitment is relatively informal with personal approaches dominating, particularly word-of-mouth recruitment and social networks. As the event volunteering will be short-term, there is lot of scope to encourage those volunteering or participating in related activities to also donate time to the event. These can be volunteers and members of sporting clubs or art societies, or any specialist group that shares a community of interest with the event organization. In comparative research at cultural festivals, Smith and Lockstone (2009) identified two main sources of new volunteers: individuals and groups. Individuals tend to be recruited through word-of-mouth and special interest groups, with some events outsourcing their volunteer recruitment to third parties such as volunteer centers or bureaus. Events can also involve groups who often volunteer together in a particular role, for example, taking responsibility for a functional area such as stewarding or ticket sales. Event managers can work in partnership with community organizations, education institutions and businesses (including sponsors and employer-supported volunteering programs) to supply or even manage a group of volunteers at an event.

Newham Volunteers (Chapter 17) illustrates a program where a local council has used the future hosting of a mega event, the 2012 London

BOX 6.2 ANNUAL RECRUITMENT CYCLE FOR MARBLEHEAD FESTIVAL OF ARTS, UNITED STATES

The Marblehead Festival of Arts is an all-volunteer not-for-profit organization in Marblehead, Massachusetts. The annually elected board of directors comprises a president, 2 or 3 vice presidents, a treasurer, a secretary and 6 to 12 directors, all of which are voluntary positions. Over 40 committees cover art exhibits, events and various support functions and involve several hundred volunteers. Established in 1962, the organization produces the annual summer Arts Festival that takes place over the Fourth of July holiday, and sponsors other arts events throughout the year.

'Being a Festival volunteer is a way to support the arts that enrich our lives, give back to our community, make new friends, and have a lot of fun' (www.marbleheadfestival.org). Volunteers can be involved all year round or just when they are available for specific events. Details of festival committees and volunteer opportunities are described online, and there is an annual cycle of volunteer recruitment events:

September	Annual General Meeting: election of officers and Board of Directors
January	Logo Premiere and Volunteer Information Party
March/April	Volunteer Information Booth one evening a week at a local restaurant and pub
	Friends-of-the-Festival Mailing
	Volunteer Recruitment Parties: Board of Director members and committee chairpersons discuss Festival activities and greet new volunteers. For veteran and new volunteers this is a chance to 'Join the camaraderie of the Festival family!'
July	Summer Festival of Arts
	Volunteer Appreciation Party: a few weeks after the festival the Board of Directors holds a Volunteer Appreciation Party for Festival volunteers and their families

Volunteer information sessions are integrated with other public events so that volunteering is promoted at every opportunity. For example, at the Logo Premiere Party where the Festival Logo Contest winner is announced, the Board of Directors and Committee Chairpersons are on hand to provide information on volunteer opportunities.

While most of the volunteering is at the summer Festival, other events and activities enable all year round involvement, and Easel, the volunteer e-newsletter, keeps supporters informed about upcoming events and volunteering opportunities. For example, the Friends-of-the-Festival Mailing event in March is the Festival's major fund-raising campaign. Volunteers get together to prepare 15,000 information packs; the presence of key personnel mean 'this is a good time to learn about the Festival while helping out. Bring a friend!' (www.marbleheadfestival.org)

www.marbleheadfestival.org/

Olympic Games, to create a pool of trained volunteers whom local event organizers can draw on for their voluntary workforce needs. Manchester Event Volunteers, a legacy of the 2002 Manchester Commonwealth Games, is a similar program (www.mev.org.uk).

While many periodic events have a loyal pool of volunteers and are able to fill all their volunteer positions, some struggle to recruit and few are in a position to actively reject volunteers due to an oversupply of applicants. Like recruitment, there is often an informal approach to selection. For these events, selection involves screening volunteers for suitability and role allocation rather than choosing between different candidates (Smith and Lockstone, 2009). Given the short-term nature of the volunteering, the volunteer's availability also needs to be taken into account (see Chapter 2).

New events, periodic roaming events that change location and one-off events need a different approach to recruitment. They have no pool of veteran volunteers to draw on, although there is some evidence of a very small band of volunteers who follow events on a global basis essentially becoming event volunteer tourists (e.g. the Olympic Games, Fairley et al., 2007). To attract new volunteers, a recruitment drive approach is needed. Publicity is required to raise awareness of the event and its need for volunteers. Many mega events use the volunteer program launch to generate hype in the host community about the forthcoming event. The recruitment drive is often in stages; the Australian Sports Commission (2000a) recommends a two-phase approach: recruiting supervisory positions first, and then operational level volunteers.

The timing of the recruitment process is critical: the larger the event, the sooner recruitment should start. For example, at the 2002 Salt Lake City Winter Olympics the recruitment drive for the 35,000 volunteers required began two years before the event and incorporated publicity on television, radio, newspapers, flyers and the Internet (Walker, 2002). Chapter 16 maps the recruitment and selection process for Melbourne Commonwealth Games volunteers as part of the 'volunteer's journey'. It is also important not to have too much lead time as volunteers see their psychological contract with the event beginning as soon as their application has been accepted (Ralston et al., 2004). Communication and preevent activities, often relating to training, team building and socialization, need to be in place to keep volunteers motivated in the event buildup. Many events also overrecruit in anticipation that some attrition will occur between recruitment and event delivery (Volunteering Australia, 2006b).

High-profile events can be extremely popular, and despite the substantial number of volunteers required, mega-event volunteer programs are typically massively oversubscribed (Baum and Lockstone, 2007). For example, the 2002 Manchester Commonwealth Games received over 22,000 applications for just over 10,000 volunteer positions (also see Web Resource 5.1: 2004 Athens Olympic Games). For these events, a structured selection process and clear selection criteria are required. Stages of selection can include:

- a registration of interest linked to the recruitment drive publicity – this can be done through newspaper supplements and online;

- a written application – online applications facilitate the processing of the data but older applicants still prefer writing a postal application;

- an interview – ideally individual face-to-face contact but for a large-scale program this can be logistically challenging. Telephone or group interviews can be used, as can the interviewing skills of other volunteers. For example at the Sydney Olympic Games, organizers trained 500 university students studying human resource management to conduct many of the volunteer selection interviews.

As with other settings, legislative and ethical requirements may require police/criminal record checks to be carried out. Appropriate selection criteria vary depending on the nature of the event, but the 'Count Yourself In' recruitment program at the 2002 Manchester Commonwealth Games has typical qualifying criteria for large-scale events where there is competition to gain a volunteering position:

- a willingness to work for at least 10 days of the two-week event;
- attendance at an interview and training sessions;
- aged 16 years or over; and
- able to provide own accommodation (Manchester 2002).

Language skills and visa requirements may also be important, particularly for high-profile events that attract overseas applicants who are event volunteer tourists.

GUESTS: VOLUNTEER TOURISM

Volunteer tourism participants are recruited differently from most other tourism volunteers, not least because they are usually paying customers. Volunteer tourism organizations use many of the same distribution channels for marketing their products as other tourism providers, including brochures, Web sites, and travel agents. Dedicated guidebooks (e.g. Hindle 2007;

Ng, 2006), online referral portals (e.g. www.goabroad.com and http://www.charityguide.org) and umbrella organizations (e.g. www.yearoutgroup.org and www.volunteerinternational.org) promote volunteer tourism opportunities, and gap years more generally (e.g. Bindloss and Hindle 2005; Griffith, 2008). Alternative/ecotourism and adventure travel shows are particularly important in the UK market, and volunteer tourism providers also attend university fairs and events to target the student market. Word-of-mouth is a crucial promotional and recruitment tool, particularly involving returned volunteer tourists, and many providers put testimonials in their marketing materials (including online), and facilitate the interaction of past and potential volunteer tourists.

Volunteer tourism products are complex and a study of youth travelers (Richards, 2007) found they were most likely to be purchased directly from the product supplier, typically the sending organization. Most travel agency bookings were through a student, youth or other specialist rather than a general travel agent. Regardless of distribution channel, booking online was most popular. Where a host organization directly runs their own program, distribution is largely though word-of-mouth, the organization's Web site or online portals (Mustonen, 2005). Large providers such as i-to-i distribute their products direct to tourists through their Web site (www.i-to-i.com) and via agents (see Web Resource 2.4).

Selection can be considered in two ways: we will first look at the factors influencing volunteer tourists' selection of a volunteer tourism project and provider, then consider how the organizations themselves select project participants. In an increasingly competitive volunteer tourism market, potential travelers can select between a huge choice of experiences, products, providers and destinations. Jones (2004) presents the decisions facing gap year participants as two-fold. First, there is the choice between traveling overseas or staying in one's home country, and deciding whether to plan the gap year independently or to use one or more organizations (including sending and servicing organizations and travel companies) to help facilitate the gap year experience. Second is the choice of what combination of activities to do: paid work, volunteering, learning, travel and leisure.

The choice of specific gap year volunteering organization and project is driven by a complex interplay of factors (Söderman and Snead, 2008) including: the influence of peers; the variety offered by the organization's project (e.g. its length and the combination of volunteering with a language course and/or travel); and the image and assurances offered by the organization. Söderman and Snead's research with British gap year volunteer tourists in South America found that being a charity or other not-for-profit provider was appealing and some volunteer tourists deliberately avoided using a profit-making company. Fees and available finances also govern participation in volunteer tourism and the selection of a particular provider and project. While fund-raising to finance a trip can be part of the experience, the substantial costs of many volunteer tourism products mean that this remains a niche market and, particularly for the gap year, remains the preserve of the more affluent (Jones, 2004). This theme will be further discussed in Chapter 9.

From the providers' perspective, whether they select participants depends on the nature of the volunteer tourism project and participants. Callanan and Thomas' deep to shallow spectrum of volunteer tourism programs (2005. Also see Chapter 2) can be used to discuss approaches to selection by different volunteer tourism providers. At the shallowest level, for VolunTourism there is no selection on the part of the provider as the participants are simply booking a holiday. Shorter volunteer vacations are likely to have minimal skills/qualification requirements due to the nature and duration of the volunteering activities. Self-selection is likely to be in place whereby the sending or servicing organization gives details about the project and any associated requirements (e.g. physical fitness), and the participant can make their choices based on this information.

With longer intermediate volunteer vacations, there may be some skill requirements or other preferences that the provider wants to target in selection. On shallower and some intermediate programs participants typically volunteer as a group. For deeper programs sending volunteers on individual placements, selection procedures have more importance (Power, 2007) as the skills, experience and personality of the volunteer play a major role in the project's effectiveness. As the deepest form of volunteer tourism program, gap year volunteering placements should have the strictest selection requirements as without certain skills, qualifications or experience, the ability to make a positive impact at the destination is limited. This is a reason for the move away in international volunteering and gap year programs from unskilled young people toward sending professionals on a career break or in early retirement. As the volunteer tourism program deepens, there is an increased need for selection so that the volunteer tourist can make a genuine contribution to the project, host organization and destination.

As with other settings, volunteer management best practice and some legislation requires background checks on prospective volunteers. However, Power's research (2007) found a concerning number of UK-based volunteer tourism organizations do not conduct Criminal Record Bureau checks even for roles working with children. He also found that just over a quarter of volunteer tourism providers in the United Kingdom did not meet their volunteers before sending them overseas. While volunteer tourists may be tourists as well as volunteers, Power highlights that organizations are sending volunteers who they have not even met face-to-face but will be representing their organization and may be working with vulnerable people.

REFLECTIONS ON RECRUITING AND SELECTING VOLUNTEERS

The recruitment methods used by most organizations, regardless of the tourism setting, typically result in a homogenous group of volunteers. Homogeneity can actually be beneficial as volunteers will have shared interests and social networks (Smith and Lockstone, 2009) and this can help reduce turnover. A homogenous volunteer group works particularly well for popular, high-status and high-profile programs. Of course, homogeneity also brings limitations, such as lack of diversity and cliqueyness, which can be offputting to new volunteers; diversity management will be discussed further in Chapter 9. A reactive rather than proactive approach to recruitment may stifle the organization's development over time.

Membership development as a means of recruiting volunteers offers lots of potential to organizations and may be of particular benefit to attractions and events. Members have an interest in the organization and have already donated their money and can be persuaded to donate their time as well (see Web Resource 6.1: Scotney Castle). As members are a part of the organization's clients or audience, recruiting volunteers from the membership association can also be considered a form of audience development, building a new relationship between the organization and the member.

Screening offers benefits to both the volunteer and the organization as it allows the organization to assess the volunteer's motives and skills and match them to a suitable and satisfying role. Selection is dependent on

- the role the volunteers will take;
- the demands of the post;
- the flexibility of potential volunteers and their previous skills (efforts to minimize training requirements);
- the level of competition for volunteer places; and
- the availability of potential volunteers.

Selection and screening can result in the rejection of an applicant, possibly due to excess demand or a lack of fit between the organization's and the volunteer's needs. Few texts address the potential problems associated with this outcome, such as negative word-of-mouth recommendation. Chapter 16 considers this issue with regard to the Melbourne Commonwealth Games.

PRINCIPLES FOR GOOD PRACTICE

- Recruitment of new volunteers is a two-way activity, with volunteers selecting the organization as much as the organization selects the volunteers.

- Active recruitment is better than reactive recruitment as it enables organizations to target specific volunteer markets.

- Organizations should consider active recruitment to target under-represented groups as this is also a means of widening the client base or audience and managing diversity (see Chapter 9).

- Recruitment needs to be honest about what the volunteer role involves, what is expected from the volunteer and what the rewards will be (see Chapter 8).

- Open days or information sessions are a good way to meet potential volunteers face-to-face and to enable them to meet current volunteers or returned volunteer tourists who can give their perspective.

- Organizations should seek to minimize formal procedures such as individual interviews or complex application forms but at the same time they need to demonstrate that their volunteers are fully appreciated and treated professionally.

- Organizations should also seek to minimize the paperwork involved or smooth the process for new volunteers, such as application forms, police checks and volunteer agreements (see Chapter 4) but at the same time they need to ensure they are not putting anyone at risk.

DISCUSSION QUESTIONS

Q6.1 How does practice vary between recruiting ongoing, seasonal and episodic tourism volunteers?

Q6.2 Why might a tourism volunteer program want to complete a background check on a potential volunteer?

Q6.3 How far are tourism volunteers selecting a program rather than the organization selecting them?

FURTHER EXAMPLE

Web Resource 6.1: Volunteer Recruitment Drive at Scotney Castle House and Garden, UK.

RESOURCES

Dyer, F., & Jost, J. (2006). Recruiting Volunteers. Directory of Social Change.

Ellis, S. J. (2004). The Volunteer Recruitment (and Membership Development) Handbook. Energize Inc.

Energize Inc. www.energizeinc.com/art/subj/recruit.html

Online Volunteering Databases: see Q2.1 in Chapter 2.

CHAPTER 7

Training and Developing Volunteers

INTRODUCTION

Once volunteers have been recruited, they need induction (or orientation) and training. Training should set and manage the expectations of volunteers and impacts on their satisfaction, effectiveness, retention and a volunteer's sense of competency in their role. Like new paid employees, volunteers need to be introduced to the organization, event or activity with which they will be assisting. Indeed, training can be even more important for volunteers as the opportunity to learn about the organization or its subject matter can be a key motivator and reward (Stamer, Lerdall, & Guo, 2008). Orientation and training prepares and supports volunteers to perform their role effectively; development goes beyond this and enables a volunteer, if they choose, to pursue a career within their chosen activity (Stebbins, 1992).

Training has a social role and contributes to the development of a strong volunteer team. This social role is particularly important for bringing together new groups of volunteers, for example, on a volunteer tourism project, a new attraction or a one-off event. At seasonal attractions and destination services and at periodic events, a training session can bring back together a group of returning volunteers and also facilitate the integration of new volunteers. It is also important to consider the training needs not only of the volunteers but those of staff and managers working alongside them or in supervisory and management roles, as well as those from the volunteer tourism host organization. This training can set expectations for all involved. It should contribute to developing a team spirit across the attraction, destination service or event workforce, and the integration of volunteer tourists into the local community and host organization.

Training can also be a source of dissatisfaction. This can be a lack of training so volunteers feel unable to fulfil their role confidently, or a perception

Managing Volunteers in Tourism
Copyright © 2009 Elsevier Ltd. All rights reserved.

of poor quality or inappropriate training. For example, Nogawa (2004) found that a considerable number of 2002 Football World Cup volunteers later complained that sessions in the extensive phased training program were 'often rather meaningless and a waste of their time' (p. 232) when the procedures practiced were not later used when volunteering at the event.

The induction and training offered by an organization depends on the size of the volunteer program, the complexity of the volunteer role and the supply of volunteers. These factors will also influence the timing of training delivery. For short-term episodic experiences, such as events and volunteer vacations, much, if not all, of the training will be up front and volunteers will have to learn rapidly on the job. For ongoing volunteering, induction is important to orientate the volunteer but training can be delivered over a longer period and becomes part of the ongoing development of the volunteer. Good practice in volunteer management states that volunteers should at the very least receive an induction including an introduction to the organization, health and safety information, particularly if the volunteer role includes an element of visitor management and instruction on how to perform the required tasks (McCurley and Lynch, 1998). Any training program needs to include a range of learning methods and styles, and aim to foster and nurture volunteers' sense of community (Green and Chalip, 2004). Volunteers as experiential learners (who learn by doing) has been highlighted in attractions (Holmes, 2006), events (Kemp, 2002) and volunteer tourism (Leigh, 2006) settings.

For those motivated by the desire or need to gain work experience through volunteering, especially younger people, students and sometimes gappers on a career break, training is a key part of both motivation and reward. Internships are time-limited volunteer positions (which often include a stipend) expressly for supporting experience-seeking volunteers. Training therefore needs to be integral and there is often the opportunity to gain recognized qualifications.

HOST VOLUNTEERS: ATTRACTIONS

The induction and training offered by attractions varies. Seasonal attractions, which close over an off season, typically hold a training session for all volunteers near the start of the open season. This preseason briefing is usually short and focuses on changes that have taken place over the closed season such as new exhibits or a reminder of health and safety regulations. It also serves a social function for the volunteers to get together after the closed season. Training can be compulsory or voluntary, although the former is recommended, particularly for health and safety issues.

As noted in Chapter 6, attractions with large volunteer programs often prefer to recruit annually or have regular intakes, which means that there will be a group of new volunteers all starting at the same time. As such, many attractions hold an annual induction combined with the training program to coincide with the new intake. In Australia, Canada and the United States, training can be extensive, lengthy and even include the award of formal qualifications. Chapter 11 details the 6- to 8-month training program for new guides at the Australian War Memorial; on completion, the guide is awarded a Statement of Attainment in collaboration with the Canberra Institute of Technology. Volunteers at the National Museum in Thailand undertake 2–3 hours training a week over 2 months (Stamer et al., 2008). These formal and lengthy training programs may seem excessive to non-volunteers but the opportunity to learn about the attraction can be a major factor in volunteers' motivation (Chapter 5) and training can therefore also be a reward for volunteers (Chapter 8).

There may also be a charge to the volunteer for training (see Box 7.1: Denver Zoo). This can reduce the expenses for the attraction and may ensure volunteers are committed but it can also act as a barrier to some potential volunteers and may reduce the diversity of the volunteer program

---

BOX 7.1 DENVER ZOO VOLUNTEER TRAINING PROGRAM, UNITED STATES

Denver Zoo in Colorado involves volunteers in a range of areas including public interpretation, community outreach, education programs, administrative duties and special events; there is a separate Zoo Crew program for teen volunteers. Denver Zoo offers a program of continuing training and development to volunteers.

Potential volunteers can attend a Volunteer Open House event, then complete an application form and interview and attend a two day 'ZooU' induction program. Volunteers have to pay $25 toward training and recognition costs, pay for their uniform and be a member of the Denver Zoological Foundation (individual annual membership $45).

New volunteers become Zoo Ambassadors and perform a variety of functions, from meeting and greeting visitors to assisting at events and with education programs as well as helping keepers with various animal programs. A Zoo Ambassador must commit to 50 hours of volunteering each

year and attend five general meetings or further education sessions. New volunteers are on probation for their first year.

A Zoo Ambassador can apply to become a Zoo Guide. These volunteers are based at guide stations throughout the zoo and engage in basic interpretation of the zoo exhibits for visitors. Guide training is offered each spring, costs an additional $25 and potential guides must participate in three full days of training. Finally, a Zoo Guide can apply to become a Zoo Docent on completion of the docent training program. Zoo Docents are also involved in interpreting the exhibits to visitors but have more autonomy, can develop their own material and roam around the zoo, lead tours or be involved in outreach programs. Docent training is the largest commitment; it begins each autumn and lasts for seven months.

www.denverzoo.org/involved/volunteer.asp

(see Chapter 9). In some cases, there are legal requirements regarding the training and qualifications volunteers need to complete. This is most common where there are health and safety restrictions. For example, volunteers operating a preserved steam railway need to comply with transport safety legislation (Wallace, 2006).

Programs that require ongoing training also offer development opportunities for volunteers who wish to take their volunteering further and improve their knowledge or skills. This may be of particular value to serious leisure volunteers wanting to pursue a career in their volunteering (Stebbins, 1992). Denver Zoo volunteer program (Box 7.1) offers three levels of training, each progressing from the previous level, in order for volunteers to move from being a Zoo Ambassador to Guide to Docent. There is no requirement, however, for volunteers to progress through these levels so the degree of development opportunities is up to the volunteer.

Research by the British Association of Friends of Museums (BAFM, 1998) found some disparity in managers' and volunteers' perceptions of training, with 74% of managers at heritage attractions in the United Kingdom reporting that they delivered induction training and only 34% of volunteers at the same attractions reporting that they received this. One factor may be different expectations of training and delivery. Induction delivered one-to-one by a manager or experienced volunteer may not be viewed as formal training by a volunteer. However it is delivered, good practice requires training to be accompanied by supporting documentation, for example, an induction handbook.

Attraction volunteer training programs are most commonly organized in-house and delivered by managers and experienced volunteers (and therefore become part of these volunteers' development too). In-house organization may explain why many training programs are short as they rely on staff time and expertise. Large organizations such as Conservation Volunteers Australia (see Web Resource 7.1) are more likely to have the resources and numbers to develop in-house qualifications to give their volunteers the opportunity to obtain a certificate recognizing their contribution, skills and knowledge. Other attractions involve outside agencies, as at the Australia War Memorial (Chapter 11), and Birmingham Back to Backs, a National Trust attraction in Central England (www.nationaltrust.org.uk), which offers new volunteers a certificate in tour guiding taught in conjunction with a local college.

Another model for training programs is when the volunteer program operates as a separate association from the attraction (see Chapter 4). Existing volunteers organize the training in partnership with paid staff at the attraction. Kings Park and Botanic Garden is one of the leading attractions in Perth, Australia. Kings Park Guides is a separate, entirely voluntary association to the Botanic Garden and Parks Authority (BGPA) who manage the park and garden. The training program for new guides is organized and administered by Kings Park Guides but in partnership with BGPA. Organizing and conducting training for new volunteers also serves as a development opportunity for existing experienced guides (www.bgpa.wa.gov.au).

HOST VOLUNTEERS: DESTINATION SERVICE ORGANIZATIONS

Destination service organizations also need to provide orientation and training as most roles involve information delivery so volunteers need a good level of knowledge about the destination, matched with customer service skills. As with attractions, there is considerable variation in the length of training programs even for volunteers undertaking similar roles. For example, in the United States, North Carolina's Charlotte Douglas International Airport requires new volunteer meet-and-greeters to undertake just one day's training, which addresses customer service, security and the layout of the airport (www.charmeck.org/Departments/Airport). In contrast, Hong Kong's Airport Ambassador Program requires participants to undergo 10 days of initial training (Box 7.2).

BOX 7.2 TRAINING AND DEVELOPMENT OF AIRPORT AMBASSADORS AT HONG KONG INTERNATIONAL AIRPORT, HONG KONG

The Airport Ambassador Program was launched in 2002 to enhance customer service standards at Hong Kong International Airport. Airport Ambassadors provide information, directions and assistance to travelers and approximately 200 new volunteers are recruited each year. Senior Ambassadors (aged 55 and above) and Student Ambassadors are all volunteers. Youth Ambassadors (18- to 24 year olds who do not hold a degree) receive a small stipend and on-the-job training. This latter program is for those wanting to develop a career in aviation and tourism; it is highly competitive, receiving 300 applications in the first 6 months of 2008 alone.

Ambassadors are required to undergo 10 days of training on the airport's operations, emergency response and customer care. Further development opportunities are offered to high-performing Youth Ambassadors who are promoted to leadership roles to train and manage other Ambassadors. The Airport Authority also hosts 20 summer internships where participants receive training and experience in a variety of departments including passenger terminal management, retailing, corporate communication and human resources.

---

www.hongkongairport.com/ see Airport Services/Facilities.

Hong Kong Airport Authority (2007) *Annual Report 2006/07.* HKAA.

As with other settings, the level of training required depends largely on the role that volunteers will undertake as well as practical considerations. Campground hosts are usually supported by paid staff, such as national park rangers, to whom problems can be referred. However, postings may be spread out geographically and training sessions can provide important team building and social opportunities for otherwise isolated volunteers. Surf life-savers, on the other hand, are entirely responsible for the safety of swimmers on their shift, emotionally if not legally. Training for surf life-savers is ongoing and follows national minimum standards, for example through passing exams. At Surf Life-Saving South Africa's 118 clubs, training begins for junior club members at age 8 and continues until they receive their Life Saving Award at the age of 18 years. Surf life-savers are then expected to maintain their skills and demonstrate this proficiency regularly and club activities such as competitions are designed to facilitate this (www.lifesaving. co.za). This again highlights the difference between training to perform a role and development to pursue a career within an activity (Stebbins, 1992).

HOST VOLUNTEERS: EVENTS

For events, the timing of training delivery is crucial and training can be a way of maintaining contact and motivation in the build up to an event. Monga and Treuren (2001) established that positive early experiences through training can significantly improve volunteering effectiveness. Training can include orientation about the event, venue/site training and role-specific training. Training should set out the volunteer's role and responsibilities as well as logistical and practical information (see Web Resource 7.2: The Great American Beer Festival).

The intensive nature of event volunteering means that while volunteers will certainly be learning on-the-job, there is little time for formal on-the-job training and training sessions should occur before the event is held. The induction and training for events again depends on the size and frequency of the event. For periodic events relying on a returning group of volunteers, training may take the form of a preseason briefing as discussed above in relation to seasonal attractions. For new volunteers, new and one-off events, training will need to be more comprehensive. For small-scale events and festivals, the training can largely take place on the day, although a pre-event training session is preferable and can also play an important social role in creating a team spirit among volunteers and other staff.

The large number of volunteers at mega events means that the training program is a more serious undertaking and requires a structured approach. The long lead-in period means training can be staged and used to keep recruited volunteers motivated and involved (see Chapter 16: Melbourne Commonwealth Games). A preevent training program can also be used to support under-represented and socially excluded groups to volunteer (e.g. see Chapter 17: Newham Volunteers). In the lead up to mega events, other events can be used to test various aspects of event planning and operation, including volunteer management practices. These events give volunteers the opportunity to develop their skills, knowledge and experience, and build team spirit and anticipation. For example at the Sydney Olympic Games in 2000, volunteers were involved in 43 test events (Lynch, 2001). Through training and volunteering at test or other events, a pool of trained and experienced volunteers can be built up. Chapter 17 discusses Newham Volunteers, a program set up by a local council in anticipation of the 2012 London Olympic Games.

As with other host settings, volunteering in roles involving contact with event visitors, including international tourists, has implications for training requirements, particularly customer service skills. At events attracting a range of spectators and competitors, training needs to incorporate learning not just about the event but also the host location (Kemp, 2002). Training can also increase volunteers' capacity to deal with public health, emergency management roles and security aspects of events (Earl, Parker, Edwards, & Carpa, 2004; Walker, 2002).

GUESTS: VOLUNTEER TOURISM

To maximize the positive outcomes for all involved, it is crucial to support volunteer tourists before their trip (pre-departure preparation), in the destination (in-country orientation) and when they return home (debriefing) (Raymond, 2007). Chapters 18 and 19 detail the training offered to volunteer tourists at each stage by BTCV and Greenforce, with the BTCV case study also emphasizing the role of training to prepare and support the volunteer leaders of conservation holidays.

Pre-departure information and training is important to set the expectations of volunteers, including providing a realistic idea of what they will be able to achieve in their limited time on a project. Raymond (2008, p. 56) highlights the importance of developing an appropriate attitude so that volunteer tourists arrive at their destination 'with an open mind and a willingness to learn'. In their report on international volunteering, NGO Tourism Concern recommends that volunteer tourism organizations require all volunteers to participate in appropriate preplacement training and preparation (Power, 2007). However, the amount and structure of training will differ depending on the type of volunteer tourism experience (Callanan and

Thomas, 2005). This is particularly evident in variations in pre-departure preparation. For a shallow VolunTourism trip, extensive pre-departure training is unlikely to be cost-effective or even required due to the short duration of the trip and the volunteering component, the tasks undertaken by the volunteer tourists and the lack of skills required. Nevertheless, information is still required pre-departure and is typically delivered online or through a printed itinerary. In contrast, a deep volunteer tourism program will involve extensive pre-departure training. This can start at the selection stage and continue through a briefing course delivered before a volunteer travels to their placement. For example, for their two-year volunteer placements in developing countries VSA Aotearoa New Zealand has a two-day interview process, which includes information about VSA, volunteering and the proposed assignment. Successful candidates then attend a comprehensive four-day briefing course (www.vsa.org.nz).

As with event volunteers, training enables the volunteer tourism organization to keep in touch with episodic volunteers in the build up to the actual volunteering activity. This lead up period can be both 'exciting and scary' (McGehee and Santos, 2005, p. 773) and volunteers who have signed up (and paid) 'craved support from the organisation in which they had placed their faith and resources'.

Background information on the destination and project are continued during in-country induction, which should include input from the host organization and project partners. There are further parallels with episodic event volunteers who also need to develop knowledge and skills in a relatively short time. This period may include extensive skills training and even qualifications to enable volunteers to undertake their allocated role safely and effectively (see Chapter 19: Greenforce). The orientation may be the first time a group of volunteer tourists have met each other and so has an important socialization and team-building function. The personal and skills development gained through training are important rewards derived by volunteer tourists (see Chapter 8).

While volunteer tourism is an episodic experience, participants are also likely to require support after their volunteering is completed. Debriefing can be seen as part of the longer-term development of volunteer tourists. Many participants, even those on shorter trips, find leaving a project can be hard (Hindle, 2007). Not only can volunteer tourists experience culture shock after arriving at a destination, reverse cultural shock can also occur where volunteers find it difficult to adjust following their return home (Broad, 2003; Leigh, 2006; McGehee and Santos, 2005).

In-country debriefing should be followed by contact with the returned volunteer (Raymond, 2007). While the Tourism Concern study (Power,

2007) found many organizations provide this, it is often by telephone, email or even a postal follow-up, rather than in person. Again, the form of the debriefing will differ depending on the nature and duration of the volunteer tourism experience. It can help the volunteer to reflect on their volunteering experience and should be part of an organization's monitoring and evaluation of their program. This feedback should also be passed on to host and partner organizations. Debriefing can develop alumni networks and encourage participants to continue their volunteering either at home or as returning volunteer tourists. These issues are discussed further in Chapter 8.

REFLECTIONS ON TRAINING AND DEVELOPING VOLUNTEERS

The research reviewed in this chapter highlights the important role that induction and training play within any volunteer program. If volunteers' time is to be utilized effectively and their role performed well, then they need to be properly briefed and trained in whatever that role might be. Added to this, learning about the organization and its services is frequently an important motivator for volunteers. Induction for new volunteers and ongoing training also help in building a volunteer team. The need for volunteers to complete their activities as a team varies depending on their role and the tourism setting. For example, volunteer tour guides typically operate alone whereas a volunteer tourism program may require volunteers to complete a task together, such as building a school.

A volunteer's need for training may also relate to their motivation. A younger volunteer seeking work experience leading to paid employment, such as the Youth Ambassadors at Hong Kong airport (Box 7.2), may relish opportunities to gain skills and qualifications, which will help them in this. Leisure volunteers may prefer training which is combined with social activities. Leisure volunteers may also seek a career in their volunteering and look for opportunities for further development, whether through knowledge acquisition, skills development or promotion to a more skilled role.

Training can be delivered in a variety of forms: as a one-off induction; regular briefings; on the job or as a lengthy introductory training course. Mentoring can play an important role in development. Internally this can be a buddy system between experienced and new volunteers but for small volunteer-run organizations, managers and trustees can also benefit from professional development and mentoring opportunities (Hede and Rentschler, 2007). Managers must ensure that whatever and however training is offered, any legal requirements are met, for example with health and safety briefings. As many tourism volunteers have a visitor management role, they can be responsible for the health and safety of the visitors and spectators and other clients as well as themselves.

Volunteer programs, which seek to create a longer legacy for an event or attract a more diverse group of volunteers, will need to tailor their training programs to the needs of nontraditional volunteers. Examples of these programs are presented in Chapter 9. Volunteers at the Imperial War Museum North (Box 9.1) need help with basic skills such as literacy and numeracy as well as building their confidence. Chapter 17 presents a case study of Newham Volunteers where the actual volunteer program serves as a lengthy experiential training course in preparation for the 2012 London Olympic Games.

Entry to a profession or at least postgraduate study can often require experience that is most commonly gained through volunteering. This is largely the case in the museum and conservation management professions, but in other areas (e.g. event management) commitment and experience demonstrated through volunteering is often seen as desirable if not essential. While these motivated volunteers can be beneficial to their host organization, it raises questions of whether the volunteer effort is compulsory, rather than voluntary (see Chapter 1), and not being able to volunteer (or afford to volunteer) may act as a barrier to a career (also see Chapter 9).

While regular and seasonal volunteers may seek ongoing development opportunities, episodic volunteers need debriefing at the end of the event or volunteer vacation. Debriefing helps volunteers to reflect on what they have learnt and also provides feedback to the program organizers. There is also a social element to debriefing as it brings together the volunteer team for one last meeting. This debriefing can aid with retention either by encouraging volunteers to bounce-back or to volunteer for another program, for example, volunteer tourists may volunteer in their home location (see Chapter 8).

PRINCIPLES FOR GOOD PRACTICE

- New volunteers should be given an introduction to the organization and their role as part of an orientation program.

- Returning volunteers should be given a refresher induction to the new season, event or program.

- Training sessions should involve a social element to help build team spirit among volunteers.

- Managers should try to involve experienced volunteers in induction and training as this provides development for these volunteers as well as benefiting new recruits.

- Managers should provide development opportunities for those volunteers who seek them.

- Training can be used to maintain contact and interest from volunteers between seasons or reoccurring events and, for episodic volunteering, in the period between recruitment and the event or vacation.

- A debriefing session should be provided for episodic volunteers after the event or volunteer tourism program has finished.

DISCUSSION QUESTIONS

Q7.1 Choose a tourism volunteering organization (an attraction, event, destination service or volunteer tourism provider). What would you include in an orientation or induction session for new volunteers?

Q7.2 What is the difference between training and development for volunteers?

Q7.3 How can training be used to ensure retention of a group of volunteers in the downtime between an annual event?

FURTHER EXAMPLES

Web Resource 7.1: Conservation Volunteers Australia Certificate in Active Volunteering, Australia

Web Resource 7.2: Training New Volunteers at the Great American Beer Festival, United States

RESOURCES

Energize Inc. www.energizeinc.com/art/subj/train.html

Volunteering Australia training resources. www.volunteeringaustralia.org

Volunteering England training resources, see Good Practice Bank. www.volunteering.org.uk/Resources/goodpracticebank

CHAPTER 8

Rewarding and Retaining Volunteers

INTRODUCTION

Volunteering is based on the principle of reciprocity, so recognizing and rewarding volunteers is an integral part of satisfying their motivations and retaining their services. Recruiting, selecting, and orientating new volunteers can be time consuming and costly (see Chapters 6 and 7); it is therefore important to consider rewarding and retaining the volunteers already involved. This can keep ongoing volunteers engaged but is also important for getting seasonal and episodic volunteers to re-engage, or bounce-back, each season or each time the event is held. Research on volunteers' length of service shows that with good reward and retention policies, organizations can hope to gain many years of support (BAFM, 1998; Holmes, 2003). Few studies, however, collect data on retention rates, turn-over or length of service, focusing rather on snapshot surveys.

Reward is the outcome of understanding volunteers' motivation by seeking to meet their needs. As volunteering is a discretionary activity—that is volunteers are relatively free to enter and leave the relationship—they will usually continue volunteering if they find the experience rewarding and satisfying. Good practice in volunteer management recommends that although volunteers are not paid, they should be provided with appropriate rewards (McCurley and Lynch, 1998). Rewards are a way of informing volunteers that the organization recognizes their contributions, and can include:

- special events such as a Christmas party or end-of-season celebration;
- special access such as behind-the-scenes tours at an attraction or tickets to an event;
- volunteer of the month or year awards or outstanding contribution awards at an event or volunteer tourism project;

CONTENTS

Managing Volunteers in Tourism
Copyright © 2009 Elsevier Ltd. All rights reserved.

- certificate of service, presented by a member of the senior management team;

- showcasing volunteer contributions on the organization's website or newsletter, or in external publications such as newspaper coverage; and

- tangible ways of identifying with the organization, such as T-shirt/ uniform.

Unfortunately, some organizations concentrate on tokenistic tangible rewards such as a tiepin or small gift. However, studies show that volunteers value intangible rather than direct tangible rewards (Goodlad and McIvor, 1998). Material rewards such as free admission and discounts are the least important reasons for volunteering (Caldwell and Andereck, 1994; Williams et al., 1995); the most valued rewards are verbal or written appreciation (Low et al., 2007), such as simply saying 'thank you'. In 1985, the United Nations General Assembly created an annual International Volunteer Day on 5th December; this can be used as a time to publicly thank, recognize, and promote volunteers' contributions. Opportunities for development, further responsibility, and promotion can also serve as important rewards (Chapter 7).

While a verbal 'thank you' from managers, staff, other volunteers, or visitors is both effective and free, most other rewards involve costs to the organization (see Chapter 3). For this reason, rewards are frequently offered in return for a minimum level of service (typically a specified number of hours over a set period; see Box 8.1: National Trust Volunteer Reward Scheme); this should ensure that the organization receives a cost and time-effective return on the investment in recruitment, training, development and rewards. Organizations involving ongoing, seasonal and episodic volunteers will need to consider how they value all these contributions. While it may be appropriate to tailor rewards to different groups of volunteers, or scale rewards on an incremental basis, this must be balanced with clear recognition of all contributions. So, for example, only inviting ongoing but not seasonal or episodic volunteers to an annual volunteer recognition event sends the message that there is a hierarchy of service, which is incompatible with volunteer trends toward more flexible volunteering. Inviting all volunteers could also inspire some episodic volunteers to become more involved.

Just as volunteers have their own personal set of motivations, each volunteer will also value rewards differently. Given the costs involved, it is important to implement a recognition program that is appropriate and effective as well as continually reassess volunteers' motivations, rewards and levels of satisfaction, as these are likely to change over time (Green and

Chalip, 1998; Pearce, 1993). Reward is also about managing volunteers' expectations and as such is part of recruitment, training and support so that volunteers' expectations are met. Indeed the recruitment process and training strategy should be used to 'inspire volunteers with positive, albeit realistic, expectations regarding their entire experience' (Ralston et al., 2004, p. 17).

Managing volunteers' expectations is a crucial part of maintaining their psychological contract with the organization. A psychological contract is the term used to describe the informal reciprocal agreement of a work environment, between a (paid) employee and their employing organization from the perspective of the individual (Rousseau, 1995). This is separate from their actual contract of employment. Researchers have argued that as volunteers are not paid they have a different psychological contract to paid employees (Holmes, 2003; Taylor, Darcy, Hoye, & Cuskelly, 2006), but the nature of the volunteers' psychological contract has rarely been investigated (also see Chapter 17: Newham Volunteers). It is clear, however, that volunteers do develop psychological contracts with their organizations and they will respond to perceived breaches in these contracts by changing their behavior by, for example, reducing their hours (Starnes, 2007). Ralston et al. (2004, p. 24) warn 'there is a fine line between perception of breach of the psychological contract and violation'.

Retention is a form of relationship marketing that 'requires building a relationship with the volunteer, monitoring the benefits volunteers seek, and continually marketing those benefits back to the volunteer' (Green and Chalip, 1998, p. 19). Retention may seem more important for organizations involving volunteers on an ongoing and seasonal basis, but it is equally important for periodic events. Indeed the intention to return is a sign of an event's success (Williams et al., 1995). Successful retention has a number of benefits: returning volunteers will be familiar with the organization and their role and high retention rates mean lower recruitment costs and reduced training requirements. Retaining experienced volunteers has the potential to impact on volunteer's effectiveness and levels of service delivery.

Retention is not simply about having an appropriate reward scheme. The rewards have to be balanced against inevitable downsides, with volunteers evaluating whether, overall, the volunteering experience satisfies their motivations. The UK *Helping Out* study (Low et al., 2007) highlighted downsides including criticisms of how volunteering is organized, the amount of bureaucracy and not being able to leave as there is no one to take over. Despite this last point, it is also vitally important that the organization does not place demands on the volunteer that become too onerous. These could include expecting the volunteer to bear increasing costs, such as travel, which makes it too expensive for them to volunteer or demanding more in terms of time contribution or activities from the volunteer. The latter can lead to volunteer burnout, where the activity or the organization's demands become too stressful (McCurley and Lynch, 2005) and volunteers can develop a feeling of lack of accomplishment, emotional depletion and adopt a negative attitude toward their activities (Maslach and Jackson, 1986). Mellor et al. (2008) found that volunteers who contributed more than 15 hours a week were at risk of developing such feelings and reported reduced levels of personal well-being. Chapter 13 (St John River Society) demonstrates some of the difficulties that can arise when volunteers take on multiple volunteering responsibilities, for example, as board members and operational volunteers.

Recognizing the reasons why someone might decide to leave is also part of volunteer management. Sheard (1995) identifies four factors in a volunteer's decision to withdraw: a change in personal circumstances (e.g. ill health or moving home or job); overinvolvement; disenchantment; and reasons connected with the organization such as poor administration and inadequate support. Low et al. (2007) found that most ex-volunteers stopped volunteering as a consequence of changing life circumstances, particularly lack of time due to changing home or work commitments, rather than a deep dissatisfaction with the organization. Nevertheless, internal organizational factors can be a source of dissatisfaction (see Chapter 15: Kongsberg Jazz Festival).

For episodic volunteers, their involvement with the organization may have a predetermined set time period; for example, for the duration of the event, project, or trip. Volunteers who start with a particular goal may leave when this is achieved; for example, a volunteer intern wanting to gain work experience leaves when they gain paid employment. Withdrawal is not necessarily negative and a turnover of volunteers can be desirable to maintain the vibrancy of the program. As Millar (1994, p. 278) points out: 'even good volunteers do not stay forever'.

It cannot be assumed that volunteers who are unhappy or dissatisfied will choose to leave; they might remain but withdraw and become less reliable, drop their standards or spread their dissatisfaction amongst other volunteers. More rarely discussed is when an organization wants to initiate the end of the volunteering relationship. Managers can find dismissing a volunteer a difficult decision, which requires sensitivity and diplomacy, but it is important to deal with problems in order to maintain standards and the health of the overall program and organization. Ideally, evaluation of the program and individual volunteers should be built in at the program design stage (see Chapter 4) and made clear at recruitment (Chapter 6). This could be an annual meeting where volunteer and manager discuss the volunteering relationship, or volunteers can be trained and encouraged to undertake self and/or peer evaluation, for example of their performance as a guide.

Unfortunately, our research has found that with seasonal and episodic volunteers managers dodge the issue and simply do not invite back a volunteer that is deemed unsuitable, which usually means someone who 'doesn't fit in'. While this is a somewhat understandable response to a difficult situation, it devalues the volunteer and their contribution. However difficult, managers need to be open with their volunteer and could suggest other opportunities within or outside the organization. 'Not fitting in' may also reflect a wider need for the organization to consider their approach to managing diversity (Chapter 9).

HOST VOLUNTEERS: ATTRACTIONS

Volunteers at attractions are generally attracted to volunteering because of their interest in the subject at the attraction (Smith, 2003), their love for the site itself or because of the volunteer activity, for example, guiding (Holmes, 2003). They are therefore self-motivated (see Chapter 5) and this partially explains the high retention rates at, for example, museums and heritage attractions.

As well as thanking volunteers and ensuring they do not incur out-of-pocket expenses, reward strategies need to focus on the reasons why volunteers become involved with the organization. If they are motivated because of their interest in the attraction's subject matter, then they need to be offered opportunities to learn more. This could be through training opportunities, talks from paid staff, a volunteer library or trips to similar attractions. If volunteers are motivated by their love for the site, then they should be offered opportunities to get to know the site better or to see parts of the site, which are not available to visitors. This again recognizes that volunteers may be part of the audience as much as part of the staff (Holmes and Edwards, 2008) (see Chapter 5).

Opportunities for social interaction are also a frequent motivator for those in front-of-house roles and these volunteers derive rewards from interacting with other volunteers, visitors, and other staff members and managers (Smith, 2002). On busy days with lots of visitors, this is easily achieved but managers also need to consider opportunities for social interaction on quiet days, particularly if single volunteers are stationed at different points over a large site. Volunteer guides may only come to the attraction when there is a tour scheduled and may rarely meet other volunteers. Social activities such as trips, talks and dinners can help facilitate team building, in a similar way to training (Chapter 7). Volunteers are often more committed to each other than to paid staff and building a sense of camaraderie among volunteers who have completed their training program together or who regularly volunteer on the same day can greatly facilitate retention.

Vancouver Aquarium, for example, summarizes its volunteer rewards as opportunities to learn, grow and have fun (www.vanaqua.org). Learning may involve working with experienced aquarium staff, delivering education programs and having access to the aquarium library. Growing, that is expanding one's horizons, could include helping a range of visitors and schoolchildren and contributing to volunteer publications. Lastly, opportunities for fun include socializing with other volunteers in the volunteer lounge, spending more time with the marine life at sleepovers and receiving a discount at the gift shop and for special events. These rewards also highlight the importance of providing appropriate facilities for volunteers to ensure that they feel a valued part of the organization. Facilities can include car parking, a volunteer room, and reference materials to aid volunteer development. Providing these rewards will bring costs to the organization (see Chapter 3) that need to be factored into program planning and design (Chapter 4). Box 8.1 demonstrates the range of rewards offered to National Trust volunteers.

Attractions often focus on providing rewards that satisfy their ongoing volunteers and keep them involved. However, seasonal and episodic volunteers offer different challenges. Many attractions are open on a seasonal basis and operate their volunteer programs accordingly. This means an organization needs to maintain their relationship with their volunteers over the closed season to maximize the likelihood of their return. Volunteers can be kept involved through closed season activities, including social events that can also serve as training opportunities (see Chapter 7). There can also be additional volunteering; for example, many National Trust properties involve seasonal room stewards in cleaning projects during the closed season. This grants them special access to the property and collection, which can be an important reward, and the knowledge gained also enables them to perform their core interpretation role more effectively. Ongoing communication with volunteers during the closed season is important, and a similar approach can be used with episodic volunteers, who may be required to assist at an attraction's special events, such as educational workshops on an as-needed basis.

BOX 8.1 NATIONAL TRUST VOLUNTEER REWARD SCHEME, UK

The National Trust for Places of Historic Interest and Natural Beauty is the UK's largest membership charity and preserves, protects and opens to the public built and natural attractions across England, Wales and Northern Ireland. Their 52,000 volunteers gave 2.3 million hours in 2007/08.

The National Trust highlights three key motivations and rewards to potential volunteers:

'What's in it for you? Volunteering with the National Trust, you can:

- Strengthen your CV and help to develop your career
- Learn new skills and develop new interests
- Make new friends and help us to protect our beautiful places' (www.nationaltrust.org.uk)

With the exception of working holidays (an example of volunteer tourism where participants pay to volunteer), National Trust volunteers can claim reasonable expenses such as travel. Chapter 12 illustrates the range of rewards for attraction volunteers, including refreshments, social events, trips to other National Trust sites and free parking. Volunteer activities and achievements are also showcased in *Active*, the National Trust's magazine for volunteers.

Volunteers who complete 50 hours of service during one year receive a Volunteer Card. Many property-based volunteers are involved as Room Stewards during the seven- to eight-month opening season, so 50 hours equates to volunteering once a fortnight. The card gives the holder free entry to all National Trust sites and a 20% discount in their restaurants and shops. If the recipient is already a member of the National Trust, which most are, then they can use their card so an accompanying friend gets free entry. The Volunteer Card is a reward that will be of value to the National Trust volunteers and reflects the volunteers' interests and motives for volunteering.

www.nationaltrust.org.uk/volunteers/

HOST VOLUNTEERS: DESTINATION SERVICE ORGANIZATIONS

With local knowledge and the development of specialist skills (e.g. emergency rescue) central to the volunteering roles and high investment in training and development, many destination service organizations recognize the importance of rewarding and retaining good volunteers. Recognizing and promoting volunteers' knowledge and skills can be a part of their rewards. This can include offering opportunities to gain qualifications, be involved with training other volunteers, writing material for publications, or giving talks to visitors or community groups. Partnership organizations can also offer opportunities for recognizing volunteer service, for example, through a familiarization program for visitor information centre volunteers. At Chicago O'Hare and Midway International airports in the United States, local attractions, shops and services show their appreciation of the Volunteer Airport Ambassadors by donating gift certificates, complementary passes and discount vouchers that are then awarded to randomly selected volunteers (www.flychicago.com/aboutus/VolunteerAmbassadors.shtm).

While some destination service organizations operate all year round, many, including campground hosts, visitor centres and surf patrols, are seasonal. Surf life-saving clubs offer a model for volunteer reward and retention, which is enabled by their club setting. Their system of continuous training ensures that volunteers develop their skills further and also increases commitment as many volunteers have invested time and effort in their training to date. While most beach patrols only operate seasonally, the club system also ensures that members are kept involved through social activities all year round. Competitions between clubs help with team building, assist with retention, as well as promoting the teamwork needed in rescue situations. Indeed, surf life-saving clubs fit well within the dimensions of serious leisure (see Introduction to Part B).

HOST VOLUNTEERS: EVENTS

In event organizations, recognition strategies often focus on the tangible rewards (such as certificates, pins, tickets to the event) although Williams et al.'s (1995) study of volunteers at Whistler's Men's World Cup skiing event found material benefits were the least important reward for volunteers. As with other settings, reward needs to be matched with the volunteer's motivation. Of more importance are those rewards which clearly identify the volunteer's affiliation with the event's prestige and reputation. These rewards can be tangible (souvenirs and uniforms) and intangible (being a valued member of the event team and the sense of camaraderie and shared purpose (Green and Chalip, 2004; Williams et al., 1995). For volunteers who are primarily interested in the subject of the event (e.g. a sport or art form), then the opportunity to participate in behind-the-scenes aspects may be rewarding. Meeting the event participants, whether they are athletes or artists is something which may not be available to an audience member. This rewards volunteers with entry into a particular subculture, and feeling and being seen as an 'insider' (Green and Chalip, 2004).

Volunteers identify a range of reward factors that contribute to a satisfying event volunteering experience, including being part of a unique event, celebratory atmosphere, social interaction and networking, public appreciation and recognition, achieving job skills and desired level of job competence (Elstad, 1997b; Kemp, 2002; Ralston et al., 2003; Solberg, 2003). While volunteer managers cannot directly control many of these external factors, they can influence them and build them into their volunteer management strategy. For example, giving volunteers the space and time to socialize and feel involved or enabling more experienced volunteers to pass on their expertise to newer volunteers.

Unlike ongoing volunteering where retention focuses on the commitment to remain a volunteer with the organization, the episodic nature of event volunteering presents different challenges. The event and volunteering can end abruptly and a lesson from the 2000 Sydney Olympic Games was the need to let people down gently and give opportunities for public recognition and continued socialization; for example, the volunteers' tickertape parade through the city (Lynch, 2001). Meeting expectations and rewarding motivations are important but the actual volunteering experience during the event itself is also crucial, including being satisfied with facilities and the organization of the event (Ralston et al., 2004; Green and Chalip, 2004; Farrell et al., 1998).

Different event volunteering retention strategies are required in the preevent, during and postevent stages (Hanlon and Jago, 2004; Cuskelly, Taylor, Hoye, & Darcy, 2006):

- *Preevent*: Once investment has been made in recruiting and training a volunteer, it is important to retain their commitment in the build up to the event delivery, which for a mega event could be a number of months (see Chapter 16: Melbourne Commonwealth Games). Attrition rates, the volunteers leaving before the event, can be high and one strategy, particularly for mega and major events, is to overrecruit in anticipation of volunteers withdrawing (Australian Sports Commission, 2000b, Volunteering Australia, 2006b), although this can mean a waste of resources. The emphasis here is on the prestige and timing of the event and the involvement of volunteers in the planning stages to engender a sense of ownership. For periodic events, this preevent period targets those who have previously volunteered and getting them to return or bounce-back to the event, much like reengaging seasonal volunteers at attractions and destination service organizations.

- *During the event*: While the event itself may be short, it is vital to retain volunteers as the nature of the psychological contract (see p. 121) means they are able to easily leave their post if they are not satisfied. During the event, volunteers require support and encouragement and the chance to debrief on issues relating to their role; this is particularly important in multiday events.

- *Postevent*: Immediately after the event, all volunteers should be thanked and recognized. This is also a chance to debrief the volunteers and gather feedback to evaluate the event's organization and the volunteer program.

At all stages, retention can be enhanced by fostering and maintaining a strong event team who are involved and interested in the subculture of the event (see Green and Chalip, 1998).

For periodic events, volunteers committed to the event can be retained and encouraged to bounce-back and re-engage with the organization in a series of episodic contributions (Bryen and Madden, 2006). Periodic events can build up a strong returning band of loyal volunteers (see Box 8.2: Honda Classic). Postevent, the retention strategy should focus on maintaining an ongoing relationship with the volunteers. As with seasonal attractions, in the period between volunteering the organizers should keep in touch through newsletters and other personal communications, and perhaps by promoting other volunteering opportunities. Elstad's research on Kongsberg Jazz Festival (2003; see Chapter 15) found that the most significant influence on retention was years as a festival volunteer: the longer a volunteer had contributed to the event, the stronger their intention to remain in the future. How the event organization treats its volunteers is important not only for rewarding and retaining existing volunteers but also creating positive word-of-mouth in the wider community about the event and volunteering, which can lead to recruitment of new volunteers (see Box 8.2: Honda Classic).

For one-time events or a roaming periodic event that moves between locations, the opportunity to volunteer at the event is a one-off, but it is possible to build on a volunteer's commitment and retain them as an active volunteer. Follow-up research with World Ice Hockey Championship volunteers (Solberg, 2003) found that while many event volunteers have good intentions toward further event, sport and other volunteering, actual rates of volunteering were lower, partly because of an absence of other major sporting events in the study area. Event legacy strategies therefore need to include a retention element that identifies and promotes alternative opportunities for volunteer participation. This can be opportunities to volunteer with other events or associated activities or voluntary activities in other areas. This longer-term legacy of increased volunteering capacity is discussed in Chapter 3.

GUESTS: VOLUNTEER TOURISM

In comparison to other forms of volunteering, volunteer tourists rarely receive the same kinds of rewards for their efforts. Chapter 3 detailed the main personal outcomes volunteer tourists gain, including personal and skills development. As paying customers, it would perhaps seem strange

BOX 8.2 RETAINING VETERAN VOLUNTEERS AT THE HONDA CLASSIC, FLORIDA, UNITED STATES

The Honda Classic is a Professional Golf Association (PGA) tournament held annually in Southern Florida since 1972. The event attracts over 90,000 spectators and over 1200 volunteers are involved, mostly during tournament week. Volunteers generally do daily shifts of between four and six hours. They are organized into 27 committees, including caddies, child care, communications, greeters, hospitality, locker room, leader-board and scoreboard, marshals, player registration, spectator information, transportation, tournament office, TV liaison, and volunteer headquarters.

Tournament Volunteer applications can be mailed or completed online and have to be accompanied by a fee (US$65 in 2009). In return for the fee and completing three shifts volunteers receive a reward package valued at US$300, including a tournament shirt, hat and name badge (with discounts for additional shirts); two weekly ticket books for admission; breakfast and lunch each day of volunteering; and two coupons to play a round of golf at any of the courses at the host venue (the PGA National Resort and Spa) at a discounted price. The event organizers also emphasize the wider beneficiaries of volunteering and the rewards this brings:

'Who benefits from the work I do?

Of course, the players and spectators greatly appreciate the efforts of our volunteers - it's no secret that the success of the event depends on our volunteer force. An enhanced experience for players, spectators and sponsors ensures our charitable giving increases. The Honda Classic has many charitable partners, though our main benefiting charity is the Nicklaus Children's Health Care Foundation' (www.thehondaclassic.com).

Coyne and Coyne (2001) investigated the recruitment, motivations and retention of volunteers at the 1997 Honda Classic. There was a high retention rate and 79% of their survey respondents were returnees or 'veteran' volunteers.

A database records volunteer's details and they are contacted each year by letter and a phone call from the committee chair. Retention strategies focus on keeping experienced volunteers as this minimizes recruitment costs and their previous involvement means they are experienced and need less training. Getting volunteers to bounce-back is 'a function of their perceptions of expectation-fulfilment from prior Honda Classic volunteering' (p. 207). The threshold motivation was 'love of golf'; without this people did not volunteer. The free round of golf was also a valued reward. These were important for both new and veteran volunteers, but otherwise motivations differed:

'the attraction for the [veteran] volunteer to re-enlist turns strongly to the interpersonal relationship areas of wanting good volunteer supervisors and enjoying the camaraderie, in addition to the satisfaction of supporting the community'. (p. 213)

Having satisfied volunteers not only bounces them back but they also act as the main recruitment method for getting new volunteers involved as they encourage and support friends to start volunteering at the event too.

---

www.thehondaclassic.com/Volunteers.aspx

Coyne, B.S., & Coyne, E.J. (2001) Getting, keeping and caring for unpaid volunteers for professional golf tournament events. *Human Resource Development International, 4*, 199–214.

---

to spend their money on tangible rewards, rather the experiences offered by the program form the basis for the volunteer rewards, such as the opportunity to meet local residents, take part in local events or to participate in close encounters with wildlife. Returned gap year volunteer tourists surveyed by Power (2007) identified the best things about their experience, the rewards, were learning about another culture, the feeling of doing something good, getting to visit another country, good experience for their CV and making new friends. In contrast, the worst things were more diverse and often criticisms of the organization and project they participated in, for example feeling unsupported, lack of organization and the attitude of local staff. Feeling out of my depth and seeing poverty were also mentioned, and there were more general criticisms of gap year volunteering and questioning of its benefits to destination communities.

The time commitment means deeper volunteer tourism, such as a gap year or a long-term volunteer vacation, is likely to occur only when a participant's circumstances mean they can donate a significant amount of time (e.g. posteducation, after retirement) or as a deliberate decision to take a break from paid employment. Shorter volunteer vacations and VolunTourism offer more opportunities to re-engage participants and attract repeat custom either through the same organization or more generally (see Chapter 18: BTCV). Each year approximately one-third of Earthwatch's 4000 volunteers are repeat volunteers, with some serial volunteers having been on more than 50 expeditions (www.earthwatch.org). Coghlan (2006) divides conservation volunteer tourists into two markets: younger volunteers (18–24 years old) may be a fast growing market and able to undertake long-term expeditions but they are not likely to be repeat volunteer tourists and are less interested or involved in conservation. Mature volunteers (50 years plus) are a more stable market but are likely to be repeat volunteer tourists who have demonstrated commitment to volunteering, conservation and travel. Although the importance of experience is alluded to (see p. 130), the notion of bounce-back volunteer tourists has received little acknowledgement in the volunteer tourism literature.

Chapter 7 has discussed reverse culture shock and the difficulties some volunteers face returning home. In addition to debriefing (Raymond, 2007), promoting opportunities for future volunteering can potentially help overcome these reassimilation challenges. This could be using skills developed through volunteer tourism in their own community, which can help with re-integration and enables returning volunteers to continue contributing and developing the sense of purpose that typically develops from longer-term volunteer tourism (Leigh, 2006). There is little discussion of the option to volunteer again internationally and become a bounce-back volunteer tourist.

The potential of volunteer tourism to change and enhance social consciousness and act as an agent of change after returning home has been discussed in Chapter 3. As well as further volunteering, *The Lonely Planet Guide* (Hindle, 2007) also promotes other ways of maintaining longer-term links with a project or destination, including starting a charitable project;

this has been an outcome of some BTCV international conservation holidays (see Chapter 18). Returned volunteers can also be retained as supporters who offer financial donations rather (or as well as) time. As with other forms of volunteer tourism, word-of-mouth is a key recruitment tool (Chapter 6) and most advice sites for would-be volunteer tourists suggest talking to returned volunteers as a way of learning about the experience and organization.

REFLECTIONS ON REWARDING AND RETAINING VOLUNTEERS

This chapter has emphasized the importance of providing appropriate rewards and recognition to maintain volunteers' motivation and aid in retention. There is, however, debate around what kinds of rewards can or should be offered. Tangible rewards tend to be less important for volunteers than intangible rewards and rewards also need to be matched to the volunteer's motivation. As retention is closely linked to motivating volunteers and meeting their needs, retention strategies should start with program design, in creating attractive volunteer roles and rewards and properly resourcing the volunteer program (see Chapter 4).

It helps to separate out rewards, such as behind-the-scenes tours and Christmas parties, and recognition, such as an acknowledgement of length of service or a volunteer's particular contribution. While rewards are about meeting the volunteers' needs, recognition is about showing how important the volunteers are to the organization. These two factors are interrelated but not interchangeable. Some rewards, such as travel and out-of-pocket expenses, may be considered by volunteers as more of a right than a reward. Indeed, good practice recommends that these should be provided. Both reward and recognition must be fair to all volunteers.

A further way of both rewarding and recognizing volunteers is to involve them more in the organization, particularly in decisions or areas which affect them. Changing the opening hours of an attraction, for example, can have a major impact on the volunteers and should not be done without consulting them. Furthermore, volunteers are often the people most likely to come into contact with the visitors and they are therefore well placed for commenting on any proposed changes to the visitor experience or service. Asking volunteers for their input shows that their experience and perceptions are valued beyond their immediate role. This is particularly important when volunteers have been recruited because of a particular skill; this needs to be recognized and full use made of the volunteer's experience otherwise they may become frustrated and disenchanted with their role.

Traditional forms of reward and recognition may need to be adjusted in response to the changing climate for volunteering. While a minimum contribution can ensure a return on the organization's investment, it is also important to acknowledge that rewards and recognition based on long-service (such as the National Trust Volunteer Card, see Box 8.1) may not be as appropriate if volunteers are more likely to be episodic and short term. Organizations may need to reward volunteers based on specific activities or may need to devise group rewards for family, employee or team volunteering. Bounce-back volunteering can be encouraged by offering first choice of roles to previous volunteers or development opportunities such as supervising an event team in subsequent years or undertaking training to become a volunteer leader on a volunteer tourism program.

While we have focused on retention in this chapter, leaving a program can be a positive (and unavoidable) step for many volunteers. Frequently, volunteers leave for personal reasons such as family commitments, starting or leaving full-time study or moving to a new area. Ideally the organization will facilitate their departure in such a way as to encourage the volunteer to join a new program, which better suits their new circumstances. An alternative, if the volunteer is not moving out of the area, is to offer a sabbatical rather than require them to leave the organization completely. The volunteer manager should try to conduct a brief exit interview with the volunteer, which can be useful in identifying problems with the program but is also a final opportunity to thank the volunteer for their contribution to the organization. For volunteer tourists, leaving a program can be difficult and debrief training can help the reassimilation into their home environment (see Chapter 7). Completing their holiday can be just the first step in an ongoing relationship with the organization, cause, destination, or volunteering. Repeat custom can be encouraged, particularly for shorter volunteer tourism, and returned volunteers can be directed towards home-based volunteering and becoming monetary donors.

Finally, discipline and dismissal are often seen as difficult and sensitive areas where organizations are reluctant to exert authority. Nevertheless, this is an essential part of the good management of volunteers. Poor morale and other difficulties can have social and personal repercussions (Wilson and Pimm, 1996), which can quickly spread through an organization as the result of ignoring a disciplinary issue. A poorly handled, or avoided, problem can breed resentment, engender bad publicity, and can ultimately lead to decreased support, both in terms of volunteers and donations.

PRINCIPLES FOR GOOD PRACTICE

- Reward and recognition are closely linked to motivation and should aim to meet volunteers' needs.

- Bringing the volunteers behind-the-scenes emphasizes the special relationship they have with an organization.

- Organizations should offer volunteers intangible rewards, which are more highly valued than tangible rewards.

- Reward can be used to keep in touch with volunteers over closed seasons, between events, or encourage repeat custom from volunteer tourists.

- Organizations need to be flexible and allow volunteers to come and go, rather than lose them completely.

- The exit of a volunteer from an organization needs to be positively and sensitively handled.

DISCUSSION QUESTIONS

Q8.1 For a tourism volunteer program you are familiar with, what are the rewards and recognition offered to volunteers? Divide these into tangible rewards, intangible rewards and recognition.

Q8.2 How can the closed season be used to encourage retention from seasonal volunteers?

Q8.3 What can tourism volunteer organizations do to increase their level of bounce-back volunteers or repeat customers?

RESOURCES

McCurley, S., & Lynch, R. (2005). Keeping Volunteers: a Guide to Retention. Fat Cat Publications.

Volunteering Australia (2009). *Recognising and Awarding Volunteers*. Available: www.volunteering.com.au

Volunteering Canada (2009). *Volunteer Management: Recognition – Recognition Guidelines*. Available: volunteer.ca

CHAPTER 9

Managing Diversity

INTRODUCTION

Managing the diversity of volunteers should be an integral part of program design and management. We have placed this chapter toward the end of the management part of this book in order to reflect on how current management practices in tourism organizations largely fail to address issues of diversity at either a sectoral or organizational level. This chapter will first review the reasons for a diversity management approach before looking at a number of best practice cases of tourism volunteer programs that have targeted nontypical populations and successfully widened participation in tourism volunteering.

In Chapter 1 we highlighted that volunteering participation rates are not consistent across a population, with particular groups of individuals more likely to volunteer than others. While there is some variation in age, the people who are most likely to volunteer are in employment, have higher levels of educational attainment, occupational status and income levels and are from the dominant ethnic group (see Table 1.1). Under-represented groups include ethnic minorities, immigrants, (both of which can incorporate people with culturally and linguistically diverse (CALD) backgrounds), those with a disability or long-term illness and people with no formal qualifications (Finlay and Murray, 2005; Low et al., 2007; Zappalà & Burrell, 2001). These are groups often facing 'social exclusion' from full participation in economic, social and political life (IVR, 2004). Yet volunteering can be particularly beneficial for these individuals and communities and has the potential to combat social exclusion through empowerment, ending personal isolation, developing skills, improving employability and generating a sense of satisfaction and well-being through helping others (IVR, 2004). At a government, sector and organizational level, there have been attempts to target these groups and address barriers to volunteering (see Chapter 1) in order to increase the diversity of volunteers.

Diversity management is a strategic approach which values individual differences beyond the basic variables of age, ethnicity, disability, gender, race and sexuality (Mavin & Girling, 2000) and seeks to enable individuals to achieve their full potential (McDougall, 1996). Diversity management, and its forerunner equal opportunities, has a long history in paid employment but its application to unpaid voluntary staff is relatively recent. The drive for diversity management within volunteer programs can be summarized into four key arguments:

- The *ethical case* argues that diversity is morally right, that volunteering opportunities should be available to everyone;

- The *economic case* is also known as the *business case* for diversity (Cassell, 2001), whereby an organization whose workforce reflects that of their market is likely to be more successful;

- The *legal case* is simply that all organizations should ensure that they comply with antidiscrimination legislation but also, in the case of organizations in receipt of public funding, the legal case cites the statutory duty of public bodies to promote equality and eliminate discrimination; and

- The *social case* advocates the benefits of a pluralist society, where different cultural groups can 'co-exist and interact without conflict of assimilation' (Hylton, 2004, p. 5). The social case draws on social capital discourse, whereby the whole of society benefits from a broad range of individuals volunteering.

Many Western governments stress the social case, seeing volunteering as a means of engaging people in public life and engendering a sense of civicness, with voluntary activity being a key contributor to social capital (Putnam, 2000. Also see Chapter 3). National peak bodies for volunteering typically use business case arguments for promoting diversity within volunteer programs. They have developed resources to encourage diversity within volunteering; for example, Volunteering Australia have resources for involving Indigenous Australians, those from CALD backgrounds (particularly Australian Muslim communities), people with a disability, those living in remote and rural areas, young people, baby boomers, families, and corporate volunteers. Similarly, Volunteering England's resources include support for involving refugees, asylum seekers and migrants; ex-offenders, offenders and prisoners; and volunteers who are lesbian, gay, bisexual or transgender.

In each case, organizations need to consider the specific needs of these groups and individuals in order to be inclusive, welcoming and supportive to potential and actual volunteers.

Managing diversity can bring positive outcomes not just for individuals and society more widely, but also for the organization, its clients and community. These include a wider pool of volunteers for an organization to draw on; new perspectives and experiences that volunteers from diverse backgrounds can bring; improved relationships with the wider community, not least by hosting an accessible and inclusive program that reflects the diversity of that community; and increased awareness of the needs of clients and communities and enhanced service provision (Volunteering Australia, 2006a). The Institute for Volunteering Research (2004) identifies how organizations can work toward overcoming barriers to volunteering by making the organization and opportunities more flexible and inclusive. Strategies include:

- targeted recruitment campaigns and making recruitment and selection 'user-friendly' (e.g. minimal form filling);

- building capacity for volunteering among those who lack the confidence to get involved (e.g. open days and prevolunteer training);

- a flexible approach to job allocation and developing roles that match the individual volunteer's capabilities rather than trying to fit them into an existing position;

- creating an inclusive environment (e.g. through training staff and current volunteers, and improving physical accessibility); and

- supporting volunteers once they have joined an organization (e.g. through peer support, training and recognition).

We have seen in Chapters 1 and 2 that tourism volunteering has proved attractive to younger and older volunteers, groups who typically have a lower propensity to volunteer. While there are some substantial differences in volunteer profiles between tourism organizations, this is largely related to the type of activity or interest they encompass and at the level of the individual volunteer program, there is considerable homogeneity. For example:

- Volunteers at the West Somerset Railway are predominately older white males, many of whom are retired (Rhoden, Ineson, & Ralston, 2009), which reflects the profile of preserved steam railway volunteers more generally (Holmes, 1999);

- A study of volunteers who rescue tourists in difficulty in the Israeli desert (Uriely et al., 2002) revealed that they were male, mostly aged under 45 years, highly educated and had served in the army (see Box 5.1: Fast Israeli Rescue and Search Team volunteers);

- Queensland 500 V8 supercar race volunteers are mostly male, blue collar workers, who are educated to high-school level (Harrington, Cuskelly, & Auld, 2000);

- Volunteer tourists on a Habitat for Humanity project in South Africa (Stoddart & Rogerson, 2004) were diverse in terms of age, although the largest groups were early retirees and young people. Many had professional and managerial backgrounds and most were from the United States. Habitat for Humanity is a grassroots ecumenical Christian organization and most respondents identified with a Christian denomination.

A homogenous profile is not unexpected given the reliance on word-of-mouth and membership development recruitment strategies (Chapter 6). The availability of different groups is also determined by the times (of the year, week and day) when tourism organizations require volunteers (see Chapter 4). This can limit tourism volunteering to those who have free time during the week (e.g. retired volunteers dominating in attractions) or can devote longer periods to volunteering (e.g. young people dominating volunteer tourism). A homogenous group of volunteers, not least one that has a shared interest, can make bonding, socialization and team development relatively easy, which can be attractive to both managers and volunteers. However, for the reasons discussed above, tourism organizations are encouraged to pursue diversity management, although this is likely to require additional time and financial resources, such as investment in training (see Box 9.1: Imperial War Museum North). This is a big ask for organizations who have limited resources, capacity and volunteer management expertise. Organizations who are struggling to recruit enough volunteers can find that incorporating a diversity management approach can lead to a redesign of the volunteer program to widen their recruitment pool and bring new volunteers that invigorate their program and organization.

VOLUNTEER HOSTS: ATTRACTIONS

In countries such as the United Kingdom, diversity management in attractions is driven by a social inclusion agenda and the business or economic

BOX 9.1 TARGETING VOLUNTEER DIVERSITY AT THE IMPERIAL WAR MUSEUM NORTH, UK

The Imperial War Museum opened a new site in Manchester in 2002. The Imperial War Museum North (IWMN) is situated in an area that has a higher than average proportion of residents with a limiting long-term illness or describing their general health as 'not good'; a lower proportion holding qualifications at degree level or higher; and a higher proportion of households without a car or van; all indicators of deprivation.

Various IWMN initiatives aim to involve the local community in the museum and give local people a sense of ownership. The volunteer program focuses on people who have not previously considered volunteering and are not regular museum goers. Target groups are: long-term unemployed; people with low skill levels and outdated skills; nonlearners – people who have been out of the education system for a number of years and/or have become disengaged with learning; young people (older than 16 years) at risk of exclusion and or/offending; and asylum seekers and refugees (north.iwm.org.uk).

Volunteers are recruited in small intakes three times a year. Opportunities for learning and skills development are central to the program and new volunteers follow a training schedule with a local further education college, which can include English skills if required. Initially recruitment to the program was through outreach and the Volunteer Co-ordinator visited community groups and libraries. Currently, social-care professionals refer many participants as the target populations often do not have the confidence to apply directly to the museum and are unlikely to even know about the program. Volunteers receive expenses for travel, lunch and childcare so they are not left out-of-pocket; this is important in order attract the target population for whom the costs of volunteering can be a major barrier (Teasdale, 2008).

While the museum supports the volunteer program (e.g. the Volunteer Co-ordinator position is core-funded), it is financially independent and funding is the biggest challenge (IWMN, 2006). IWMN has been able to access various national government, European Union and lottery funding schemes designed to support at-risk groups and this has meant that the program has had to evolve in response to changes in the availability and priorities of funders. The program is also supported by a number of sponsors. Most recently, the IWMN has partnered with Manchester Museum (www.museum.manchester.ac.uk) and secured three years funding from the Heritage Lottery Fund to deliver the 'In Touch' volunteer program. This integrates 'culturally and socially excluded individuals into the Museums' Learning and Access teams, giving them the confidence and skills to become lifelong learners, museum users and contributors to the Museums' delivery and development' (north.iwm.org.uk).

IWMN (2006). *Imperial War Museum North's Volunteer Program.* Available: north.iwm.org.uk/upload/pdf/SummaryReport.pdf

Teasdale, S. (2008). *Volunteering among Groups Deemed at Risk of Social Exclusion.* Institute of Volunteering Research.

north.iwm.org.uk/server/show/nav.2524

case. This is most evident in audience development strategies targeting the diversity of visitors, but has also fed through to workforce diversity programs. For example, it is argued that there is a clear link in museums between a diverse workforce (including volunteers), a diverse program of exhibitions, and attracting and meeting the needs of a diverse audience (Sandell, 2001). Traditionally, in the United Kingdom, museum workforces and audiences have been white, middle class and highly educated (DEMOS, 2003; MORI, 2001). This homogeneity is also evident in the profile of volunteers (Howlett et al., 2005), with the majority also middle-aged or retired (IVR, 2005).

Many human-made and natural attractions receive a substantial part of their funding from public sources and so are under pressure to attract an audience more representative of the wider population and contribute to addressing social exclusion amongst disadvantaged communities. A criticism of many museum workforce diversity initiatives is their almost exclusive focus on cultural diversity and the outcomes for audiences. One museum that has adopted a much broader approach to volunteer diversity is the Imperial War Museum North (Box 9.1). Their approach shows how a volunteer program can be developed to create wider benefits for the participants and society and also illustrates the need for active recruitment to target nontraditional volunteers.

Diversity has also been identified as a challenge facing those involving volunteers in the natural outdoors, including natural attractions, with a clear lack of ethnic and age diversity (e.g. an absence of data on disability and sexual orientation) (Ockenden, 2007). Again, there are illustrations of good practice; for example, conservation organization BTCV (whose volunteer vacations are discussed in Chapter 18) also run local volunteering schemes. In 1999 BTCV set up the 'Environments for All' program to recognize that 'many black, minority ethnic and marginalised people were not taking part in [environmental] volunteering because they felt excluded' (www2.btcv.org.uk/). The program aimed to recruit more people from diverse communities and involve them in conservation and volunteering, and diversity management is now integral to BTCV's overall strategy.

VOLUNTEER HOSTS: DESTINATION SERVICE ORGANIZATIONS

Little attention has been paid to diversity issues within destination service organizations. As with attractions, this is partly a resources issue and also a customer service concern. While few destination service organizations have actively sought to increase the diversity of their programs, they are usually keen to involve as many interested and capable volunteers in their programs as are needed. Surf Life-Saving South Africa, for example, states that 'A lifesaving qualification is open to everyone, irrespective of age, gender, ethnic/cultural background and you don't need to be a champion swimmer to be one, all you have to know is how to swim' (www.lifesaving.co.za).

The importance of local knowledge for many destination service volunteering roles has been discussed earlier (see Chapter 6) but our ongoing research with destination service organizations has revealed that they can also appeal to immigrants who are actively looking to build networks. New migrants are attracted to meet-and-greet programs or tour-guiding services because they have pride in their new home and want to promote the area to visitors. The language skills of CALD volunteers can be utilized within the provision of tourism services.

VOLUNTEER HOSTS: EVENTS

Events can attract a wide variety of people as volunteers, but again the profile of volunteers at a particular event is often quite homogenous and typically reflects the profile of the participants, spectators or members of the associated sport, art form or community (see Chapter 2). Mega events have the most diverse profile of volunteers because of their international and often intercultural appeal (Downward et al., 2005). Events can play a role in social inclusion strategies, and episodic volunteering can be attractive because it does not require a longer-term commitment that may put off potential volunteers.

Central to event diversity strategies is recruitment targeted at socially excluded groups and offering training both for event volunteering roles and for developing transferable skills, which can possibly lead to employment or further training or qualifications (Warrior, 2007). In the lead up to the 2002 Manchester Commonwealth Games, a Pre-Volunteer Program (PVP) aimed to address social exclusion by offering people from the most disadvantaged areas in the region the opportunity to participate as sports and event volunteers, undertake accredited training and gain experience, skills and confidence that could serve to develop their employability, move them into education and training or apply for volunteering roles at the Games themselves (Jones and Stokes, 2003; Warrior, 2007). Chapter 17 on Newham Volunteers is a program with similar goals and aligned with the 2012 London Olympic Games. A lack of longitudinal data means the success of such event programs is hard to judge, nevertheless, encouraging ongoing volunteer behavior is a stated intention of many mega-event legacy strategies (see Chapter 3). In the 2002 Commonwealth Games example, a legacy is the Manchester Event Volunteers service that recruits, trains and organizes volunteers for community, regional, national sporting and nonsporting events in the Manchester area (www.mev.org.uk).

GUESTS: VOLUNTEER TOURISM

The previous chapters in this book have demonstrated how volunteer tourism is maturing as a form of both niche tourism and international volunteering. While some commentators argue that international volunteering is involving a wider range of individuals globally (Davis Smith et al., 2005), others contend that cross-national volunteering is still the preserve of the developed world global citizen (Simpson, 2004). Whether volunteer tourists originate within North or South countries, they still tend to come from the higher socio-economic groups (Jones, 2004; Sherraden et al., 2008), not least because of the costs of paying to participate (see Chapter 2). Many volunteer tourism programs also have selection criteria which, often unwittingly, prohibit recruitment of a more inclusive cohort; for example skill, language and age criteria will limit who is able to apply for these programs. From a demand side perspective, Sherraden et al. (2008) identify a number of reasons for the lack of diversity for longer volunteer tourism programs:

- The high cost of programs prohibits those on low income;

- Older adults and those on low income may not be able to (or afford to) take time away from paid work to participate in a program; and

- Older adults may be more concerned about tax issues and health coverage should they take time off from paid work.

For people with disabilities there are the added challenges they may experience while traveling to some countries as a volunteer; international travel in itself presents several problems (see Yau, McKercher, & Packer, 2004). We have also discussed barriers to formal volunteer participation for people of certain ethnic backgrounds who are more likely to volunteer informally within their own cultural community (Chapter 1).

Domestic volunteer tourism programs are likely to be less expensive and involve less travelling. The move toward shorter volunteer tourism opportunities (see Chapter 2) may also make participation more accessible and increase the diversity of applicants by becoming more affordable in terms of time and financial commitment. Some volunteer tourism programs have made efforts to offer more flexible and inclusive opportunities. For example Earthwatch (see Web Resource 3.2) offers projects from upwards of five days, which can fit into a normal holiday period and they have projects designed specifically for families and teenagers. Raleigh International (Box 9.2) offers subsidized places on its projects to local volunteers in destination communities.

Advocates of volunteer tourism have promoted programs as a means of fostering intercultural exchange and understanding (Wearing, 2001). Research has shown, however, that host organizations need to actively promote cultural exchange (Raymond and Hall, 2008). Methods for doing

BOX 9.2 MANAGING THE DIVERSITY OF RALEIGH INTERNATIONAL VOLUNTEERS

Raleigh International is an international volunteer program launched in 1978 that aims to 'develop self-confidence and leadership in young people, through their participation in adventure, scientific exploration and community service' (www.raleighinternational.org). Raleigh International organizes five- and ten-week programs for young people aged 17–24 years in the United Kingdom and overseas (currently Borneo, Costa Rica, Nicaragua and India). Each program is divided into three phases: environment, community and adventure.

Raleigh International takes young people out of their comfort zone and this includes designing programs with a diverse group of project participants. Raleigh International works with youth groups in the United Kingdom, Bermuda and Australia to recruit and enable disadvantaged young people to participate in their programs. To further increase the diversity of volunteer groups and build closer links between the project and the local community at the destination, young volunteers are also recruited from the host country. For example, the Borneo project seeks to recruit participants from both mainland Malaysia and Sabah. The Raleigh International Kuala Lumpur branch runs introduction weekends to introduce potential volunteers to the Raleigh International ethos and help prepare them for the project. Potential volunteers from Sabah are invited to meet with the Host Country Participant Co-ordinator to find out about the Raleigh project. Sabah participants are eligible for government support to help them participate in the project. While the projects are all conducted in English, participants need to have only a little English language proficiency to participate or be willing to learn.

www.raleighinternational.org

so include role-play and diary-keeping to encourage reflection by volunteer tourists; and providing opportunities for volunteers to mix with local people in the destination, such as homestays and designing projects, which involve both volunteer tourists and local volunteers (see Box 9.2: Raleigh International). While mixing tourist and host volunteers is one way to ensure a more diverse program and also facilitate cultural exchange between participants, there is a danger that different treatment of volunteers on the same program can reinforce dependent relationships (see Chapter 3).

REFLECTIONS ON MANAGING DIVERSITY

Increasing the diversity of a volunteer program requires intervention and can involve significant resources in terms of staff time and money for training that may not be readily available. For an organization with limited resources, traditional sources of volunteers are often more attractive and cost-effective. These volunteers can usually be recruited through word-of-mouth, which encourages further homogeneity or they approach the organization themselves (see Chapter 6). In contrast, nontraditional volunteers need to be proactively recruited, may also need training, may not stay as long, especially if they are using volunteering as a route to further study or employment (see Chapter 5), and often require expenses to be paid so that they are not out-of-pocket. It may not be financially viable for an organization to implement the changes necessary to develop a more diverse volunteer group. External funding for developing volunteer programs may be available, but often only for fixed periods, which makes a program such as that at The Imperial War Museum North (Box 9.1) difficult to sustain. This is a problem when trying to build relationships with people and communities who may have needed some persuading to become involved.

Given these challenges, it is perhaps not surprising that many volunteer-involving tourism organizations have not yet embraced diversity management. This is despite the positive outcomes that can result for the organization, individual, clients and communities. For tourism organizations, this can mean visitor experiences that are more relevant to a diverse audience, which could increase visitor numbers and satisfaction, and organizations and programs that relate more closely to the needs of the local community or host destination. Developing diversity within episodic programs such as events and volunteer tourism may also lead to subsequent volunteering both within tourism and more widely.

Managing diversity within a volunteer program is complex and the easiest way to create a diverse group of volunteers is to start at the design stage (see Chapter 4). Many managers will, however, be working with an existing volunteer program. First of all, the manager needs to assess the diversity needs of program - what are the aims for diversity management? Is it so that the program can reach a more diverse audience? Is it because the local market for traditional volunteers is limited? Is it to build better connections with the local community? Diverse volunteers can have different needs and expectations and this may result in a need to change the expectations of the organization. This can include reviewing the required time commitments of volunteers and redesigning volunteer roles to be more flexible. Active recruitment strategies (Chapter 6) need to target potential volunteers, perhaps as a group who already know each other, and promote opportunities that meet their interests and needs (e.g. training and skills development).

A further barrier to developing a more diverse volunteer group can be existing volunteers. The same benefits which keep existing volunteers committed, such as their social networks, can be discouraging to new volunteers and managers will need to work with their existing volunteers to break down cliques and potentially change the culture and perceptions of existing volunteers. It may be easier to initially involve new groups of volunteers on different tasks or roles than to try and break up existing volunteer networks. Managers also need to consider the rewards that will attract and continue to motivate a diverse range of volunteers, which may mean offering different rewards to different individuals depending on their motivation (see Chapters 5 and 8).

PRINCIPLES FOR GOOD PRACTICE

- There needs to be a clear rationale for diversity management within any volunteer program.

- Volunteer managers should ensure that they understand any barriers to involving the target group of new volunteers.

- Any diversity initiative needs to be sufficiently resourced. Diversity management is likely to require more resources to support active recruitment, provide adequate training and to ensure volunteers are not left out-of-pocket.

- Diversity initiatives need support from management, paid staff and current volunteers, and the purpose of diversity initiatives should be explained to current volunteers.

- Diversity management may require a redesign of volunteer roles to meet the needs of the target group of volunteers.

- New sources of volunteers may be easier to target as a group and engage on group activities.

- Any diversity initiative should be evaluated as to its effectiveness.

DISCUSSION QUESTIONS

Q9.1 What are the barriers to recruiting a more diverse range of volunteers at a visitor attraction, destination service organization or event?

Q9.2 Why would a commercial volunteer tourism program wish to recruit a wider range of participants?

Q9.3 What benefits do you think the following groups of people will be looking for from their volunteering?
- a. A group of school students who have to complete 20 hours of community service

b. A company which wants to organize a corporate volunteer day for a group of 15 office workers

c. A recent migrant to a new country

RESOURCES

Publications by Volunteering Australia and Volunteering England for involving diverse groups as volunteers (see Section 9.1).

www.volunteeringaustralia.org

www.volunteering.org.uk

CHAPTER 10

Conclusions

INTRODUCTION

The objectives of this book were to bring together the diverse forms of tourism volunteering within one framework; to examine trends and underresearched forms of tourism volunteering; and to review research and good practice in managing volunteers. We will now review each of these topics in turn.

TOURISM VOLUNTEERING IN ALL ITS FORMS

In Chapter 2, we conceptualized tourism volunteers as either hosts or guests. We classify as host volunteers those individuals who volunteer in their local community, that is residents of the destination; and guest volunteers as those who volunteer on holiday, that is volunteer tourists. As well as two major groups of tourism volunteers, we identified four main settings for volunteer activities. Volunteer hosts are predominantly involved at attractions, destination service organizations, and events. Volunteer guests are predominantly involved in volunteer tourism. There is of course further diversity within these settings, for example, with volunteer guests engaged in VolunTourism, volunteer vacations, or a gap year. We also stress the fuzziness of the boundaries between these groups and settings, and particularly the overlaps. For example, volunteer tourists (guests) may undertake their actual volunteering in an attraction, destination service organization, or event at their destination, although most volunteers in these settings will be hosts. Finally, we classified these two groups of volunteers and four tourism volunteering settings against three different time contributions made by volunteers. These time contributions are ongoing, seasonal, and episodic. As we note, traditionally volunteering has been seen as ongoing, regular and sustained, but there has been a rise in episodic volunteering, as

Managing Volunteers in Tourism
Copyright © 2009 Elsevier Ltd. All rights reserved.

described in Chapter 1 and this is reflected in event volunteering and volunteer tourism.

We bring all these forms, settings, and contributions together in Table 2.1, our model of tourism volunteer engagements. This model also helps to identify where the gaps in current research lie, as reviewed in Chapter 2. Some settings such as attractions, events, and volunteer tourism have received significant attention, while others such as destination service organizations, which include visitor information centers, meet-and-greet programs, and rescue services, have been largely ignored. We hope that our typology will enable researchers to take a more holistic view of tourism volunteering rather than focusing solely on one form or setting in isolation, or at least recognize the commonalities between those volunteering in different settings and making similar contributions.

Previous research has focused on the positive outcomes of tourism volunteering mostly for the volunteer. In Chapter 3, we examined the benefits and costs of volunteering to the volunteer, the organization, the client, and wider society. There has been surprisingly little research on the impact of volunteering on the clients such as visitors to an attraction, users of visitor information centers, spectators or participants at events, and community beneficiaries from volunteer tourism projects and we call for further studies on all these groups.

Having set out a typology of tourism volunteering engagements, we must, however, emphasize that volunteering is not static and there are significant trends impacting on the nature and forms of volunteering internationally.

TRENDS IN VOLUNTEERING AND THE IMPLICATIONS FOR TOURISM VOLUNTEERING

In Chapter 1, we identified six forms of volunteering, which have grown in importance in recent years. These are: international volunteering, volunteer tourism, episodic, virtual, family, and corporate or employee volunteering. We note that several of these forms are interrelated; for example, volunteer tourism can be described as both a form of international and episodic volunteering.

As part of the growing recognition from governments of the importance of volunteering as a contributor to a society, various researchers and commentators have examined the future of volunteering. While there are common themes identified, there are also differences, which may be in part due to the national setting within which each study was conducted. The key themes that emerge across these studies include demographic change, increased choice and time pressures, advances in information and communications technology (ICT), employee volunteering, and diversity (Finlay and Murray, 2005; Merrill, 2006; nfpSynergy, 2005). For each, we will review the trend more broadly before considering some of the implications for tourism volunteering.

Demographic change

Demographic change offers both possibilities and limitations for volunteerism. Many commentators point to the impact of the large baby boomer generation (those born between 1946 and 1961/1962) who are nearing retirement. The most educated, affluent, and discerning generation to retire, they are likely to expect more from their retirement activities than previous generations. Nevertheless, declining pensions, increased retirement ages, and labor shortages in some sectors mean that volunteer organizations will need to compete with each other, continued paid work, other leisure options, and family commitments for volunteers' time (Finlay and Murray, 2005). This includes caring for grandchildren and intergenerational volunteering can at least attempt to combine both volunteering and time commitments (Commission on the Future of Volunteering, 2008). There is recognition of the need to engage this cohort as they set their priorities for retirement (Esmond, 2001; Volunteering Australia, 2007a).

The impending retirement of the baby boomer generation may appear to offer a ready pool of volunteers for tourism organizations but these individuals have high expectations that will need to be understood and met. Episodic roles such as campground hosts and volunteer vacations are more likely to appeal to them than ongoing, regular volunteering. Tourism organizations dependent on ongoing volunteers will need to redesign roles to be more flexible and volunteer-centered to attract and keep volunteers in the future. Programs can also be designed with ongoing and episodic opportunities that enable baby boomers to volunteer with their family in their home community or on holiday.

Demographic change will also mean that many developed countries have fewer young people as a proportion of their population. While a growth in university education, which is usually associated with a higher propensity to volunteer could be beneficial for volunteering, students are completing their studies with increasingly higher debts. Young people are likely to view volunteering as a means to gaining skills or work experience, rather than as a social service.

A reduction in young people with disposable income is potentially a problem for all forms of tourism volunteering and organizations will need to diversify their market further (see Chapter 19: Greenforce). In contrast, tourism organizations that can offer episodic roles that involve learning new skills or gaining valuable work experience will be more attractive to younger volunteers. Tourism organizations will need to emphasize the learning elements in their recruitment material and will need to build mentoring and training opportunities into their volunteer programs (Volunteering Australia, 2007d).

Increased choice and time pressures

Increased choice among the various free-time options available to people today means that volunteering is in competition with a multitude of other activities. This has been exacerbated by a reduction in many governments' services and an increased reliance on volunteering, which leads to increased competition among organizations for the pool of willing volunteers. Volunteers are likely to seek more flexible roles and commitments (nfpSynergy, 2005) and also desire more enriching volunteer experiences (Finlay and Murray, 2005). In order to achieve this, volunteering needs to improve its image as research shows that the word most strongly associated with volunteering is 'commitment' and tomorrow's volunteers are likely to be cause-driven rather than time-driven (nfpSynergy, 2005).

While tourism settings which have been reliant on more traditional forms of volunteering, such as attractions, may have to adapt to changes in the volunteer market, other settings, such as volunteer tourism or other episodic opportunities, may benefit from these trends. For example, affluent baby boomers are likely to want to use their retirement for travel and may be persuaded to participate in VolunTourism projects while they do so. Episodic programs, which involve travel and social opportunities such as campground hosting, are also likely to appeal to this cohort; for example, the Grey Nomads program in Australia (Box 4.2). Volunteers may still commit to an organization but will want the relationship to be more flexible. For example, choosing to become a bounce-back event volunteer or a repeat volunteer tourist rather than assisting at an attraction every week throughout the year. Tourism organizations will need to respond to these trends by organizing their volunteer roles differently, which may mean rethinking how they operate. Organizations could pool their resources and share a group of volunteers, therefore offering a variety of volunteer experiences, in a similar way to Newham Volunteers (Chapter 17). Attractions and destination service organizations may look at designing more episodic roles and encouraging volunteers to take 'sabbatical' breaks rather than leaving an organization altogether.

Advances in information and communications technology

ICT offers opportunities for virtual volunteering and for individuals to assist an organization remotely but ICT also has implications for the management of volunteer programs. ICT tools offer a means to engage new volunteer markets, for example using social networking sites to reach young people (Commission on the Future of Volunteering, 2008). ICT can enable people with disabilities or mobility problems to get or stay involved in a volunteer program and as there is a documented link between personal well-being and volunteering (Mellor et al., 2008), and ICT increases the contribution a volunteer program can make to society.

Many tourism organizations are reliant on ICT for their operations and these could be used to involve volunteers remotely, whether school students volunteering in their classroom or an individual volunteering at home. Volunteer projects could involve updating web site material for a visitor information center or designing a new visitor trail for an attraction, substantive parts of which could be completed off-site. Having a presence not just online but also through social networking sites will reach potential volunteers, not least through online word-of-mouth. ICT can facilitate maintaining social contact with volunteers between their shifts, during a closed season, between events, and with returned volunteer tourists, and can assist with retention and encourage bounce-back and repeat volunteering.

Corporate or employee volunteering

Employee volunteering has also been cited as both a trend and an opportunity, which has hitherto been underexploited (Commission on the Future of Volunteering, 2008). While employees may be keen to volunteer, there is still restricted support from employers and this has typically been limited to corporate social responsibility programs in large commercial companies and public sector agencies. There is the potential, however, for volunteer organizations to devise programs that both appeal to and are flexible for individuals and groups of employees who seek to fit their volunteering within or around their working day. Employee volunteer programs do, however, favor activities that impact on child welfare, disability, or health in preference to those which benefit the environment or developing countries (nfpSynergy, 2005), which may limit the potential impact of this trend on tourism volunteer programs. Employers can also support long-term volunteer commitments as trustees and by offering their employees career breaks.

Corporate volunteering programs can often provide large numbers of employees as volunteers but they often want a distinct project that can be completed in a short period of time. Tourism organizations with flexible and/or episodic opportunities are thus likely to benefit most from employee volunteering, although many employers want volunteering that takes place within and benefits their local community. Volunteer vacation and gap year volunteer tourism providers can target career breakers as another market for their programs. Tourism organizations may also benefit from employees volunteering their services as trustees.

Increased diversity

Researchers also argue that volunteering should and will become more diverse (Commission on the Future of Volunteering, 2008; Finlay and Murray, 2005). This does not just mean more diverse in terms of the individuals involved but also in the ways in which they become involved with an organization. We have highlighted in our chapters examples of organizations with varied volunteer programs, which require different contributions from their diverse volunteers, which is illustrative of this trend. As such, volunteering and volunteer management will become more complex and demanding for the organization and coordinator but with potentially much greater rewards for all involved.

As stated above, tourism organizations will need to offer a range of volunteer roles requiring different time contributions in order to attract and retain volunteers. This will require active recruitment in order to promote these opportunities to the most appropriate market. Increasing diversity will require resources and interventions (Chapter 9) but can bring rewards to the volunteer and organization, as well as have positive impacts for visitors, communities, and society more generally.

These trends do suggest that there will be an increasing and continued market for tourism volunteering opportunities if these are designed appropriately to meet the volunteers' rather than the organizations' needs.

AN ORGANIZATIONAL APPROACH TO TOURISM VOLUNTEERING

We have taken an organizational perspective within this book and this has enabled us to examine the volunteer experience holistically to include not just the volunteers but also the organization, the clients, and the wider community within which these are situated. An organizational approach does not, however, mean treating volunteers as unpaid employees. Indeed, Davis Smith comments that the move toward a more professional approach to volunteer management means that 'we have basically imposed a workplace model on volunteers' (nfpSynergy, 2005, p. 24), which may serve to denigrate the role of volunteering both within an organization and wider society.

The key trends in volunteering discussed above will have significant impacts on the way in which volunteer programs are organized. The UK's Commission for the Future of Volunteering (2008) emphasizes the potential of the modern volunteer to evolve beyond traditional models of volunteering but they also state that volunteer programs need to take a more strategic approach and plan volunteering as an integral part of the organization. The trend toward more diverse forms of volunteering and greater competition for volunteers' time means that organizations need to redesign volunteer programs that better meet the needs of potential volunteers, clients, and the organizations. Reconceptualizing volunteers as clients rather than unpaid employees will help organizations to design appropriate volunteer roles (see Chapter 5).

Volunteer programs need to be flexible and diverse in order to adapt to changes within an organization's activities and the volunteers' lives. Organizations will need to reconsider the time contributions they require from their volunteers. Volunteers are still likely to offer long-term support to an organization but not necessarily as an ongoing contribution. Management of recruitment, motivation, and training needs to be both proactive and pluralistic (Finlay and Murray, 2005; Merrill, 2006), in order to attract a more diverse group of volunteers and maintain their interest. Volunteer roles, their motivation, and training needs should be revisited over the life span of the volunteer program to respond to changes in the volunteers' interests and lifestyles. Organizations need to ensure that they provide adequate introductory training to all volunteers, whether ongoing, seasonal, or episodic, and further training must be made available to enable development opportunities for those volunteers who seek them. Training opportunities are likely to be particularly attractive to younger volunteers seeking work experience or skills development.

All of these factors are likely to mean that volunteer programs will grow more complex and volunteer management will require more time. As such, it will be essential that volunteer programs are sufficiently resourced; that volunteer management ceases to be only a part of a person's job and full-time volunteer coordinators are appointed and supported professionally; and that organizations need to seriously reconsider how far they can require volunteers to bear the costs of the program. These costs include training, uniforms, transport, and refreshments and it is these costs that may hinder efforts to appeal to a wider market for volunteers, as well as create barriers to individuals with lower income, including retirees and university students. Properly resourcing a volunteer program also means ensuring appropriate recognition for volunteers, which links to their motivations and emphasizes the reciprocal nature of their relationship with the organization. This is likely to be of increasing importance to potential volunteers, for whom volunteering is just one of many leisure options.

ETHICAL ISSUES

This book has also highlighted the ethical issues that surround tourism volunteering. Volunteer guest programs have received the most attention in previous studies both in relation to the payments made by volunteer tourists and also the impact they have on the communities within which they volunteer. These issues have received significant media attention (see Chapter 19: Greenforce) and it is likely that volunteer tourism organizations will need to be more transparent in how they spend tourists' payments in future (see Chapters 2 and 3). There also needs to be careful consideration of whether volunteer tourism projects are the best means of solving some of the problems in these destination communities. Chapter 3 noted that many volunteers, not just guests, incur expenses through their volunteering and this can serve as a barrier to volunteering for under-represented groups and hinder diversity (Chapter 9). In addition to this is the dilemma as to whether commercial business should benefit from volunteers. Increasingly, volunteer tourism providers are profit-making and commercial events can also be reliant on volunteers, giving their time for free to the financial benefit of others (see Ferdinand, 2008).

We have discussed the conceptualization of volunteering as leisure, in contrast to volunteering as unpaid work. This conceptualization fits with predicted future trends for volunteering, particularly the need for organizations to devise meaningful yet enjoyable roles for volunteers, which fit into the free time that they have available. Good practice in managing volunteers will still be important as although volunteers may be engaged in leisure, they still want their time to be properly organized. However, devising volunteer programs, which recognize that volunteering can be a form of leisure, also means that care needs to be given to avoid too much bureaucracy and too many formal and work-like requirements.

Finally, we have noted that there are forms of volunteering which may be described as marginal or even compulsory volunteering, called voluntold by nfpSynergy (2005). These can include internships or volunteering for work experience; volunteering for service learning at school or university; or compulsory community service. Evidence suggests that these forms of volunteering will continue and, in the case of service learning, may even increase in the future. While there is debate as to whether some or any of these activities can be truly considered as 'volunteering', due to the participants' lack of free will, these offer new sources of mostly episodic volunteers for tourism organizations (see Chapter 14 for the Vancouver International Children's Festival's response to government policy requiring student community service) and these marginal forms of volunteering may serve as a precursor to leisure volunteering.

CONCLUDING COMMENTS

Throughout Parts A and B of this book we have urged readers to think more holistically about the forms, settings, and time contributions of volunteers within tourism. We have sought to provide a comprehensive overview of volunteering and volunteer management issues within tourism, which recognizes the vital, varied, and extensive contributions of these individuals. We have brought together existing research and practitioner literature from the range of tourism settings and noted commonalities and differences, and shown how the different time contributions made by volunteers can impact on the way their activities are organized. The organizational approach has involved all stakeholders within the volunteer experience: organizations, clients, communities, society and, of course, volunteers themselves. The final section of this book consists of ten case studies which are illustrative of the range of tourism volunteering settings, forms, and management issues. Finally, we hope that our readers may even be inspired themselves to volunteer and reap the personal, social, and career benefits that volunteering in tourism can offer.

Managing Tourism Volunteer Programs: Case Studies

INTRODUCTION

The final part of this book contains a series of invited in-depth case studies of volunteering across different tourism settings. The authors include both academic researchers and volunteer program managers and thus bridge the gap between the academic and practitioner literature. Each case study stands alone but also illustrates the management issues highlighted throughout the book. Common themes explored include: motivating and recruiting volunteers, allocating roles, training, rewarding and retaining volunteers; managing expectations; the importance of partnerships; the potential legacies from episodic tourism volunteering; and the importance of leadership as a crucial factor in the success of a volunteer program.

The case studies are organized into three groups: attractions, events and destinations.

In the first attractions case study, Edwards and Foley (Chapter 11) examine the volunteer programs at three large Australian museums. All employ formal volunteer management procedures and the scale of these volunteer programs highlight the need for appropriate training and support for the volunteer managers. Holmes and Yasuda (Chapter 12) compare the volunteer programs at two small heritage attractions: Smallhythe Place, England, and Dr Komai's residence, Japan, each managed by their country's National Trust organization. Despite organizational differences, the attractions are similar with regard to recruitment, training and the relationship between the managers and volunteers. Turning attention to a Canadian natural attraction,

Fresque and Plummer (Chapter 13) examine the role of volunteer trustees, a frequently neglected group of volunteers, at the St John River Society and how the organization has responded to change over a period of 15 years.

The next set of case studies focuses on events, with two long-standing annual festivals followed by two volunteer programs developed for sport mega events. Burley and Stewart-Imbert (Chapter 14) examine the volunteer program at the Vancouver International Children's Festival in Canada. Issues covered include the expansion of the volunteer program, allocation of volunteer roles, the role of the volunteer coordinator and their leadership style. Elstad (Chapter 15) focuses on volunteers at the Kongsberg Jazz Festival in Norway. She analyzes their motivation, recruitment, continuance commitment and sources of dissatisfaction among the volunteer cohort.

Baum and Lockstone (Chapter 16) examine the volunteer program at the 2006 Melbourne Commonwealth Games in Australia. They follow the volunteer's journey through recruitment, role allocation, rostering and training. They consider how to manage disappointment among unsuccessful volunteer applicants, a common challenge at high profile and oversubscribed mega events. The issue of a volunteering legacy is also reviewed and this theme continues in Nichols' Chapter 17 which analyzes a volunteer program established in anticipation of the 2012 London Olympic Games. In order to develop a cohort of experienced volunteers, the London Borough of Newham has established a pool of volunteers for events currently running in the locality. Nichols appraises the recruitment and training of these volunteers, the flexibility of the program and the relationship between event managers, volunteers and the program managers.

The final group of case studies focuses on destinations and volunteer tourism programs. Jefferies (Chapter 18) reports on the partnerships developed by BTCV (formely the British Trust for Conservation Volunteers) in order to run an international conservation volunteering vacation in Lesotho. The management of both the volunteer leaders and the volunteers themselves is considered, particularly managing the expectations of volunteers. Next, White and Smith (Chapter 19) evaluate a Bahamas-based volunteer tourism project run by gap-year provider Greenforce. They appraise the development of the gap-year market for volunteer tourism, how Greenforce has adapted to market changes and also address the issue of managing volunteers' expectations. Lastly, McIntosh (Chapter 20) examines a developed world volunteer tourism program: WWOOF (Willing Workers on Organic Farms). Unlike the other volunteer tourism case studies, WWOOFing is largely organized by the individual volunteer through the WWOOF network. McIntosh analyzes the motivations of both WWOOF hosts and guests and the factors which lead to a mutually successful volunteer tourism placement.

CHAPTER 11

Australian War Memorial, Australian Museum, and the Art Gallery of New South Wales

Mutually Satisfying Relationships: the Secrets of Successful Volunteer Programs in Australian Museums

Deborah Edwards and Carmel Foley
University of Technology, Sydney, Australia,
Deborah.Edwards-1@uts.edu.au,
Carmel.Foley@uts.edu.au

KEY POINTS

- At three large museums in Australia, the Australian War Memorial, Australian Museum, and the Art Gallery of New South Wales, volunteers undertake a range of tasks both front-of-house (e.g. guiding) and behind-the-scenes (e.g. conservation projects).

- The management of these volunteer programs is different yet each is successful as the organizations match task requirements with volunteer skills and abilities, and have recognition systems, which reward the volunteers while meeting the operational needs of the museums.

- The process of recruitment, selection, induction, and training results in volunteers joining their museum knowing what to expect and the organization's expectations of them in terms of their role, obligations, and commitment.

- The volunteer programs could be further improved by greater integration of the volunteer programs into the institutions, including

CONTENTS

Managing Volunteers in Tourism
Copyright © 2009 Elsevier Ltd. All rights reserved.

increased access to resources, and improved training and support for volunteer coordinators and managers.

- A model for volunteer management conceptualizes the volunteer program as an integrated part of the organization, which brings benefits for volunteers, volunteer coordinator, and the organization.

OVERVIEW OF THE MUSEUMS

This case study tells the story of how three large museums in New South Wales and the Australian Capital Territory in Australia manage their volunteers. Each museum operates a successful volunteer program for which there is a waiting list of volunteers. The volunteers at each museum are well managed, happy, and doing a valuable job for their respective organizations. We can learn something from their success. The volunteer coordinators from each organization have also identified areas in which their volunteers could be better managed in terms of the volunteer programs' integration into the larger organization and the ongoing support and training of the managers and coordinators who supervise volunteers. These are significant insights from practitioners in the field, which provide valuable learning opportunities. The case study provides an overview of the three organizations and their successful volunteer programs, and identifies key issues and a model for successful volunteer management.

Three prominent Australian museums are the center of this case study: The Australian War Memorial (the Memorial), located in Canberra, the capital city of Australia, in the Australian Capital Territory; the Australian Museum (the Museum), located next to Hyde Park in the center of Sydney, New South Wales; and, also in central Sydney, the Art Gallery of New South Wales (the Gallery), located in The Domain.

Australian War Memorial

The idea of a war museum for Australia was conceived in 1916 by Charles Bean, an official war correspondent, and the Memorial opened in Canberra in 1941. The Memorial's purpose is to commemorate the sacrifice of those Australians who have died in war. Its mission is to assist Australians to remember, interpret, and understand the Australian experience of war and its enduring impact on Australian society (Australian War Memorial, 2007). The Memorial houses the largest collection of war artifacts in Australia and is open daily except for Christmas Day. Admission and tours are free and there are six tours offered every day.

Australian Museum

The Australian Museum was founded in 1827 and is Australia's oldest museum, with unique and extensive collections of natural science and cultural artifacts. The objectives of the Australian Museum are to 'propagate knowledge about the natural environment of Australia and to increase that knowledge, particularly in the natural sciences of biology, anthropology and geology' (Australian Museum, 2007, p. 5). The Australian Museum has an international reputation in the fields of natural history and indigenous research, community programs, and exhibitions. The Museum is open daily except for Christmas Day. Although there is a general admission charge guided tours are free.

Art Gallery of New South Wales

The Gallery is an art museum that houses an extensive collection of national and international artworks. The purpose of the Gallery is to 'maintain and develop a collection of works of art, and to promote understanding and appreciation of art' (Art Gallery New South Wales, 2007, p. 5). The Gallery's mission is to 'maintain a reputation as an energetic, outgoing and accessible art institution, and at the same time strive to be a major international gallery of the world, continuing to inspire, interest and provide enjoyment to increasingly diverse audiences' (Art Gallery of New South Wales, 2007, p. 5). The Gallery is open daily except for Good Friday and Christmas Day. Admission and tours are free but entry to special exhibitions attracts a fee.

OVERVIEW OF THE VOLUNTEERING PROGRAMS

Each organization employs a proactive management approach to their volunteer program. This approach generates a high level of satisfaction that both the volunteers and the organization have with the volunteer program and contributes to a positive corporate image of the organization in the wider community. This section provides details of the volunteer programs in each organization.

Australian War Memorial

Volunteers participate in many areas within the Memorial the major areas being the voluntary guides, the Discovery Zone (a hands-on education space for visitors), Treloar Technology Centre, and the Online Gallery. Within all these areas, volunteers are involved in a range of activities including conducting interpretive guided tours for the general public, VIPs, and special interest groups; assisting the public with research enquiries; assisting with functions and formal ceremonies; assisting conservators in preparing relics for storage; and working in laboratories treating textiles and paper-based artifacts. There are two Volunteer Managers and one Assistant Volunteer Manager who conduct all administrative work relating to volunteers. Volunteers are supervised by the staff working in their area of activity. The largest of these areas is Education and Visitor Services, which employs two staff full time specifically to supervise the volunteer guides.

Recruitment is conducted on an 'as-needed' basis. When required, the volunteer manager will advertise through local newspapers. People can also register their interest online or by contacting the volunteer manager directly who then records their enquiries and when intakes begin, forwards an information package and application form. Applicants are invited to an interview by the volunteer manager and two guides. Selection criteria includes their interests, skills relevant to the area in need of support, age (at certain times, the Memorial seeks either a younger or a more mature cohort to maintain an age diversity of volunteers), and applicant's willingness to undertake training and to commit to volunteering for a minimum of one year following recruitment and training. All volunteers must undergo a security check and are required to sign a confidentiality agreement. Successful applicants are given a Volunteer Guides Manual that outlines the policies, rules, and procedures regulating volunteer involvement and a teamwork agreement document that sets out guidelines to which volunteers must adhere.

New guides are trained by two experienced guides for a period of six to eight months. During this time, the volunteer is required to present a paper to the training team on how they intend to conduct tours through the Memorial and to conduct this tour 12 times on which they undertake a self-assessment. On completion of the 12 tours, they are accredited by two reviewers selected from a panel of experienced guides and/or Memorial staff. Guides are evaluated three times a year to ensure that they are maintaining a professional standard. Completed training is formally recognized with the award of a Statement of Attainment, jointly badged by the Memorial and the Canberra Institute of Technology (CIT).

The recruitment process for conservation volunteers is less formal than for visitor services volunteers. The initial point of contact is over the phone. If the applicant's skills are required, the applicant is invited to an interview/orientation. This session acts as a culling tool as some applicants withdraw their interest when they understand that the environment in which they will be volunteering is not always a comfortable one. The volunteer is placed on a probationary period of 50 hours.

Volunteer benefits include full access to the research center and facilities; discounts at the bookshop and kiosk; concessionary entry to other museums, galleries and institutions in Canberra; invitations to ceremonies and presentations by curators, services, and other activities organized by the Memorial; insurance cover for injury or illness arising out of volunteering at the Memorial; and payment for guides to be members of the Association of Australian Gallery Guides Organization (AAGGO). The institution also pays the full cost for the Memorial's representative to attend the AAGGO biennial conference.

Certificates of appreciation are presented to online, gallery, and discovery room volunteers following 2000 hours of service. Conservation volunteers receive certificates of appreciation on the completion of a project, and badges indicating 200, 500, 1000 or 2000 hours of service. The gallery guides have a separate Christmas function.

Australian Museum

The volunteer program at the Australian Museum in Sydney is situated within Visitor Services under the Division of Public Programs. It comprises two areas: Public Programs and Behind-the-Scenes. Public Programs volunteers meet-and-greet Museum visitors, help visitors feel welcome and oriented within the Museum, take guided tours, interpret Museum content, and assist in special events. Behind-the-Scenes volunteers assist in a wide variety of roles, supporting scientists, and other Museum staff in clerical and other duties such as cataloguing, researching, and classification.

The management of volunteers at the Museum has been somewhat disjointed. The program from 2000 to 2004 had numerous coordinators. Sometimes this has been one person and at other times up to three people. At the time of data collection, the major duties fell to the Front-of-House manager who also has other duties to fulfil within the Museum. This person enjoys managing the volunteers but recognizes that the program deserves the time and commitment of a full-time manager.

There are separate recruitment processes for Public Programs volunteers and the Behind-the-Scenes volunteers. Public Programs volunteers are recruited approximately once a year. Those people interested in guiding are invited to an information day at which they are informed of the Museum's expectations, commitment required, activities they can be involved in, and training requirements. Participants are then asked to fill in an application form. These are reviewed and prospective volunteers are invited in for an interview conducted by the volunteer coordinators. The applicant is asked to bring with them an object from nature on which they are to give a three-minute talk. Interviews are similar to a job interview but not as formal.

Public Programs volunteers are required to volunteer a minimum of 22 days a year as well as attend regular meetings and training days. New volunteers attend a four-day induction course that covers customer service, basics of museum interpretation and education, museum content, and conducting guided tours. Volunteers are expected to commit for a period of 12 months and are appraised once a year. Training for Public Programs includes undertaking tours with trained volunteers and paid front-of-house staff. When the volunteer feels comfortable with their knowledge they are assessed by the volunteer coordinator. If the coordinator does not think the volunteer is ready, they will make suggestions for improvement in their guiding skills. The volunteer is also required to evaluate themselves after 50 hours of volunteering.

For Behind-the-Scenes volunteers the recruitment process is less formal. A scientist will make a request to the volunteer coordinator for a person to fill a particular task. Commitment for Behind-the-Scenes volunteers varies with the type of task performed. Ongoing projects will require regular attendance, while short-term projects will require volunteers for a specified period. Training for Behind-the-Scenes volunteers is provided by the respective supervisor.

Volunteers have their own room, which contains a small library and resource center, coffee and tea facilities, and a pigeon hole for messages. On recruitment, volunteers are given a T-shirt (uniform), which must be returned if they leave within six months. Volunteers have free access to the Museum and special exhibitions and receive a free subscription to Nature Australia magazine, the Museum's own publication, which is sold in the Museum shop, discounted attendance for any public and staff lectures, discounts at the Museum shop, and honorary membership of the Australian Museum Society.

Art Gallery of New South Wales

Volunteers in the Art Gallery come under Public Programs within the division of Curatorial Services. The Art Gallery currently has four volunteer bodies: Volunteer Guides, Task Force, Community Ambassadors, and Contempo. The Gallery's annual report states that the value of volunteer services to the Gallery is AU$1.6 million (Art Gallery of New South Wales, 2007).

The guides provide guided tours of the Gallery's collections and major exhibitions for the public, schoolchildren, and special groups. The Volunteer Task Force is a group of Australian Museum Society members who provide voluntary support to both the Gallery and the Australian Museum Society.

It is a multifunction support group that undertakes a variety of activities such as ticket and catalogue sales, assisting in the members' room, mail outs, opening mail, counting votes, clerical and library assistance, and serving at a variety of day and evening functions hosted by the Gallery.

The Community Ambassadors program introduced in 2005 was designed to expand the Gallery's audience into non-English-speaking communities. Community Ambassadors are Japanese-, Mandarin-, Cantonese-, and Vietnamese-speaking volunteers who offer regular tours of the Gallery and on special projects. Contempo is a membership category of the Art Gallery of New South Wales designed specifically for those interested in Sydney's contemporary art scene. The Contempo volunteers program is a small program created to engage younger people in the museum. The role of Contempo volunteers is to assist in planning, organizing, and managing Contempo events and promote fund-raising opportunities for the Gallery's contemporary art acquisitions program.

Management of the Guides and Task Force is not dissimilar to that of self-managed teams. The Volunteer Guides are self-managed by an unpaid Coordinator and an Assistant Coordinator. The coordinators are in the position for one year. The position of Volunteer Guide Coordinator is the most senior. When the Coordinator vacates the position, they are replaced by the Assistant Coordinator, who in turn is supported by a new Assistant Coordinator. The Coordinator and Assistant Coordinator are invited into the position by a Volunteer Guides Committee. The Guide Coordinator works in conjunction with a volunteer committee.

The volunteer committee is comprised of the Guide Coordinator, the immediate past Coordinator, the Assistant Coordinator, the Children's Coordinator and assistant, the Lecture Program Coordinator and assistant, and the Treasurer, Secretary, and assistant. People are nominated to the committee by committee members. Four of the committee members have the additional role of liaison guides who act as a mediator between the curators and the Volunteer Guides and are the only guides allowed to speak to the curators. Liaison guides also gather materials that support specific exhibitions that can be used by the Volunteer Guides. The Community Ambassadors also come under this management structure. Contempo volunteers are self-managed by a Contempo volunteer committee similar in structure to the Volunteer Guides Committee.

The Volunteer Task Force is managed by the Volunteer Coordinator Task Force, and a committee of eight members. The Volunteer Coordinator Task Force is elected from the current sitting committee and is in position for two years. The duties of a Task Force volunteer are carried out on a roster basis. There are also five project officers who are responsible for a number of social activities and a Task Force news letter. To be a Task Force member a person is required to pay an annual subscription of AU$10.

There are two separate recruitment processes for Volunteer Guides and Task Force volunteers. Gallery guides are recruited through advertisements in a major Australian newspaper and the Gallery's monthly magazine once every four years. Applicants are sent an information package that explains the guiding commitment including: a minimum of 42 hours guiding per year, children and adult guide training for one year, three years of children's guiding, followed by the option to take adult tours. These explicit expectations act as a culling tool as people tend to withdraw their interest if they feel they are unable to fulfil these commitments.

Interviews are conducted by a panel that includes a representative of Public Programs, the guide coordinator and two members from the volunteer committee. Volunteers are required to pay AU$25 a year to be a guide. People who have previous guiding experience in other museums or overseas and have a second language will be interviewed outside the normal recruitment period. Guides are expected to attend 75% of lectures which are aimed at educating the guides about art. Guides are also invited to participate in presentation workshops, which can cover a range of topics such as health and safety issues, care of children, and presentation skills.

The Task Force recruits volunteers on an 'as-needed' basis and at the time of data collection, they had a waiting list of two years. Task Force volunteers must commit to volunteering a minimum of 48 hours a year or 4 hours a month. New members are given a folder with explicit instructions for all Task Force activities and rules of membership. For the first six months they are rostered alongside a senior Task Force member who shows them what to do and 'keeps an eye on them'. New recruits are on a six-month probationary period and must demonstrate satisfactory performance to the committee to be accepted as Task Force Members.

Task Force volunteers and Volunteer Guides each have their own facilities with tea, coffee, milk, and biscuits. The benefits of being a guide include attending lectures by curators, special exhibitions, and seminars at reduced cost; a small reduction in parking fees; Christmas luncheon; free access to exhibitions; and a badge. Task Force volunteers are also given a lunch at the Annual General Meeting.

KEY ISSUES FOR VOLUNTEER MANAGEMENT

While the organizations manage their volunteer programs successfully, there were two issues identified as requiring more attention: the extent to which the volunteer programs are integrated into the larger organization; and the ongoing support and training of the managers and coordinators who supervise volunteers.

Integration of the volunteer program into the wider organization

In this section, the case study organizations will not be named as interviewees requested anonymity. The integration of the volunteer programs into the institutions is different at each organization. In one organization, the program is given equal member status to other departments within the institution. In another institution, the manager's role is less valued, evidenced by a difference in resources the volunteer program receives as compared to other areas within the organization. While in the other, the self-managed volunteer program tends to function outside the normal operations of the institution, any involvement is on an 'as-needed' basis. The practices in the latter two organizations have served to isolate volunteer managers and coordinators, which can leave them feeling undervalued. All volunteer programs are expected to be self-supporting with the expectation that they will not cause a strain on the organization's resources. This may be because the volunteer programs are not seen to be critical to the continuity of the organizations.

Volunteers at each institution participate in highly structured environments and have specific job functions. They operate under an explicit agreement similar to a contract of employment. The role of the volunteer is to support and/or supplement the work of paid staff, by undertaking activities for the organization, in the form of predetermined and specific tasks. However, the distinct separation of the volunteer programs from other departments in two of the museums can lead to miscommunication and gaps in the delivery of services.

In each museum, a top-down approach to management is employed, where decisions are made further up the line to ensure control of members at the bottom of the organization. Some horizontal linkages occur through interdepartmental meetings with direct, formal, reporting relationships. It could be said that volunteers are at the very bottom of the organizational hierarchy. This functional structure is even in place where the volunteers are self-managed.

In two of the institutions, changes, issues, and ideas are discussed at the volunteer committee level before they are presented to the volunteers for consideration; in effect, controlling the direction of the outcome. None of the paid volunteer coordinators are at a level where they can go to a departmental or management meeting. All coordinators rely on representation through their immediate supervisors. Therefore, volunteer managers can only indirectly influence decisions that affect their volunteer programs.

Each volunteer program achieves its assigned objectives although access to resources is constrained. A coordinator in one museum suggested that volunteers were less valued than paid staff and would have liked more resources for both the management and operation of the program.

Ongoing support and training for volunteer coordinators

All volunteer coordinators believe they have a personal understanding of their volunteers, but did not feel this was shared by many staff outside the programs. Paid coordinators, however, were challenged by their own insecurities; in contrast, unpaid managers (who are also volunteers) were confident in their abilities but felt somewhat alienated from other departments. There are two reasons for this. Firstly, although the volunteer programs have been around for a number of years, the formal management of these programs has not been a priority for the organizations; essentially they have been left to look after themselves. Consequently, the programs have evolved through a process of trial and error.

Secondly, paid volunteer coordinators and managers have gained their positions not because they have the specific skills and training necessary for volunteer management but because the role has been an add-on to their other responsibilities. The skills they brought with them came from experiences gained in previous organizations that were not volunteer-related. Therefore, they feel inadequately prepared to meet the challenges of the position regardless of whether these perceptions are well founded. For these reasons, the paid coordinators believe that 'things could be done better' and look for other models as to how this could be done.

A model for volunteer management

The volunteer programs at the Memorial, the Gallery, and the Museum are, on the whole, well managed and successful and can be explained with reference to a model for volunteer management (see Figure 11.1). Each of the programs attempts to match the skills and abilities of the volunteers to organizational tasks and each program has a recognition system in place. In this way, the organizations are attempting to create environments where the contribution of volunteers is recognized in a meaningful way and the recognition system fits within the operational needs of the organization. The programs vary in their integration within the organizations and this causes some tension for volunteer coordinators. Integration is important if the program is to continue to develop and is valued for the contribution it can make to organizational objectives.

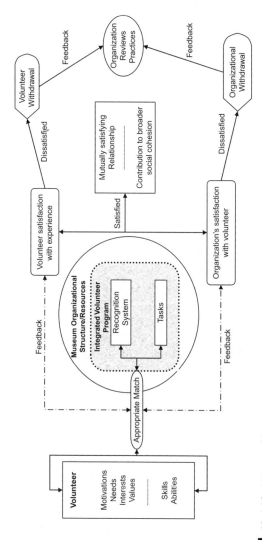

FIGURE 11.1 *Model for Volunteer Management.*
Source: Adapted from Pearce (1980)

The extent to which each organization matches task requirements with volunteer skills and abilities, and recognizes volunteer needs and interests, has resulted in the high level of satisfaction that both the volunteer and the organization have with the volunteer program.

The strength of a volunteer's satisfaction will be moderated by the volunteer's perception that their serious leisure interests are being met through their participation in the organization. The strength of an organization's satisfaction with its volunteers will be moderated by the organization's perception of the volunteers' ability to complete assigned tasks. Organizations should strive for the strongest match in both areas in order to realize a mutually satisfying relationship. Task requirement and recognition system should be embedded in the organization's structure. Should the volunteer or the organization be dissatisfied, the organization may need to review their practices in relation to the volunteer program.

This model suggests that the volunteer program be considered as part of a whole, rather than an extra add-on, that it be seen as one of operational areas of the museum to be taken seriously by all staff. There are a number of benefits to be derived from this level of integration. First, it ensures that volunteer coordinators are present at meetings where key information is communicated and they are able to input into the decision-making process. Second, a more equitable and efficient distribution of resources can occur as the needs of the program are considered alongside the needs of other operational areas. Third, it is an inclusive approach that draws staff and volunteers together, which is likely to facilitate a greater understanding between volunteers and staff. Finally, recognition as an operational program will provide those within the volunteer program with a sense that what they are contributing is meaningful and valued within the organization.

CONCLUSION

In summary, each of the institutions in this study has explicit transactional contracts that direct volunteer participation in the organization. As these volunteers join their respective institutions they know what to expect and what is expected of them. Volunteers have a clear understanding of where they fit into the organization and are well informed of the organization's expectations of them in terms of their role, obligations, and commitment. However, each of the programs would benefit from greater integration into the respective institution, increased access to resources, and improved training and support for coordinators and managers. These are issues that require reflection and exploration.

DISCUSSION QUESTIONS

Q11.1 In relation to this case study, suggest ways in which the volunteer programs can be more fully integrated into the organizations in which they operate?

Q11.2 This case study has recommended that volunteers be given the opportunity to take on more diverse roles within museums. How might managers address the problem of paid staff potentially perceiving volunteers as a threat to casual and full-time positions?

Q11.3 How can the museums address the insecurities felt by the paid coordinators?

FURTHER INFORMATION

Australian Museum. www.austmus.gov.au

Australian War Memorial. www.awm.gov.au

Art Gallery of New South Wales. www.artgallery.nsw.gov.au

CHAPTER 12

Dr Komai's Residence, Japan, and Smallhythe Place, United Kingdom

A Comparison of Volunteer Management at Small Heritage Attractions

Kirsten Holmes[1] and Izumi Yasuda[2]

[1]*Curtin University, Australia,*
K.Holmes@cbs.curtin.edu.au
[2]*World Bank, Japan, Izumi.Yasuda@gmail.com*

KEY POINTS

- The National Trust for Places of Historic Interest and Natural Beauty is the largest national trust organization, manages over 350 properties, employs over 6000 paid staff, and involves over 52, 000 volunteers in England, Wales, and Northern Ireland. The Japan National Trust is a much smaller organization, which currently manages 11 properties, with the assistance of 8 paid staff and 150 volunteers.

- Volunteering is much more prevalent in the United Kingdom and has a longer history than in Japan where 16% of the adult population volunteer compared to 43% in the United Kingdom.

- Dr Komai's Residence in Japan and Smallhythe Place in the United Kingdom are both small visitor attractions owned and managed by their respective national trust organizations. As small properties, they have limited resources due to staffing and the size of the building.

- Recruitment at both properties is important but time consuming and the property managers employ a range of recruitment techniques,

Managing Volunteers in Tourism
Copyright © 2009 Elsevier Ltd. All rights reserved.

mostly focusing on visitors and national trust members, rather than the wider community. Selection processes are more formalized at Smallhythe Place than at Dr Komai's Residence.

■ Training at both properties involves matching new volunteers with existing and experienced volunteers and is largely on-the-job due in part to the small numbers of volunteers at each site.

■ The relationship between the manager and the volunteers at both properties is informal and this is partly due to the way the program is organized but also a consequence of the facilities at each site.

OVERVIEW OF THE NATIONAL TRUSTS

National trust organizations around the world are found in Australia, Bermuda, England, Wales and Northern Ireland, Fiji, Japan, Malaysia, Netherlands, New Zealand, Scotland, United States, and Zimbabwe, all established for the preservation of heritage. While all national trusts are concerned with heritage preservation, they all operate differently and independently. The Bahamas National Trust is discussed briefly in Chapter 19.

The oldest organization is the National Trust for Places of Historic Interest and Natural Beauty (the National Trust), which covers England, Wales, and Northern Ireland (there is a separate National Trust for Scotland), established in 1895 by an Act of Parliament for the acquisition and protection of threatened coastline, countryside, and buildings. The National Trust owns and opens to the public in excess of 350 historic properties including large areas of countryside and coastline. The historic sites include castles, country houses, pubs, historic gardens, other buildings of historic interest such as John Lennon's childhood home, rock houses carved into the foot of the cliff at Kinver Edge, and even entire villages. The National Trust has one of the largest volunteer programs in the United Kingdom, with over 52,000 volunteers engaged in a range of activities from environmental conservation to information stewards in historic houses and volunteer tourists on National Trust working holidays.

The Japan National Trust for Cultural and Natural Heritage Organization (Japan National Trust) was established in 1968 under the Ministry of Land, Infrastructure, and Transport in response to concern in the media about threats to the natural and cultural heritage of Japan. The Japan National Trust has three aims: to conduct research on historic and natural heritage sites; to conserve natural and cultural assets; and education. It is a not-for-profit, public-benefit organization and is supported by its members and contributions from industry, government, and private foundations. Since 1984, the Japan National Trust was granted tax exemption and began to acquire properties for restoration and maintenance so that they are suitable for opening to the public for educational purposes. The Japan National Trust currently owns and manages six historic properties and five heritage centers. These sites are varied and include heritage railways such as the Nagahama Railway Heritage Centre, traditional or architecturally important buildings such as Shirakawa Village Gassho-style Houses, and historic gardens and parks, such as Old Daijoin Temple Garden with Daijoin Garden Heritage Centre. The Japan National Trust involves 150 volunteers across three properties, one conservation project, and in central administration roles.

The Japan National Trust is therefore a considerably smaller organization than its sister organization in the United Kingdom. This size is also reflected in the salaried workforce. The National Trust has around 6000 paid staff (both full and part time) compared to the Japan National Trust's eight paid employees. The rest of the Japan National Trust's activities are delivered by volunteers, local nonprofit organizations, and local communities. In addition, the Japan National Trust has only 3000 members compared to the National Trust's 3.5 million members.

OVERVIEW OF DR KOMAI'S RESIDENCE AND SMALLHYTHE PLACE

This case study compares the volunteer programs at two small historic attractions. The first is the Japan National Trust property Dr Komai's Residence, the former home of Dr Taku Komai, a zoologist and a professor of Kyoto University (1886–1972). The second is the National Trsut property Smallhythe Place, the former home of the English actress Ellen Terry (1847–1928). These properties offer comparable attractions in that, while the actual building has historical or architectural merit, their interest for tourists is the proximity to the personalities who lived there.

Dr Komai's Residence has been open to the public every Friday and Saturday since 1994. The property is interesting architecturally as well as its associations with Dr Komai. It was built in 1929 by the American architect William Merrell Vories, whose designs contributed to the development of Japanese modern-style houses. Dr Komai's Residence was registered as 'reserved-cultural-heritage' by Kyoto City Council in 1998 and is a unique Spanish–Japanese style historical house located in Kyoto, the ancient capital of Japan. While this style of building is found elsewhere in

Japan, it is unusual in Kyoto, which is known for its traditional architecture. Dr Komai's residence received 3150 visitors in 2004 and is open all year round.

Smallhythe Place was given to the National Trust by Ellen Terry's daughter in 1939. While it is well known for its association with the actress Ellen Terry who lived there from 1899 to 1928, it is also architecturally interesting in its own right as an early sixteenth century half-timbered house, set within a rural village in southeast England. The property hosts a number of events, particularly in its barn theater, built in 1931, and also has a display of Ellen Terry's costumes. The property is Grade 1 listed, as a building of exceptional historic or architectural importance. Smallhythe Place received just under 22,000 visitors in 2007. As with most other National Trust built attractions, Smallhythe Place is open seasonally, from March to October each year.

OVERVIEW OF THE VOLUNTEER PROGRAMS

The National Trust, as noted above, is a very large organization involving significant numbers of volunteers. Policies are set at a national level but there are also regional offices, which provide support for individual properties and implement policy at a regional level. The organization has a national policy for volunteer management. The resources at each site, such as the number of paid staff and facilities, vary significantly across different properties, which means that although there are national guidelines on volunteer management, volunteer programs do vary across different properties. As a smaller organization with more limited resources, the Japan National Trust does not have the same centralized policies and procedures.

Both of the properties examined in this case study are small buildings and have small numbers of volunteers and paid staff. Both are also restricted in the support and facilities they can offer to their volunteers by resources such as staffing and the nature of the site itself.

At Dr Komai's Residence, there are 20 volunteers who are managed by a part-time Property Manager, who also has several other responsibilities, which is symptomatic of the wider voluntary sector where volunteer management is often under-resourced. While the typical profile of Japanese cultural volunteers is older, many of the volunteers at Dr Komai's Residence are younger university students aged 20 to 29 years, who are studying arts subjects. Most volunteers at Dr Komai's Residence are female. In contrast with student volunteers in other countries, who tend to be instrumentally motivated (Haski-Leventhal et al., 2008), the student volunteers are motivated by their interest in art, not by the career benefits that volunteering could offer.

At Smallhythe Place, the volunteers are managed by the Property Manager and again the volunteers are only one of their responsibilities. The property has approximately 60 volunteers on its register but most of the shifts are taken by 20 regular volunteers. The property needs between three and six volunteers each day, with three room steward stations (the admissions desk, the upstairs room and the barn theater) spread out throughout the property and two shifts – a morning and an afternoon session. There is often a shortage of volunteers, however, and the Property Manager has learnt to cope with only two volunteers for each shift. The shortage of volunteers has been dealt with in two ways: firstly, the Property Manager assists in extreme cases and frequently takes over a steward station to enable the volunteers to have their tea break. Unfortunately, this takes the Property Manager away from other tasks. Another temporary solution has been to host an international exchange student for a few months. This in itself raises some problems as there is no on-site accommodation for the student.

KEY ISSUES FOR VOLUNTEER MANAGEMENT

Cultural volunteers in two countries

Volunteering has different meanings in Japan and the United Kingdom. While there is a standardized definition of volunteering in the United Kingdom, provided by Volunteering England (the peak body for volunteering), volunteerism has no such standardized meaning in Japan. This may be the result of low volunteer participation levels in Japan across all sectors, with only 16% of the population volunteering compared to 43% in the United Kingdom, according to the World Values Survey (www.world valuessurvey.org; see Figure 1.1 in Chapter 1). Regular volunteering in Japan is therefore a minority activity. The World Values Survey figures illustrate the comparative histories of the voluntary sectors in both countries. The United Kingdom has a long history of philanthropy dating back to the nineteenth century, the period in which the National Trust was established. In Japan, volunteer participation is much more recent and it was the 1995 earthquake in Hanshin Awaji, which prompted a surge in volunteer activity initially within emergency and support activities but also more widely (Makoto, 2003).

In Japan, volunteers are most likely to be aged 30 to 50 years, be affluent and well educated and live in a rural area (Nakajima, Nakano, & Imada, 2004). In the Japanese cultural sector, volunteers are older (the 50–60-year age group accounts for over half the volunteers), and are twice as likely to be female than male and studying art (Agency for Cultural Affairs, 2003). Furthermore, the largest volunteer roles in the Japanese cultural sector are hosts, arranging meeting places and group visits (47%), guides (21%) and front desk assistants providing information or selling tickets (27%) (Agency for Cultural Affairs, 2003). This data emphasizes the important role that volunteers play in welcoming visitors and enhancing their experience.

This profile compares with cultural volunteering in the United Kingdom, which is also more popular among older people with a high level of educational attainment (Holmes, 1999). A survey of 723 volunteers conducted by the National Trust in 1997 found that 56% of respondents were aged 60 years or older and 82% of respondents described themselves as permanently retired (National Trust, 1998). In addition, research by the UK government found that 63% of museum volunteers were aged more than 55 years, while 36% were aged more than 65 years (Resource, 2002). The front-of-house roles undertaken by cultural volunteers in Japan also compare with the most well-known and most visible volunteer role within the National Trust: the room steward. These volunteers are stationed in a particular room or part of an historic property and assist with the visitor experience by greeting the visitor and answering questions, although they also have a security role. Volunteers are, however, involved in a wide range of behind-the-scenes and front-of-house roles in the National Trust.

Recruitment

Recruitment for the volunteer program at Dr Komai's Residence is informal, with no interview for prospective volunteers and no tangible rewards offered. The Japan National Trust does not receive many enquiries about volunteering and this is supported by comments from the volunteers that they were initially unaware about volunteer opportunities at the property. Recruitment methods used include regular advertisements in the Japan National Trust membership magazines and mailshots to members. There is also an advertisement on the property's web site, but this has not resulted in any inquiries. The Property Manager has also

- talked to some visitors about volunteering at Dr Komai's Residence,

- asked an arts university to put a volunteer advertisement on their notice board, and

- placed an advertisement in the property's brochures, and distributed these at a citizens' activities center, which has a recruitment office for volunteers.

The biggest recruitment difficulty is getting participants from the local area, who may become longer-serving volunteers than university students.

While there is a shortage of volunteers at Smallhythe Place, there is a low turnover among the existing volunteers, with only two to three leaving each year and they are easily replaced by individuals offering their services. Recruitment is usually through advertisements on the National Trust Web site, enquiries through the regional office or leaflets and enquiries at the property itself. In order to address the overall shortage there is a need for a specific recruitment campaign. One method, which has been tried by the Property Manager, is offering free guided tours of the property, which included a recruitment talk about volunteering at Smallhythe Place. This method successfully recruited six new volunteers from 43 tour participants. Other methods such as direct mail and partnership with a local Volunteer Information Centre have not yielded results. It is particularly difficult to find volunteers at weekends and during holidays, which coincides with the busiest visitor times for the property. This is because of family commitments – most volunteers are retired and looking for something to fill their time during the week when their family is busy; their weekends are then spent with their family.

Induction and training

The induction and training processes at both Dr Komai's Residence and Smallhythe Place are similar. At Dr Komai's Residence, new volunteers have a three-week probationary period. To begin with, the volunteer manager gives the new volunteers a guide manual including a script and volunteers are recommended to remember the key facts, rather than memorize the whole script, at least at first. The new volunteers watch how the experienced volunteers guide for the first three weeks and after that, they began to do some guiding with one of the experienced volunteers. Finally, the volunteer manager gives them some advice about what points they should explain in the guide manual and script.

New volunteers at Smallhythe Place are interviewed to see if the attraction and candidate are suitably matched. New volunteers are then scheduled with an experienced volunteer for their first few shifts. The matching of new and experienced volunteers can also help build social networks between new and existing volunteers. A refresher course for all volunteers is held at the start of the visitor season, which is usually a short meeting covering news and updates on information, policy, and procedures. About two-thirds of all the volunteers attend this meeting as attendance is not compulsory. This refresher meeting is important as the volunteers at

Smallhythe Place are seasonal and this helps to bring everyone together at the start of the new visitor season.

The volunteer–manager relationship

At Dr Komai's Residence, the volunteers have lunch every day with the Property Manager in their office, which creates a friendly atmosphere. The Property Manager also tries to discuss any future plans with the volunteers and tries to ensure that they are aware of any information or news. One volunteer commented that the atmosphere there is 'like in a family'. While a high proportion of the volunteers are students, they seem to be seeking leisure rather than work experiences, with the volunteers considering their relationship with the property to be a gift relationship of time rather than one of volunteering in exchange for certain rewards. This is fortunate as there are no tangible rewards offered to volunteers at Dr Komai's Residence, although there is a small reimbursement for travel expenses. While the Japan National Trust provides guidelines for volunteers for performing their roles at the attraction, there are no volunteer management guidelines for paid staff at Dr Komai's Residence.

The management style at Smallhythe Place is also informal and this approach at both properties is largely because of their size – it is possible for everyone to get to know each other. The National Trust has a well-regarded volunteer policy, which stipulates certain rewards (as outlined in Box 8.1) including payment of out-of-pocket travel expenses and Smallhythe Place implements this reward. Other rewards, which are available to all National Trust volunteer, include the volunteer card, awarded for 50 hours of service within one calendar year, which gives free entry into all National Trust properties and discounts in National Trust shops and restaurants. Additional rewards are available at the discretion of the individual property.

At Smallhythe Place, the Property Manager organizes a couple of trips a year, such as visiting another National Trust property and also hosts a summer barbecue at their home and organizes a Christmas meal. The Christmas meal also serves as a meeting during the closed season to maintain links between the volunteers and the property. The Property Manager uses his or her own time to organize these rewards to offer volunteers opportunities to meet each other, as very few are on the same shifts. It may also help strengthen the relationship between the volunteers and the property. The informal management style at Smallhythe Place is popular with the volunteers, with one commenting that 'at Smallhythe you can do as much or as little as you want'.

As noted above, the facilities at both properties are limited by the nature of the buildings. At Smallhythe Place, the volunteers' room is a small and old kitchen. As there are few volunteers at the property at any one time, the size of the room is rarely a problem. This does mean there are limited facilities on site for reward events involving all of the volunteers, one reason why the Property Manager hosts these at their own home. There is no separate volunteer room at Dr Komai's Residence, a further reason for volunteers having lunch in the manager's office. Volunteers commented that as the Japan National Trust is dependent on donations and has limited resources, little can be expected for the volunteers although the younger volunteers were less satisfied with this.

CONCLUSION

This case study compared two small historic properties, managed by very differently sized national trust organizations in Japan and the United Kingdom. Japan and the United Kingdom have very different levels of volunteer participation and this has some impact on volunteer recruitment. Despite the National Trust as a much larger organization having more formalized procedures, both properties operate in very similar ways. The reasons for the similarities are that both attractions have limited resources in terms of staffing and the facilities available at each site. This means that neither volunteer program has formal procedures – and recruitment, selection, training, and reward are all dependent on the resources of the Property Manager and existing volunteers. While these procedures are similar at both properties, Smallhythe Place has more structured recruitment and selection and offers more rewards for the volunteers. These differences are due to the support offered by the larger National Trust and the commitment of the individual Property Manager but are also illustrative of the volunteer culture within the United Kingdom.

DISCUSSION QUESTIONS

Q12.1 How does the low profile of volunteering in Japan affect recruitment of volunteers by the Japan National Trust?

Q12.2 What are the characteristics of the friendly ad hoc relationship between the Property Managers and the volunteers at the two attractions? What problems might this approach lead to?

Q12.3 Compare and contrast the rewards and recognition volunteers receive at Smallhythe Place with Dr Komai's Residence.

ACKNOWLEDGMENTS

The authors thank the National Trust for Places of Historic Interest and Natural Beauty and the Japan National Trust for their assistance in compiling this case study.

FURTHER INFORMATION

The National Trust for Places of Historic Interest and Natural Beauty. www.nation
    altrust.org.uk
Japan National Trust. www.national-trust.or.jp/english/englishindex

CHAPTER 13

The St. John River Society, Canada

Insights from Managing a Volunteer Board

Jennifer Fresque[1] and Ryan Plummer[2]

[1]*Wilfrid Laurier University, Waterloo, Canada, fres3130@wlu.ca*
[2]*Brock University, St. Catharines, Canada, rplummer@brocku.ca*

KEY POINTS

- The St. John River Society (SJRS) began as an informal, voluntary social organization in 1992 with the purpose of providing 'a voice for the river'.

- The SJRS has evolved significantly since its formation, and is now actively involved in the provision of tourism opportunities on the St. John River, New Brunswick, Canada.

- The SJRS deals with operational volunteers and those who constitute the Board of Directors.

- The SJRS has faced three major issues associated with change: a lack of human and financial resources; Board absenteeism/inactivity; and, tensions between Board subsections.

- The SJRS has responded to these changes in novel ways, which can provide insights for other volunteer organizations.

Managing Volunteers in Tourism
Copyright © 2009 Elsevier Ltd. All rights reserved.

OVERVIEW OF THE St. JOHN RIVER SOCIETY

The St. John River Society (SJRS) was founded in 1992 and is concerned with the appreciation and wise use of the St. John River in New Brunswick, Canada. During the past 15 years, the organizational structure, number of members, and scope of programmatic offerings has expanded considerably. Tourism initiatives such as the Fredericton RiverFest and the Lower River Passage contribute considerably toward recent organizational success.

The St. John River traverses the province of New Brunswick and runs 673 km from its headwaters in Northern Maine to the city of Saint. John, where it empties into the Bay of Fundy (SJRS, 1994). The watershed encompasses an estuary, many lakes, and tributaries. It drains an area of approximately 55,000 km^2 and connects New Brunswick with the province of Quebec and the state of Maine. People living in the watershed are located in three major cities (Edmundston, Fredericton, and Saint John) and a number of smaller towns and villages. Three hydroelectric dams currently operate in the river and a number of other industries, including a significant amount of agriculture, occur on the adjacent land. Tourism and recreation activities are popular in the region due to historic wharves located throughout the river and its exceptional natural features. The majority of tourism and recreation occurs in the Lower St. John River region.

The SJRS was founded around a kitchen table by a group of concerned citizens who wanted to promote actively awareness and appreciation of this majestic river through historical appreciation and stewardship programs. The mandate of SJRS is to be 'a voice for the river' (www.stjohnriver. org/about.htm). It is a not-for-profit, river-based organization based in Fredericton, New Brunswick, Canada, and is primarily voluntary in nature. During the formative years of the organization, the primary activity was the production of a newsletter (Fresque, 2008; Plummer, 1998).

In 1993 the organization became an incorporated entity and established bylaws for guidance. Membership was initially limited to 20 members; an extensive member recruitment program saw numbers increase dramatically in the first few years of operation, but then drop off significantly following 1995. At this time, the Board of Directors began to suffer from volunteer burnout, and few new Board members came forward (Plummer, 1998). In order to address these issues while still focusing on stewardship and conservation programs, changes were made to both the general Board of Directors and the Executive (e.g. new positions were created) (Plummer, 1998).

The Government of Canada decided to divest responsibility for the wharves along the St. John River in 1998 to incorporated entities. Following several public forums and meetings, it was decided that the SJRS would be the best organization to take control of the wharves. The act of incorporation, establishment of bylaws, and focus of the organization put the SJRS in this position. At this time, ecotourism planning and a river trails network were also added to the programs being offered (Fresque, 2008).

Taking over the wharves led to a change in direction for the SJRS, as the purpose for taking over the wharves was to preserve public access. This action increased the level of activity by the SJRS and emphasized their community orientation. During this time, the activities and programs developed by the SJRS were undertaken voluntarily by the Board of Directors, general members, and individuals from communities throughout the watershed.

In 2004 the SJRS hired its first full-time staff member, an Executive Director to oversee the development and implementation of the SJRS programs. The Director undertook strategic planning for the organization and identified four 'program pillars': access, information, sustainable management, and recognition (www.stjohnriver.org/about.htm). These pillars provide direction for the current and future programs of the SJRS. It is widely expressed by many SJRS participants that the Executive Director is responsible for revitalizing the organization and shifting the Society in a new direction. Today, the SJRS is involved in many tourism and sustainable development initiatives. These include: The Lower River Passage, Heritage Steamboat Wharves Program, the Fredericton RiverFest, and the seeking of a Canadian Heritage Rivers designation for the river (Fresque, 2008; www. stjohnriver.org/canadian_heritage.htm). For more information on each of these programs, see www.stjohnriver.org

OVERVIEW OF THE SJRS VOLUNTEER PROGRAM

The structure and operations of the SJRS are volunteer-based, supported by remunerated positions including a full-time Executive Director, a part-time Technical Services Officer, and seasonal staff. The Executive Director acts on behalf of the Board of Directors and is responsible for day-to-day operations and the hiring of necessary staff and coordination of volunteers. All other positions within the SJRS are voluntary. The foundation of the SJRS is its broad membership base. Anyone may become a member of the organization through annual payment of nominal membership dues. Within the SJRS, volunteers undertake the key role of serving on the Board of Directors (Board volunteers) and assisting with operations (operational volunteers).

Board volunteers are largely responsible for contributions to the governance of the organization. These individuals are taken from the broad membership base (i.e. to be a Board of Directors member one must be a member of the

SJRS), and will typically represent a geographical region at the Board level. The role of a Board member is to contribute to discussions and participate in formal motions and voting. The Board of Directors is also responsible for general decisions concerning programming and operation of the SJRS as well as providing guidance to the Executive Director. The Board of Directors operates via a majority rule voting structure (Fresque, 2008). Board members also voluntarily take on roles/tasks in SJRS projects, as well as participate in SJRS run events. In this way, Board volunteers also at times take on the roles of operational volunteers. If staff or the Board of Directors are unable to take on certain projects or tasks, then the likelihood of these being carried out decreases substantially. In 2007 the SJRS undertook a restructuring process, which resulted in a downsizing of positions on the Board of Directors. The current Board of Directors is now made up of approximately 15 individuals who represent the diversity of communities and users along the river.

In addition, an Executive is comprised of individuals who are members of the general Board of Directors. The voluntary Executive meets once a month and is responsible for specific decisions for the SJRS that occur between regular Board of Directors meetings, including program-based decisions. The Executive was also downsized during the restructuring process, and now consists of five members. Throughout this case study, the terms Board volunteers or Board of Directors will be used to denote the entire Board structure (both the general and Executive Boards) unless specifically noted.

The SJRS also utilizes operational volunteers. Operational volunteers help during SJRS events, particularly the Fredericton RiverFest. These are the individuals at the front line, who assist in the implementation of the programming and planning undertaken by the Board of Directors, at the direction of the Executive Director and hired staff. The Executive Director and staff are primarily responsible for hiring and coordination of all volunteer positions. Operational volunteers may come from the broad membership base, the Board of Directors, and the community at large (interested civil actors). Volunteers are a necessary part of the success of events and programs such as the Fredericton RiverFest, and are welcomed by the SJRS (www.frederictonriverfest.com).

KEY ISSUES FOR VOLUNTEER MANAGEMENT

The SJRS has evolved considerably since its foundation in 1992. It has had to respond and adapt to uncertainties in the internal operating environment as well as external social, political, and environmental factors. This section highlights critical issues in volunteer management within the SJRS. During its evolution, the SJRS has dealt with several major issues, including a lack of resources, Board absenteeism and inactivity, and tensions between subsections of the Board of Directors. The SJRS has put forward considerable effort in responding to these challenges. It is from these responses that insights are gained and lessons are learned. These three key issues are discussed, then insights learned from the SJRS's responses to these issues in the context of volunteer management follow.

Lack of human and financial resources

The SJRS is a voluntary, not-for-profit environmental organization and has consistently experienced a lack of financial resources over its existence, relying on memberships, donations, and government grants for support. This lack of resources greatly impacts the SJRS as they have limited funding for core operating costs, programs, and staff. While the SJRS works to deliver and promote tourism programming, it is often faced with the reality of limited interest for tourism in New Brunswick, in comparison with the neighboring province of Nova Scotia. In 2004, 5,038,000 trips were made by Canadians to New Brunswick, while 7,066,000 trips were made by Canadians to Nova Scotia (Statistics Canada, 2006). Lack of interest in tourism can result in decreased revenues generated through events and programming. Additionally, funding for not-for-profit environmental or tourism groups in New Brunswick has been extremely limited over the last two decades and this has resulted in a lack of human and financial resources.

In order to respond to the ongoing issue of resource shortages, the staff and Board volunteers of the SJRS have had to come up with creative and novel solutions. One such solution is the utilization of operational volunteers at events such as the Fredericton RiverFest. The Fredericton RiverFest promotes awareness and appreciation of the river through three days of events, including canoe races, music, family activities, and local cuisine (salmon and fiddleheads). The festival has been successful due to the commitment of the staff and volunteers, who plan, organize, and implement the event every year. The SJRS recognizes volunteers as a critical component in the operations of the festival (www.frederictonriverfest.com). Board volunteers also act as operational volunteers during events.

Another solution is the use of collaborative partnerships with other environmental not-for-profit groups, communities, and tourism entities to maximize available funding. The SJRS also works with various government agencies to procure project-based funding, such as capital provided by the Atlantic Canada Opportunities Agency (ACOA) for the Lower River Passage. The Lower River Passage is a multistakeholder collaborative project between the SJRS, five municipalities, two cities (Fredericton and Saint John), and one additional community stewardship group; the SJRS is currently the managing partner of the project. The purpose of this project is to market the lower portion of the St. John River to increase tourism, develop common infrastructure, and establish common signage at multiple tourist sites. The SJRS also relies on community members in its Heritage Steamboat Wharves Program, through the use of community stewards at each wharf site. These local stewards assist in maintaining a critical function (reporting and maintenance) of the wharf project. The engagement of community stewards creates a link between the SJRS and the communities involved in the wharf project and helps to maintain the project's viability.

Limited availability of funding accentuates the benefits of being a volunteer-based organization. Citizen volunteers, which can include the individuals who volunteer at the Board level, are increasingly being recognized as necessary in environmental management (Plummer & Arai, 2005). Citizen volunteers and partnerships with other organizations provide novel solutions and creative synergies. Cultivating and maintaining positive relationships, connections and partnerships with individuals, organizations, and agencies is critical.

Board absenteeism and inactivity

The SJRS has had to respond to several challenges relating to its Board of Directors. Volunteer burnout on the Board of Directors was an initial challenge in the mid-1990s. During this time, many of the Board volunteers were very actively involved in promotion and implementation of the SJRS activities, which led to burnout and difficulty in recruiting new participants for positions on the Board of Directors. The response was a restructuring of the Board of Directors and its membership and the creation of new positions. This shifted the extent and scope of authority in the organization, as the Executive was now heavily involved in the majority of decision-making. The Board of Directors was also restructured to represent the diversity of the watershed, so communities and user groups were better represented on the general Board of Directors. In 2004 the scope of authority shifted again with the hiring of a full-time Executive Director. This also helped alleviate volunteer burnout on the Board of Directors by delegating day-to-day management functions to the Executive Director.

More recently, absenteeism of Board members has been a significant issue within the SJRS. While many members of the SJRS are committed to the mandate of maintaining a voice for the river, Board absenteeism and inactivity has been a significant issue, which caused problems at the Board level and within the organization (Fresque, 2008). Often Board members were difficult to locate when decisions were required or they were absent from meetings. As Board of Directors positions are voluntary, members are not required to be at all meetings. Absenteeism or inactivity can lead to loss of representation of specific community/regional interests, as well as the potential insights from Board members, which may contribute to strengthening programming. Actively engaging Board members and getting them to contribute to discussions was an ongoing challenge within the SJRS. This impacted the decision-making process, as not all Board members voiced their opinion or participated in discussions that contributed to decisions.

In order to address this issue, the SJRS proposed and implemented a Board restructuring in 2007 that was voted upon and approved by the general membership at the Annual General Meeting. This restructuring eliminated positions on both the general Board and Executive Board, in order to consolidate the efforts of individuals most engaged in the management process and in the provision of current SJRS activities. This restructuring was also designed to increase the effectiveness of community representation at the general Board of Directors level. Although this had been the intent of the earlier restructuring, it remained an issue and members describe representation as 'hit and miss' at times.

The manner in which the SJRS handled this specific Board issue is an important lesson for other volunteer organizations, as ongoing commitment and motivation has been identified as an issue in volunteer management (Boezeman & Ellemers, 2008). Weaker connections and relationships to an organization can exist at the Board level, depending on an individual's reasons for participating in volunteering, which can influence intention to stay and satisfaction (Preston & Brown, 2004). Volunteer commitment is a perennial issue and restructuring mechanisms such as a Board of Directors may be a viable option to maintain 'freshness' and commitment in an organization.

Tensions between board subsections

In the past, tensions existed between sections of the volunteer Board of Directors. These sections had difficulty communicating and sharing information, as well working together in the decision-making and implementation processes. Cohesive group features (e.g. cooperation, trust, and open communication) were not present. This tension resulted in frustration for several members of the volunteer Board, especially when information-sharing and dialogue were halted. While tensions existed between these sections of the Board of Directors, relationships with additional partners and operational (citizen) volunteers outside of the Board structure were generally described as effective and enjoyable by participants involved in the process.

The SJRS has dealt with this issue formally and informally. The previously described restructuring of the Board of Directors provided a formal mechanism to address this issue. Informally, some members of the Board of Directors work around conflicts by actively ensuring that other Board members, partner organizations, and broader community members are engaged in discussion and decision-making. This provides an important insight, as conflict among volunteer participants can exist in several types of voluntary organizations (Amis, Slack, & Berrett, 1995; Lewis et al., 1997). Conflict can result from many factors, including mistrust and differences in individual's intentions for participating (Plummer & Arai, 2005). Mitigating and managing conflict relating to volunteer Board members is a dynamic challenge that requires ongoing attention.

The role of changing processes and mechanisms for management

In order to remain a viable and effective organization, the SJRS has had to evolve its structure over time as well as the processes and mechanisms which guide management of the organization. When the SJRS was first formed, the organization was loosely structured and the roles of participants were not explicitly defined. Meetings, decision-making, and actions occurred on an ad hoc, or as-necessary basis, with limited strategic planning in place early on. The majority of the SJRS's time was spent discussing the river, promoting awareness and attempting to broaden their general membership. Overall, the processes and mechanisms used to carry out management in the SJRS were loose and unstructured. While the organization developed bylaws in 1993, it has been identified by SJRS participants that these have been changed several times over the organization's existence.

The formal processes and mechanisms used to guide the SJRS have changed as the organization has evolved. With the transfer of the wharves into SJRS authority, the development of major collaborative initiatives such as the Lower River Passage and the Fredericton RiverFest, many processes and mechanisms have become much more formalized in nature. This shift has been out of necessity, as the SJRS now deals with multistakeholder projects, increased revenue, and government funding. At this point, roles and responsibilities are more clearly defined. Meetings are now highly structured (when compared with the initial meetings) and employ a majority rule voting structure (as determined by the 1993 bylaws). Agendas are set in advance and minutes circulated to those Board members who are absent. Decisions are made by majority rule at the Board of Directors, and are discussed at length prior to voting. The Executive Director is then instructed to carry out actions on their behalf. The Executive Director is regularly required to report back formally to the Board of Directors and Executive at meetings on the outcomes of actions and status of programs. Furthermore, in order to address issues at the Board of Directors level, the SJRS undertook a formal Board restructuring process, which was voted upon by the entire membership.

At the same time, many processes and mechanisms (e.g. communication) still occur in an informal fashion. It is not uncommon for dialogue to take place over coffee, dinners, or on the street, between staff and Board members. Phone calls and emails are also regularly used when immediate feedback is required between meetings. The Executive Director is also charged with the task of carrying out daily decisions and actions, which occur on the ground; these are often informal decisions, which do not require the approval of the Board of Directors. Board absenteeism makes it difficult to locate members of the Board of Directors when impromptu decisions are required, so the Executive Director often consults informally with a few key members of the Executive.

This balance of formal and informal processes and mechanisms has helped the organization maintain its viability and promote its mandate. This balance has been especially critical in the management and engagement of the volunteer Board of Directors. In response to volunteer burnout, the need to more actively engage volunteer Board members and to address the key issues highlighted above, the SJRS has become increasingly more formalized over time. This has occurred via the creation of bylaws, the development of a formal voting procedure, and a Board restructuring process. These formalized management mechanisms also increase the structure around tourism-based program delivery, and the role of both Board and operational volunteers. The SJRS has also maintained critical informal processes and mechanisms for management from the original voluntary-led group, which are also necessary for dealing with the nature of the tourism-based programming and the utilization of both Board and operational volunteers. Informal dialogue and communication are important ways to engage volunteers of all types, in a way that is accessible, personal and comfortable. These informal processes and mechanisms are a novel way to find creative solutions through dialogue and collaboration.

CONCLUSION

It is possible for other organizations to gain insights about managing volunteers by examining how the SJRS has responded to critical challenges. In negotiating these transitions, the SJRS has changed from a small informal group with a mandate of appreciation and awareness for the river to a moderately sized formal organization that is actively involved in promoting tourism, specifically through sustainable initiatives. As the organization has evolved, several key issues in managing volunteers (primarily a volunteer Board) have arisen. The SJRS has found several novel ways to address these challenges. These include: the use of operational volunteers at SJRS events; pursuing collaborative partnerships with other organizations and community members; a restructuring of the Board of Directors and Executive; and, the use of both formal and informal processes and mechanisms where necessary. In learning from these responses, other organizations will be better positioned to manage volunteers in the face of persistent change.

DISCUSSION QUESTIONS

Q13.1 What factors have precipitated change in the SJRS?

Q13.2 What barriers might the SJRS face in the future, and how should the organization respond to these?

Q13.3 What problems has SJRS experienced with their volunteer board members and how have they sought to address these?

ACKNOWLEDGMENTS

The authors wish to thank the people of the St. John River Society, in particular, Cynthia Stacey and Molly Demma, for their hospitality and generosity. The authors also wish to acknowledge and thank the Social Sciences and Humanities Research Council of Canada (SSHRC), and the Faculties of Applied Health Sciences and Graduate Studies at Brock University for support of this research.

FURTHER INFORMATION

St. John River Society: www.stjohnriver.org

Fredericton RiverFest: www.frederictonriverfest.com

The Lower River Passage project: www.discoverthepassage.com

CHAPTER 14

The Vancouver International Children's Festival, Canada

Reflections on the Coordination of a Successful Event Volunteer Program

Peter Burley[1] and Diana Stewart-Imbert[2]

[1]*Christchurch Polytechnic Institute of Technology, New Zealand, burleyp@cpit.ac.nz*
[2]*Vancouver International Children's Festival, Canada, edu@childrensfestival.ca*

KEY POINTS

- The ability of the volunteer coordinator to motivate and insti a unique philosophy and ethos of service is what makes Vancouver International Children's Festival volunteer program special for all who participate in it.

- Government volunteerism initiatives provided a driver for the substantial growth in volunteerism at a time when the festival was in need of a boost to its volunteer numbers. The festival Volunteer Coordinator was able to utilize this Government Policy to great advantage and school students required to complete community service are now central to the volunteering program.

- Volunteer roles at the Festival are arranged hierarchically with a system of senior or 'key' volunteers doing much of the recruitment and facilitation work to ensure a much larger general volunteer base.

- The volunteer program has flourished as a result of the continuity of having one coordinator follow a model of continuous improvement over a number of years. Her style of management has influenced the effectiveness of the program.

Copyright © 2009 Elsevier Ltd. All rights reserved.

OVERVIEW OF THE VANCOUVER INTERNATIONAL CHILDREN'S FESTIVAL

The Vancouver International Children's Festival is widely recognized both in Canada and internationally as one of the premier outdoor children's festivals in the world. Since 1978, this event has enthralled the people of Vancouver with more than 1.6 million visitors from Vancouver's regional communities across British Columbia and beyond. Adults who attended as children are now bringing their own kids, creating a wonderful continuum and legacy. The Vancouver International Children's Festival Society is a trust initially set up to run this festival. It is an internationally recognized innovator in the field of arts for young people. It was one of the first Children's Theatre Trusts to take its performances outdoors and was the original destination of the now infamous Cirque du Soleil mobile truck-based circus. The Vancouver International Children's Festival Society has a clear mandate to provide performing arts to young people in a way that encourages life-long interest in the arts.

The eight-day festival is organized by eight full-time staff, a Board of Directors and an Executive Officer. The festival outputs in 2008 included: 43,000 attendees, 12,000 schoolchildren attendees, 480 performers, 139 roving shows, hundreds of hands-on arts and cultural activities, and free performances and workshops. The festival experience is also brought directly to children at the Vancouver Children's Hospital and other health centers. In 2008, the average ticket price was approximately CDN$12; however, the actual cost to the organization for one person to attend the festival was around CDN$50. This means that major fund-raising efforts, undertaken by the Festival organizers to obtain government and foundation grants, corporate sponsorships and individual donations, subsidize festival tickets by approximately 75%. Volunteer labor was valued at CDN$200,000 in 2008.

OVERVIEW OF THE VANCOUVER INTERNATIONAL CHILDREN'S FESTIVAL VOLUNTEER PROGRAM

The story of the development of this festival is also the story of the development of a unique and powerful philosophy and ethos. People who work on the festival and who volunteer their time have become a sort of brethren and they stay involved, often fondly remembering the early days and how the festival affected their development in the music industry, in theater and production, and recreation and arts management. The volunteer program was a crucial aspect of this development.

Founded in 1978, in the early years the festival site plan was substantially different from that of the present day. The initial concept was open entrance with individually ticketed performances and limited free outdoor entertainment. The festival was new, enthusiasm was high, government funding at all levels was more plentiful and, most importantly, audience attendance was high, due mostly to the lack of competition. The Children's Festival was the only event of its type and there was little other children's entertainment being marketed, so the festival had full community support. This was the situation for approximately the first 10 years. Then in 1986 Vancouver hosted EXPO86. Many local children and family performers (and the arts groups in general) flourished in Vancouver, and so the competition for audiences began. A general downsize in government funding to the arts and schools followed in the 1990s. During this time, the festival was cutting budgets and offering more activities to encourage attendance, and the need for volunteer labor was increasing. By the mid-1990s, the festival was recruiting approximately 300 volunteers annually. It was, however, getting more difficult to find the number of volunteers required.

In the late 1990s, the British Columbia provincial government brought forward a set of new requirements to encourage volunteerism, career preparation and work experience. Every high-school student was required to complete a minimum of 30 community service hours to graduate and the festival organizers targeted these school students as a source of volunteers. About the same time, the festival decided to enclose the site and charge site admission. The need for volunteers grew as more activities were added to justify the site fee. In 2000 and 2001, there were approximately 500 volunteers.

The year 2002 saw major changes in volunteer recruitment at the festival. A new Volunteer Coordinator was hired, an online volunteer sign up was created, and the in-school Key Volunteer Program was established. Key Volunteers are students interested in Arts Administration who work with Career Preparation Teachers to recruit and coordinate volunteers at their schools and who later take on key roles at the festival.

Table 14.1 indicates the growth of the volunteer program size over time. The numbers have grown according to changes in policy and changes in economic realities as labor supply shrunk or as costs increased.

KEY ISSUES FOR VOLUNTEER MANAGEMENT

Volunteer roles, allocation and choice

A key feature of the success of the festival is the scope and breadth of the volunteer and education program. In 2008 there were 1520 volunteers

Table 14.1 Growth in Festival Volunteer Numbers

Year of Festival	Total Number of Volunteers
1970–1990	100–200
1991–2000	300
2002	500
2003	650
2004–2006	1100
2007	1480
2008	1520

contributing 21,700 person-hours to help prepare for and run the festival. Some volunteers are involved in the administration office in the lead up to the festival but most volunteer only during the event. Sixty key volunteers were selected by interview to create the backbone of the program to recruit more than 1000 school-based volunteers. Another 400 or so volunteers signed up online at the festival web site. Together, this is a large and productive volunteer capability that has been steadily growing in size.

The way the festival operates demands a large labor supply. There are over 30 tents located on the site, three of which house audiences of between 400 and 1000 people at each sitting. The infrastructure is challenging with temporary seating for up to 1000 in the bigger tents, temporary power, and toilet and water supplies required for upwards of 6000 visitors per day who access 30 different tent activities, many needing volunteer help. Transportation logistics are particularly demanding with a requirement to move safely large numbers of schoolchildren via school bus to and from the site. This necessitates a large supply of marshals and a detailed marshaling operation for bus and children's movements in and out of the venue.

A fundamental ethos of the festival is 'engagement' and child-centric 'learning'. Children participate and this is facilitated through the use of 'activity tents'. This approach necessitates a large volunteer base to operate the activities around the site including a kite-making tent, an outdoor circus activities area, and dance and origami tents that would not be able to operate without the contribution of the volunteers. New volunteers are trained early on the day by those who have volunteered for this activity before and by the tent managers.

On any scale, this is a large number of volunteers who need to be found and organized each year. Volunteer roles generally correspond to the needs of different aspects of the festival: Technical, Administrative, Security, Activity Tents, Operations, Ushering and Marshaling. However, the opposite is also true and sometimes the talent of an individual can create a new volunteer

Table 14.2	Demographic Profile of the Festival Volunteers
Demographic Group	**Approximate % of Volunteers**
14–17 years and at school	70%
18 years plus left school	5%
Postsecondary/Tertiary study	20%
Adults	5%

position. Several recent volunteer positions included an origami specialist, young sound engineer, person with specialist circus skills, baby masseuse and deaf language interpreters.

Volunteers are given the choice of how they will volunteer and what activity they will choose to volunteer for. These include specific tents, marshaling duties, tent supervision, technical and 'floaters', who relieve others from stations, cover contingencies and do whatever is required. Student volunteers' positions are often related to their future career orientation, but can also be for general work experience or skills training. The range of volunteer positions is clearly defined at the outset and volunteers make their choices via the online enrolment system.

Although the mass of volunteers come from the under-17 demographic (Table 14.2), the most valuable volunteers tend to be postsecondary/tertiary students as they are often more responsible, motivated and skilled and can be used in assistant managerial positions. Adults are also generally good volunteers, depending on their physical condition, although older volunteers are more concerned about cold or wet weather as the festival takes place outdoors. It is often most difficult to find volunteers during the week when the majority of students are in school, so the festival looks for groups of volunteers, student or otherwise, who could be available weekdays: French classes for Francophone Day programming, Special Needs, new immigrants, service organizations, corporate groups.

Continuity of planning and management

An important facet of the Vancouver International Children's Festival is the continuity of management of the volunteer program. The current Volunteer Coordinator has been involved in the festival delivering the volunteer program since January 2002. Over the years, she has adapted and improved her processes and learnt from experience what works best:

> I approach it step by step. I know that I have a time line; I know things that have to be done in a certain time. I generally start off by getting my key volunteers together, which are volunteers that help me co-ordinate

and recruit in schools. At the same time I get the teachers in the schools excited about our programs to recruit students in that school. [The festival is in May] At about the end of January I start recruiting in a lot of volunteer organisations that provide volunteers and service organisations and try to get the adult population interested.

I have a plan I follow [and] I would say every year I am a week ahead of the year before. I renew material from the year before and it's usually within four to five days ahead of the schedule each year so yes there is a plan. Of course I am flexible and I do re-create my plan yearly and do a few add-ons. This year I was looking to have an assistant for the first time so I could be more creative with my job and I think that because of that it was more successful, I don't think we really had a down day at the festival or a day where we didn't have enough people or the right people for the job.

The key volunteers

With large numbers of student volunteers to organize, the Volunteer Coordinator quickly worked out that it would be impossible to manage directly the relationship with the School Administrators as there were too many of them. She also wanted the direct involvement of students in the volunteer management process; after all, this in itself would be learning about leadership for these volunteers. The Key Volunteer program was the result.

I suddenly thought that this would be a really ideal situation for any students who would like to take the initiative or who were future event managers. I thought I'd cultivate that at the same time. I love cultivating just love of the arts and future theatre goers, people who will become involved in some way or at least become people who respond to the arts. So I approached a couple of the teachers that I knew and they just thought it was a wonderful idea. So I went out there and found key volunteers and it has grown every year.

It's actually stabilized but I think what I've got now is a bit more of a handle on it because I don't have as many. Sometime I have like eight volunteers at one school and I maybe had 60 or 80 key volunteers [altogether] but they weren't as efficient as having two or three who did a really good job at each school. I have more control over them now and I know as usual if you do something for a long period of time and you fine tune it. I think it's pretty well there now

and the students always ask me from the year before, can I be a key
volunteer next year, and we talk about it a bit and I always prime
them for next year.

Style of leadership

A large part of the success of any team is based on the qualities of its leadership. Volunteerism is based on human generosity and a sense of one's
actions serving a greater good. The Volunteer Coordinator's primary objective each year is to harness this good energy and create an enthusiastic
volunteer community with clear goals and rewards. However, there is also
an underlying philosophy that defines more precisely her particular leadership style: respect for the volunteer's contribution while making the experience as rewarding as possible and awakening a volunteer's (often hidden)
strengths and talents.

Style of leadership is also demonstrated in the way the leader recruits,
organizes and evaluates his or her team. Recruiting for the next festival begins
while at the previous year's festival, where the Coordinator notes exceptional
volunteers and encourages them to keep in touch and return the following
year. In the Fall, about six months before the festival, volunteer positions are
defined and the request for Key Volunteers goes out. Key Volunteer meetings
are held monthly and recruitment progress is assessed right up to the festival.
At the same time, other volunteer sources are contacted. Three months before
the festival, the online web sign up is activated. Applicants are screened for
erroneous or missing information and potential 'exceptional' volunteers are
contacted. Volunteers are placed in requested positions as they apply. When
their requested positions are full, volunteers are signed up as 'Floaters' (contingency and extraduty volunteers which usually represent about 30% of daily
volunteer numbers). Normally all positions are filled six weeks before the
festival and final confirmations are sent out. Teachers also receive a copy of
students' schedules and pertinent paperwork as students will be credited for
their volunteer hours. Key Volunteers who take on special assistant positions
receive special training leading up to the festival, while all other volunteers
are asked to attend a training/orientation session the Sunday before opening.

During the festival, volunteers receive a T-shirt, badge and one compli-
mentary site admission for each shift. The ambience in the Volunteer Tent
is both celebratory (volunteers decorate it) and that of organized chaos. It
is everyone's second home for the week. Everyone works extremely hard,
lifetime friendships are made and everyone is sad when it's over. Volunteer
confirmations, evaluations and reference letters follow, and everything
moves into gear for the following year's festival.

To manage such a large group of people requires a specific approach. Many of the communications are brief and information-based communication is the rule. The Coordinator nurtures the key volunteers giving them guidance on a range of things, even career aspirations, and how their link to the festival may help them. Recruitment is spread to the Coordinator's other areas of interest, including language schools with which she has a relationship. The planning allows for training days for key volunteers, and for contingency planning where large groups of 'floater' volunteers are present for backup. Because of the large number of younger volunteers, the Coordinator talks about 'mothering' them and is always careful to give full attention to questions and concerns and requests for clarification. She believes that it is important to marshal volunteers in positive ways and be available to assist them as the festival runs. There is a need to provide a system of tangible rewards for volunteer participation including: formal recording of community service and the ability to attend festival shows and workshops. Through this nurturing, caring leadership approach the Coordinator maintains a smooth operational flow that is a crucial element in the operational success of the volunteer management for the eight days of the festival.

CONCLUSION

The Vancouver International Children's Festival is a large, unique and comprehensive event and a key area of success has been the substantial volunteer program. Over 1000 volunteers are needed to operate this festival successfully due to the philosophy of active audience participation and the substantial setup logistics. The volunteer program has many critical success factors that make it possible for this size of program to operate each year. British Columbia requires all its schoolchildren to do 30 hours of community service each year, and volunteering at the festival is one way to achieve this. The festival uses web-based enrolment processes integrated into a comprehensive recruitment system that allows volunteers to choose different ways of volunteering and different roles, thus giving them choice. There is a nurturing style employed by the Volunteer Coordinator and a set of tangible rewards offered. The process is under constant review, and has continuity as the Coordinator works to improve it and has done so now for a six-year period. In conclusion, this is a well-conceived, well-thought-out and well-implemented volunteer program that is a critical part of the success of the Vancouver International Children's Festival.

DISCUSSION QUESTIONS

Q14.1 Recruitment is best done by people within the immediate peer group of potential volunteers. Discuss this statement with reference to the Key Volunteers program at the Vancouver International Children's Festival.

Q14.2 How has the Volunteer Coordinator's management style influenced the effectiveness of the program?

Q14.3 For another event you are aware of, suggest how school, college, or university students can be involved as volunteers. You should consider their likely motivations, the skills they will bring, the volunteering roles they could undertake, and the likely rewards they will value. Design a recruitment campaign to appeal to this target market of potential volunteers.

FURTHER INFORMATION

Vancouver International Children's Festival Web site: www.childrensfestival.ca

CHAPTER 15

Kongsberg Jazz Festival, Norway

Motivating and Retaining Episodic and Bounce-Back Volunteers at an Annual Festival

Beate Elstad

Oslo University College, Norway, Beate.Elstad@sam.hio.no

KEY POINTS

- Social interpersonal networks are most important for recruiting new volunteers to the Kongsberg Jazz Festival;

- Analysis of motivations shows festival volunteers to be socially orientated people who love jazz music. Material rewards and fringe benefits are more important to new volunteers;

- Levels of volunteers' continuance commitment are positively influenced by feedback from managers, satisfaction with food, altruism, and connection with hobbies/interests;

- Workload, lack of appreciation, and changes in the organization and goals of the festival contribute to why a volunteer may consider quitting;

- Creative problem-solving is the key skill generated through volunteering at the festival.

CONTENTS

Managing Volunteers in Tourism
Copyright © 2009 Elsevier Ltd. All rights reserved.

OVERVIEW OF THE KONGSBERG JAZZ FESTIVAL

This case study is based on data from the Kongsberg Jazz Festival, which is among the oldest and biggest jazz festivals in Norway. It takes place in early summer during the first week of July and has been arranged since 1965. It takes place in Kongsberg, a small city with 23,000 inhabitants. The festival is arranged in different outdoor and indoor locations in the city, and the festival is dependent on cooperation with different stakeholders in the local community. The main musical profile is based on contemporary jazz music with Norwegian and famous international musicians such as Ornette Coleman, Wayne Shorter, Joe Lovano, David Liebman, and Joshua Redman. The goal is to be the most daring and border-crossing jazz festival in Norway. In 2007, the festival organizers sold 14,000 tickets and received funding from private sponsors and national, regional, and local government. In accordance with being a high-quality jazz festival, they focus on environmental issues and cooperate with the charities SOS-Children's Village and Amnesty International.

OVERVIEW OF THE KONGSBERG JAZZ FESTIVAL VOLUNTEER PROGRAM

Three paid employees work for the festival: the manager, marketing manager, and a festival coordinator; and 300 volunteers are involved. The large number of volunteers in relation to paid workers is consistent with other jazz and rock festivals such as Roskilde Festival in Denmark with 25 paid employees and 25,000 volunteers (see Web Resource 2.3). Without volunteers, these festivals simply could not take place.

To learn more about the volunteers at the Kongsberg Jazz Festival, a survey was conducted. The data collection consisted of two self-completion surveys. One questionnaire was administered before the festival and measured the volunteers' background, demographics, and motivation for participating as a volunteer. Another was administered after the festival; it measured the volunteers' evaluation of their experience as participants at the festival. Of the 300 or so volunteers participating at the festival, 278 answered the before-festival survey and 242 answered after-festival survey. In the final analysis, we only included those aged 16 years and older.

The survey showed about 30% of the volunteers were involved before, during, and after the festival, while 70% volunteered only during the festival. Most volunteered 7 or 8 days. The average volunteering hours during the festival were 73 hours; those with managerial responsibility for a group of volunteers gave on average about 130 hours, compared with the 60 hours of other volunteers.

The volunteers at the Kongsberg Jazz Festival are involved in 17 different areas. An organizational chart is presented in Figure 15.1 and shows that the volunteers are divided into many departments and there is a large degree of specialization. To ensure coordination of the festival, some groups volunteer across different departments. One example is the internal group that is responsible for food and welfare issues for all the volunteers at the festival. Another example is the Information and Communications Technology (ICT) group that has developed a technical solution, which facilitates mobile phone communications. There is also a morning meeting every day where the volunteer managers for each volunteer group, the paid staff, and other key persons meet to coordinate the main activities.

KEY ISSUES FOR VOLUNTEER MANAGEMENT

There are a variety of different challenges related to volunteer management at a festival. This case study will focus on four main themes: the recruitment, motivation, and commitment of the volunteers, and volunteering as a potential context of competence development.

Recruitment

Recruiting new volunteers is a major challenge facing many organizations which are dependent on volunteers. Organizations can choose a variety of different strategies such as advertisements in the newspapers, information meetings, information on Internet sites, or through interpersonal networks. Our survey showed that 60% of Kongsberg Jazz Festival volunteers were recruited through friends or family who were volunteers, and 14% through volunteers that were colleagues/fellow students/schoolmates. Just a very small proportion of the volunteers were recruited through advertisements in the newspapers (1%) or information meeting (0.4%). These findings are consistent with other research that indicates that interpersonal networks are essential in recruiting new volunteers (Pearce, 1993). These findings imply that the most effective pathway to recruit new volunteers is to make sure that those already volunteering are satisfied and therefore will encourage other people in their network to join in and volunteer together with them. Another advantage of this mode of recruitment is that new volunteers may be socialized and receive training and tips from the volunteers who originally recruited them.

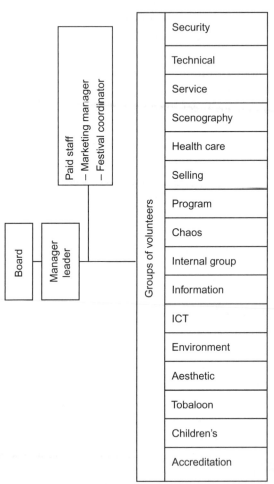

FIGURE 15.1 Organizational Chart of Kongsberg Jazz Festival.
Source: www.kongsberg-jazzfestival.no, Annual Report 2006–2007, and correspondence with the coordinator of the festival

Volunteer motivation

To increase volunteers' satisfaction, it is important to know what motivated people to be a volunteer. In other words, what reasons are perceived as important for volunteering at this festival? A review of studies of volunteer motivation identified twelve motivational dimensions (see Elstad, 1997b, p. 24). For the Kongsberg Jazz Festival research, we found that only eight of these dimensions were relevant:

1. to socialize – to be together with other people and be a part of the festival atmosphere;

2. social expectations – people around you expect you to volunteer;

3. community relations – to increase your influence and to get to know people better in your local community;

4. connected with hobby/interests – to be able to work with your hobby/interests;

5. to learn/competence development – to learn something new and increase your competence;

6. career development – a step in a career path;

7. material rewards/fringe benefits – such as festival T-shirt, free tickets, food, and beverage;

8. altruism – the wish to help.

Table 15.1 shows the motives of Kongsberg Jazz Festival volunteers. To socialize and be together with other people and be a part of the festival atmosphere is the most important motivational factor. Furthermore, volunteering being connected with hobby/interests such as interest in jazz music is the second most important factor. Thus, it seems that volunteers at the Kongsberg Jazz Festival are socially oriented people who love jazz music. A more indirectly positive effect of volunteering, for example, that to be a volunteer gives you other benefits such as improved relations to local community; and career possibility is not so important to these volunteers. It may be somewhat surprising that material rewards are not very important. Does that imply that it is not important to give volunteers free tickets and T-shirts? If the sample is split, subgroup analysis shows that material rewards/fringe benefits are more important for volunteers with less than three years of experience as volunteers (Elstad, 1997b). This implies that material rewards/fringe benefits are more important when recruiting new volunteers.

Table 15.1	Motives of Volunteers at the Kongsberg Jazz Festival	
Motive	**Mean (scale:1–7)**	**N**
To socialize	5	245
Connected with hobby/interests	4.7	248
Altruism	4.2	252
To learn/ competence development	4	246
Social expectations	3.7	250
Material rewards/fringe benefits	3.3	251
Community relations	2.5	247
Career development	2.4	247

Scale: 1 = Not at all important; 4 = Somewhat important; 7 = Very important

Table 15.1 reflects the variety of different reasons why people choose to volunteer. Consequently, it is important for managers to find out which motives are important for each volunteer so that they can provide them with tasks consistent with their motivational profile. If, for example, to socialize is most important for a volunteer, he or she should not be allocated to volunteer backstage where he or she meets few people. In contrast, for a person who volunteers mainly because of the passion for jazz music and a wish to meet some famous jazz artists, it can be very satisfying to be backstage and help a jazz artist with different practical tasks.

Continuance commitment

Because volunteers are not dependent on the event or festival economically, it is much easier for them to quit as a volunteer compared with quitting in their paid jobs. It is, therefore, quite a challenge to ensure that individuals are committed to the festival and want to continue as volunteers in the future. A key question is which factors are important to explain the volunteer's continuance commitment? In this study, the focus is on the importance of different motivational factors such as connected with hobby/interests, altruism, opportunity to socialize, material rewards, and impact/status on local community. Furthermore, different contextual factors were included in the analysis. It was expected that it was more attractive to continue as a volunteer when a job is challenging, and when one is satisfied with the feedback from their managers and the cooperation among the volunteers. In a study of volunteers at the Lillehammer Olympics, it was discovered that welfare issues were important for the volunteers' overall satisfaction (Elstad, 1997a). Thus, satisfaction with the free food and free tickets was also included to explain volunteers' continuance commitment. The following factors were discovered as significantly important in explaining volunteers' continuance commitment at the Kongsberg Jazz Festival (Elstad, 2003):

- Feedback from managers

- Satisfaction with the food

- Altruism

- Connected with hobbies/interests

Implications from these findings are that feedback from managers is important to ensure the volunteers' continuance commitment. A major challenge is to train the managers at the festival to give appropriate and sufficient feedback. The findings also indicate that only a part of the welfare system is important to ensure volunteer continuance commitment. More precisely, volunteers' satisfaction with the food was important whereas satisfaction with the opportunity to use free tickets had no impact on volunteers' continuance commitment. Thus, for the festival, it would be more important to focus on the quality of the food than on free tickets in order to ensure volunteers' continuance commitment. Among the motivational factors, altruism and connected with hobbies/interests had a significant effect on volunteers' continuance commitment. Thus, in the recruitment of new volunteers, the festival may look for individuals who want to be volunteers because it is connected with hobbies/interests or because they want to help. Individuals who volunteer because of material rewards such as free tickets and T-shirts or to improve their impact and status in local communities will be less committed to continue as volunteers in the future.

Closely related to volunteers' continuance commitment are possible reasons why they consider quitting as a volunteer. About 30% of the volunteers at the Kongsberg Jazz Festival had considered quitting. Table 15.2 lists different possible reasons.

As can be seen from Table 15.2, workload as a volunteer was the most important reason for considering quitting. Thus, it is important that the workload is at an appropriate level. Because it is subjective how much each volunteer perceives as too much work, it is a challenge for the managers to decide what is an appropriate workload for various volunteers.

It was also important for the volunteers to be appreciated. At this festival, they use more than a week of their summer holiday to volunteer for the festival without receiving any financial compensation. Non-financial rewards such as recognition and appreciation can therefore be very important. Combined with the finding that feedback from managers was important to ensure volunteers, continuance commitment, it implies a strong

Table 15.2	Reasons to Quit as a Festival Volunteer	
Reasons	**Mean (Scale: 1–5)**	**N**
Workload as a volunteer	2.90	73
That you are not appreciated enough as a volunteer	2.65	71
The organization of the festival	2.61	71
Disagreement with the festival's changing goals/ideology	2.57	68
Too little time for other leisure activities/meet friends	2.51	72
That I do not feel community anymore among the volunteers	2.48	69
Take care of my family	2.46	70
The festival has become too large	2.26	72
Are not allowed to make decisions related to own job	2.21	71
Have to do jobs I do not like	2.14	72
New paid job	2.10	65
Moving to a new place	1.54	64

Scale: 1 = Not at all important; 3 = Somewhat important; 5 = Very important

need for the management of the festival to give sufficient and relevant feedback and to express explicitly that they appreciate the volunteers' effort at the festival. Thus, to be a manager at the festival requires feedback and communications skills. This should be a focus in the recruitment and development of managers. The organizing of the festival and changing goals/ideology were also regarded as somewhat important in considering quitting. This particular festival has grown significantly during recent years, from being a small local event to being a large-scale festival. Furthermore, it has been commercialized with many private sponsors and has also been professionalized to be able to compete in the market with other festivals. Thus, those who had been volunteering at the festival for some years may perceive the values upon which the festival had been based were threatened. This may decrease their willingness to volunteer in the future.

Volunteering as a context for generation of general skills

Studies of volunteers have demonstrated that the drive to learn is an important motive for participation in volunteering (Andersen, 1996; Clary, Snyder, & Stukas, 1996; Lorentzen & Rogstad, 1994; Lynn & Smith, 1991; Ryan & Bates, 1995; Williams, Dossa, & Tompkins, 1995). At the Kongsberg Jazz Festival, learning/competence development is also seen as an important reason to volunteer (Table 15.1). Volunteering implies a challenging work situation, and therefore a potential for informal learning of new skills. General skills are skills that can be transferred across organizational

Table 15.3	Festival Volunteers' Perception of Generation of General Skills	
General skill	Mean (scale:1–5)	N
Creative problem-solving	3.2	217
Cooperation	2.9	217
Stress management	2.9	222
General management	2.7	218
Conflict management	2.7	219
Practical skills useful in my daily job/studies	2.3	211
Theoretical skills useful in my daily job/studies	2.0	207

Scale: 1 = Not at all important; 3 = Somewhat important; 5 = Very important

settings (Nordhaug, 1993). Examples are interpersonal skills and problem-solving skills. These skills can be useful in all kinds of organizations both as a volunteer and as an employee. If volunteers develop general skills as a volunteer, this strengthens the argument that volunteering is important from society's point of view. Which general skills do the volunteers perceive they develop as a volunteer at the Kongsberg Jazz Festival?

Table 15.3 indicates that to some degree people perceive that they generate general skills as a volunteer, especially creative problem-solving. A festival volunteer may often be in situations where unexpected things happen, such as bad weather, artists that arrive late at the airport, stage problems, and uncertainty regarding the size of the audience at different concerts. Consequently, volunteers must be able to respond to these unexpected situations and therefore may develop their creative problem-solving skills. This situation may also often be stressful and implies a need for cooperation to solve problems. This can be a possible explanation why volunteers, to some degree, perceive that they develop their stress management skills and cooperation skills. Thus, it seems that volunteering is a context where people can develop general skills that are also very important in their paid job such as creative problem-solving, cooperation, and stress management.

CONCLUSION

This case study of Kongsberg Jazz Festival discusses important issues related to volunteer management such as recruitment, motivation, continance commitment, and reasons for quitting, and volunteering as a context for competence development. The survey of volunteers at the Konsgberg Jazz Festival shows social networks are the most important recruitment pathway. The social dimension is also important in understanding why people choose to volunteer; socializing and being together with other people is the most important motivational factor. Furthermore, the interest in music and jazz is also an important reason, whereas material rewards, social expectations, and career development are not so important. To ensure the volunteers' continuance commitment, managers should give proper feedback and explicitly express an appreciation of the volunteers' effort for the festival. It is also important that the workload as a volunteer is appropriate. Finally, volunteers perceive that to some degree they develop general skills as a volunteer that can be useful in their paid job such as creative problem-solving, cooperation, and stress management.

DISCUSSION QUESTIONS

Q15.1 Who are the different stakeholders at the Kongsberg Jazz Festival?

Q15.2 Suggest ways of increasing the continuance commitment of festival volunteers?

Q15.3 What training do you think a festival manager needs to be able to manage volunteers?

FURTHER INFORMATION

Kongsberg Jazz Festival: www.kongsberg-jazzfestival.no

CHAPTER 16

2006 Melbourne Commonwealth Games, Australia

Recruiting, Training and Managing a Volunteer Program at a Sporting Mega Event

Leonie Lockstone[1] and Tom Baum[2]

[1]*Victoria University, Australia, Leonie.Lockstone@vu.edu.au*
[2]*University of Strathclyde, UK, T.G.Baum@strath.ac.uk*

KEY POINTS

- The 2006 Commonwealth Games in Melbourne was a very high-profile mega event, attracting far more volunteer interest than could be accommodated within the staffing requirements of the event.

- The event organizers embarked upon a program of recruitment, selection, training and role allocation that closely mirrored practice that would be used with paid employees.

- Issues of inflexible volunteer role and roster allocation were the main human resource management issues to arise during the event.

- Mega sporting event volunteers are a relatively closed 'subset' of volunteers who do not cross over to/from other volunteering activities to any significant extent.

OVERVIEW OF THE 2006 MELBOURNE COMMONWEALTH GAMES

Mega sporting events, notably those of global interest, such as the Olympic Games and the Commonwealth Games, provide a public interest agenda

Managing Volunteers in Tourism
Copyright © 2009 Elsevier Ltd. All rights reserved.

that addresses issues across a wide spectrum of concerns and opportunities. Such sporting spectacles are part of the wider and growing analysis of major events within diverse fields of urban regeneration, economic development, politics and tourism (Getz, 2005). Major events depend heavily on the participation of volunteers who undertake a wide range of tasks associated with operations and administration. Therefore, the engagement and management of these volunteers within any major event is an important consideration for organizers.

The 2006 Commonwealth Games took place between March 15 and 26 in Melbourne, capital city of the State of Victoria in Australia, and was the largest multi-nation sporting event of the year. A total of 71 countries and 4500 athletes took part in 16 sports and 24 disciplines (Brown, 2006, p. 3) over a period of 10 days. In terms of world events, it has been suggested that the Commonwealth Games are positioned only behind the Olympics and Football World Cup in terms of size and profile (Van Der Westhuizen, 2004). The story of the Commonwealth Games is presented in terms that frequently balance competitive elements with cultural and friendship dimensions (between participating countries, competitors and spectators) that are, perhaps, less emphasized by other mega event organizers. The origins of the Games begin in Hamilton, Canada where in 1930, 11 countries sent 400 athletes to take part in six sports and 59 events (www.commonwealthgames.com). Akin to its Olympic counterpart, excluding times of war (1942 and 1946), the Games have run on a continuous four-year cycle since inception. From its early beginnings, the event has seen many changes, not the least being several different names including the British Empire Games (1930–1950), the British Empire and Commonwealth Games (1954–1966) and the British Commonwealth Games (1970–1974) (www.commonwealthgames.com). It was at the 1978 Games in Edmonton, Canada that the name of the event was detached from its colonial trappings and restyled as the Commonwealth Games. The Commonwealth Games also draws particular strength from the geographical dispersion of its participating nations, something of considerable importance in tourism terms, and not evident in regional events, such as the Asian Games or the European Athletics Championships.

The Commonwealth Games takes great pride in its styling as the 'Friendly Games' and seeks to set inclusive yet challenging entry requirements for competitors in all sports. The governing body, the Commonwealth Games Federation, has a core set of values – Humanity, Equality and Destiny – that underscore every decision the Federation makes and this is further articulated as 'our vision is to promote a unique, friendly, world class Games and to develop sport for the benefit of the people, the nations and territories of the Commonwealth and thereby strengthen the Commonwealth' (www. commonwealthgames.com). As is the case with respect to all mega events, the value and benefits of hosting a Commonwealth Games is argued strongly by host cities and Games' supporters although detractors do question aspects of the cost–benefit analyses that arrive at highly positive conclusions.

The bid to host the Commonwealth Games in Melbourne commenced in 1996, with a range of benefits promulgated as likely to accrue to all Victorians if the bid proved successful. Planning in earnest began subsequently after notification in 1999 that Melbourne had been selected as the host city for the 2006 Games (State of Victoria, 2005). Evidence of such planning can be seen in the 2002–2006 Strategic Plan of Tourism Victoria, the peak government planning body for stimulating domestic and international tourism to the state. The plan details the following tourism objectives relating to the hosting of this mega event:

- Increase the national and international brand awareness of Melbourne/Victoria.

- Maximize international, interstate and intrastate visitation to the 2006 Commonwealth Games.

- Encourage visitation to Melbourne/Victoria pre and post Commonwealth Games.

- Provide tourism enhancing infrastructure and communication to visitors.

- Capitalize on the relationships that will be developed with global sporting, media and corporate partners (Tourism Victoria, 2002, p. 121).

Pre-Games estimates (cited in KPMG, 2006) suggested that the mega event would generate respectively A$100 million and A$48.5 million in international and domestic event tourism expenditure. Comparison with the official post-event study and other secondary sources form the arbiter as to whether these estimates were realistic. The official event economic impact study (KPMG, 2006) indicates that the Commonwealth Games performed favorably compared to the pre-Games estimates of total expenditure accruing to international and domestic visitors. These figures were modeled as being A$173 million and A$75 million respectively, with domestic visitors taken to include those traveling to Victoria from other states of Australia and Victorian residents who chose to holiday in Melbourne during the time of the event (that happened to coincide with school holidays) rather than leaving for another destination. Post-Games first time or repeat visitors, those expected to travel to Melbourne in the light of exposure to the event in the media or during their actual Games visit, were estimated to lead to a total inducement effect of A\$1.8 million in tourism expenditure for 2007 and 2008 (KPMG, 2006). Whilst the Games was not specifically named, recent reports suggest that Melbourne's overall events strategy is accountable for Melbourne bucking the general trend toward a leveling out in Australia's international visitor numbers (Topsfield, 2008).

Figures suggest that the Commonwealth Games attracted a total number of 157,933 people to Melbourne whose purpose of visit was collectively classed in the visitor group comprising 'spectators, visitors and business' (KPMG, 2006). Approximately, 36% of this cohort was from overseas, 38% from interstate, 23% from Regional Victoria and 3% from metropolitan Melbourne (those foregoing holidays to attend the event).

OVERVIEW OF THE 2006 MELBOURNE COMMONWEALTH GAMES VOLUNTEER PROGRAM

The official brochure for the 2006 Commonwealth Games in Melbourne (Melbourne Commonwealth Games, 2006) formally recognizes the contribution of its 'Unsung Heroes' by listing all 14,500 volunteers by name and state of origin over 12 pages of the publication. These 'unsung heroes' are probably, in numerical terms, the most significant cohort of workers at mega sporting events and are the people who are giving their time without remunerative benefits. We will now consider the phenomenon of volunteering in the context of such events.

Limited information can be gleaned about the volunteer cohort based on the available press reports. Information regarding the demographic profile of applicants to the volunteer program only emerged in relation to origin. Edwards (2005, p. 1) notes that 'nearly 70 per cent of applicants are from the Melbourne metropolitan area, almost 15 per cent from regional Victoria, nearly seven per cent from New South Wales, three per cent from Queensland, two per cent from Western Australia and between 0.6 and 1.9 per cent from other states and territories'. A smaller percentage was of overseas origin. From perusing the official volunteer listing, however, it might be concluded that none of these international applicants were actually accepted as Games volunteers to fill the 'more than 400 different types of positions across 80 venues' (Adams, 2005, p. 6).

The volunteers participating in the Commonwealth Games had a long and rich history of volunteering at mega or major sports events. Previous events that rated a mention included the Melbourne Olympics

(1956), Sydney Olympics and Paralympics (2000), World Masters Games (Melbourne, 2002) and Manchester Commonwealth Games (2002) and the Athens Olympics (2004). Attesting to the episodic nature of event volunteering, some volunteers described themselves as 'serial volunteers'. Motivation for volunteering was evidently very varied but was clearly linked to key factors relating to the 2006 Commonwealth Games – interest in sports, interest in the cultural dynamics of a multination event, pride in Melbourne and its role in hosting the Games and a wish to gain experience of the organizational and operational dimensions of the event.

KEY ISSUES FOR VOLUNTEER MANAGEMENT

The key issues for volunteer management at the 2006 Melbourne Commonwealth Games follows the volunteer's 'Journey' (volunteers.melbourne2006.com.au/journey) through recruitment, role allocation, training and rostering, and also considers the legacy of the Games' volunteer program.

The need for a long lead-in time

Despite the brevity of the actual Commonwealth Games for volunteers, the process of recruitment, role allocation and training prior to the Games followed sound practice in human resource management terms. Volunteers were recruited amid a burst of enthusiasm and publicity many months before the actual event. Keeping them alongside through communications and appropriate training activities is essential in order to avoid disillusionment, disinterest and potential drop out. The volunteer program was launched some 15 months prior to the start of the Games, on January 31, 2005 by the Australian Federal Treasurer, Peter Costello. This points to recognition of the need for a manageable lead time within which to select suitable volunteers, allocate roles and train them. Much longer would have run the risk of alienating those who were selected and losing their interest. Shorter lead time would have encountered the risk of rushing a complex process and undermining volunteer effectiveness.

Managing demand for volunteer opportunities

Demand for volunteer opportunities was very high, with over 9000 applications lodged on the first day and the self-imposed ceiling of 20,000 reached within a week. Following on from this initial stage of the recruitment process, in early March 2005 applicants who had undergone a telephone screening interview were further assessed during roadshows held in regional Victoria and all the Australian capitals. The recruitment process highlights the success of the prerecruitment publicity through, in particular, the media (Lockstone & Baum, 2009). It raises a number of practical issues, particularly relating to the disappointment of those unsuccessful in their attempts to volunteer and in the complexity of sorting through such a high volume of applications. This must have left many disappointed volunteers and may have skewed those accepted toward local participants who may have been more aware of the recruitment drive than those from further afield. This situation also provides opportunities to 'deflect' some of those disappointed into other forms of event volunteering although there is no evidence that this took place in this instance.

Training the volunteers

The training program for Games volunteers was intensive. Specific aspects included initial induction, role specific training, venue specific training and event leadership training (for those volunteers assigned to leadership roles). Volunteers were expected to attend a number of different types of training sessions, this requirement on average meaning 16 hours of training per volunteer. Elsewhere, it was highlighted that training was mandatory. This case study emphasizes the need to invest in wide-ranging training across the range of paid employment human resource management activities. This includes induction training, technical skills training, health and safety training and customer service skills training as key elements within a structured training program.

Allocating roles and responsibilities

As the Commonwealth Games drew closer, in early November 2005 focus shifted toward the allocation of volunteer roles and associated responsibilities. This phase was challenging in terms of the sheer volume of volunteers to be allocated to such diverse roles and, although some mismatches were reported, most volunteers were satisfied with their intended roles and contribution to the event. This case study points to the challenges in meeting people's 'wish list' of roles and responsibilities, especially when numbers are very high and the reality is that the most desired roles are limited in number. Nevertheless, there is a case to develop techniques that more closely match previous experience and skills with positions available.

Issues did arise in relation to a perceived lack of flexibility in the allocation of volunteer roles and this flexibility theme reappeared when the organizers began to allocate specific shifts to individual volunteers. In defense of the Commonwealth Games organizers, their challenge was to fill roles for over 15,000 volunteers and then manage a wide range of tasks at multiple venues over a two-week period so responding to specific and individual requests and needs, both in terms of tasks and rosters, was perceived to be impossible. Indeed, a lack of flexibility in these regards was emphasized to volunteers at the time of recruitment and, given the huge surplus of demand for volunteer positions over available opportunities, the organizers were in a strong position to stipulate this requirement.

At the same time, the experience raises questions about reciprocity with respect to volunteer program flexibility, encapsulated in questions along the lines of 'If I am giving of my time and skills for nothing, isn't it reasonable to expect you (the organizers) to accommodate my wishes and availability needs?'. Issues relating to roles and scheduling were undoubtedly the main causes of volunteer drop out in the period leading up to the Games. These issues relating to the role and training requirements serve to highlight the delicate balance between a volunteer's freedom to choose the activities they participate in and the Games organizer's need to fill roles and rosters. Matching rostering and volunteer scheduling in order to accommodate individual volunteer requirements and circumstances proved difficult for the organizers of the volunteer program. It would however be desirable to give greater recognition of where a volunteering commitment fits into an individual's wider working, leisure and family commitments but may be problematic to accommodate.

Managing the legacy of the Commonwealth Games volunteer program

The Commonwealth Games experience was greatly valued by the vast majority of volunteers who made it through selection and training and was reported in very positive terms in the media and by significant political and sporting interests (Lockstone & Baum, 2009). It is very clear that the Games could not have operated without the participation of the large army of volunteers who fulfilled roles ranging from low skills and 'menial' to those involving senior management, public-fronting and technical responsibility. At the same time, the overall impact on public awareness appeared to be short-lived. Perhaps it is the transitory nature of news reporting or of events themselves (the Commonwealth Games was followed closely by the launch of the 2006 Australian Football League [AFL] season and the staging of the Melbourne Formula One Grand Prix) but coverage of the Commonwealth Games volunteer program and its participants appeared to cease in the immediate aftermath of the event.

The ultimate impact on behavior of coverage of events such as the Commonwealth Games, in this instance represented by a willingness to volunteer, is also debatable given research conducted in the months following the event. Based on a general population survey of 1000 people, Ker (2006, p. 6) reported that 'despite the success of the Games volunteers, program and its 15,000-strong workforce, 59% of those surveyed reported no increased desire to join in community activities". Ker's report points to the need for further research into the relationship between episodic volunteering and participation in longer-term volunteering commitments within the community. Sporting mega event volunteering appears to attract participants who do not see themselves as candidates for other areas of volunteering but who may be keen to engage in allied areas within the sports events subset of volunteering. This finding may assist event organizers in targeting their recruitment communications strategies more effectively.

CONCLUSION

This case study offers a useful series of lessons for organizers of mega and major events. As noted above, given the often long lead times between recruitment and the actual running of these large-scale events (in the case of the 2006 Commonwealth Games over a year elapsed between these two periods), organizers must communicate regularly with their volunteer pool, a highly numerically flexible force, to maintain momentum and motivation. This communication, whether it is in the form of early recruitment materials or more structured training, should be in essence as pragmatic as possible about what volunteers should expect and what organizers will expect of them. These communications can highlight the positive motivational benefits to accrue from being involved in such events. The experience of the Commonwealth Games volunteer program highlights the importance volunteers place on these events being once-in-a-lifetime opportunities, which generate significant buzz and excitement about them. However, at the same time communications should not be sugar-coated to the extent that attrition occurs closer to the event due to a dissonance between what volunteers expect and the reality of the mega event experience.

The extremely temporal and dynamic nature of mega events, with their short time frames and large workforces, creates unique pressures for the effective management of human resources. The volunteer element associated with these events adds an extra dimension to this mix, given the need to balance volunteer expectations and motivations with the operational complexities of these events. Whilst this research has highlighted the somewhat muted control mega and major event volunteers exert over their roles and rosters, more research is required to assess how this impacts upon the overall job satisfaction, performance and turnover of volunteers in this context. Lockstone (2005) found a positive link between functional flexibility practices and the job satisfaction outcomes of volunteers in the museums sector. Testing is required to assess whether the more demand-driven numerical practices typically associated with mega and major events can deliver similar positive job outcomes for volunteers.

The timeframe of mega events is such that longitudinal studies of volunteers and their experiences, using regular data collection points or diary-based methodologies, reveal valuable theoretical and management information about the experience and point to optimum periods for recruitment and training while also recognizing the possible need for the building of postevent relationships, which can support potential bounce-back volunteering for future mega and major sporting events. The savings in terms of reduced training times and having a pool of job-ready volunteers to provide quality service to visitors are just some of the reasons why mega and major event organizations can directly and indirectly benefit from nurturing an internal labor market of episodic volunteers.

DISCUSSION QUESTIONS

Q16.1 How can mega event organizers show greater reciprocal flexibility in allocating roles and organizing rosters to meet the interests and needs of volunteers?

Q16.2 How can the disappointment of being rejected as a volunteer for a mega event be managed to the advantage of the wider sporting event community?

Q16.3 To what extent are mainstream human resource management practices relevant to the management of mega event volunteers?

FURTHER INFORMATION

The Commonwealth Games Federation: www.thecgf.com

CHAPTER 17

Newham Volunteers, United Kingdom

Developing a Pool of Event Volunteers as Part of a Mega Event Legacy

Geoff Nichols

University of Sheffield, UK, g.nichols@shef.ac.uk

KEY POINTS

- Newham Volunteers is a volunteer program run by the London Borough of Newham, which operates a pool of volunteers that event managers and council departments can draw on;

- Initially set up to support London's bid for the 2012 Olympic Games, it also aims to build a legacy of volunteering infrastructure and enrich the local community;

- Newham Volunteers recruit and train volunteers who then select which events they wish to volunteer at;

- Newham Volunteers program overcomes one of the most significant barriers to volunteers, a lack of time, by allowing volunteers flexibility of commitment. It aims to meet the needs of both episodic and long-term volunteers by matching volunteer opportunities with the time (amount and when) individuals want to give;

- The relationship between volunteers and event managers is mediated by Newham Volunteers who work with them to run preevent briefings to establish shared expectations of the volunteering experience. Newham Volunteers also manage the expectations of event managers and work to encourage good practice in volunteer management;

■ Event managers tend to adopt a 'program management' rather than a 'membership management' approach to managing their volunteers, which fits with the objectives of event organizations and works alongside Newham Volunteers' more developmental approach.

OVERVIEW OF NEWHAM VOLUNTEERS

Newham Volunteers was set up in September 2004 by Newham Borough Council to establish a volunteer program to support the London 2012 Olympic Games bid and to create a local resource to support events and services delivered by council departments. It has developed into a program that recruits volunteers and provides them with induction, training and mentoring. Newham is one of the five London boroughs that will be hosting the 2012 Olympic Games. Situated in the East of London, it is the sixth most deprived local authority in the country and the fourth most deprived in London. Within its population of around 250,000, 61% are from black and ethnic communities, compared to less than 10% nationally and there are over 100 languages commonly spoken in the borough. Forty percent of the population is under 25 years of age.

Since its foundation in 2004, the focus of the Newham Volunteers program has changed. It continues to provide volunteers with experiences that will enhance their chances of volunteering in the Olympics but it also aims to build a legacy of a volunteer infrastructure, to engage volunteers with a broader range of activities than events, and thus to enrich the local community. A volunteer manager is supported by an administration assistant, two volunteer coordinators, and another council officer helping with marketing. These are all paid roles although the number of paid officers varies in response to program funding.

Newham Volunteers have registered almost 2000 people on the program since it started and a core of about 100 people volunteer regularly. The program is promoted by the volunteers themselves who, when helping at events, wear a Newham Volunteer T-shirt. Newham Volunteers regard this as an important means of promotion, especially at events that are run by Newham Council, such as the annual Newham Show. There is also a web presence at www.newham.gov.uk/Services/Volunteering/.

The volunteer induction process involves an initial workshop and agreement to a written code of conduct. At induction, volunteers receive a 'Volunteer Journal' in which they can record their initial aspirations, the training they receive, the events they aim to volunteer at, their experience of individual events, and the impact that has had on them. Volunteers are sent a newsletter four times a year with information about future events. Volunteers can then select the events they want to be involved in. This means they may choose to volunteer as much as weekly or as little as twice a year. Volunteer training opportunities include: information technology workshops, assertiveness, disability awareness, first aid, equality and diversity training. Volunteers are encouraged to train for team leader roles where they may be responsible for up to eight other volunteers at an event. To become a team leader a volunteer must have attended at least five events, make a written case supporting their application for this role, and be a role model for other volunteers. Volunteers are offered one-to-one counseling twice a year to help them develop their curriculum vitae (CV) and can receive help with a personal development plan. For some, experience with Newham Volunteers is viewed as an important contribution to reentering the labor market after a period of unemployment, or if they are students, as a way of adding marketable experience. However, volunteers come with a wide range of motives and personal circumstances and for those who have retired from paid work gaining marketable skills for employment is not relevant. Newham Volunteers tries to maximize the developmental experience of their volunteers from volunteering at events. For this reason they may subsidize travel to an event if it is seen as particularly beneficial for the volunteers. An example is a triathlon run annually at Blenheim House; this stately home and grounds are a considerable distance outside London but offers the experience of volunteering at a prestigious event in a unique setting.

Since 2004, over 400 events have been assisted. These range from small community events, such as an after school club to national events, such as the Tour de France, charity-sponsored events and triathlons. Most events are in London, and relatively near to Newham, although some are farther away. The events include those run by the Council's Event Team and by other sections of Newham Council, such as tours of the Olympic site, health promotion programs and the Newham Show. Volunteers are also involved in other council-related roles, such as survey work to inform program evaluations. At larger events, volunteers may be accompanied by a paid member of staff from Newham Volunteers to whom event managers can delegate responsibility for a section of event administration. Newham Volunteers are aware that event organizers might regard volunteers as primarily 'making up the numbers' and they aim to change the culture of volunteer management.

The Newham Volunteers program thus aims to do more than just act as a broker between volunteers and events; it aims to develop the human capital in an area of high unemployment; to enrich the quality of life of all residents; and to be a role model of good practice.

KEY ISSUES FOR VOLUNTEER MANAGEMENT

This case study highlights key volunteer management issues for Newham Volunteers and draws on interviews with staff, event managers and volunteers.

Meeting the needs of both episodic and long-term volunteers

In general surveys of the public, the main reason people give for not volunteering is a lack of time (Atwood et al., 2003; Davis Smith, 1998; Low et al., 2007). The next most significant reasons are pressures from paid work and other family commitments, which are also related to time. Whether these time pressures are perceptual or 'real' they promote episodic volunteering 'made up of separate, especially loosely connected episodes; or limited in duration or significance to a particular episode' (Macduff, 2005, p. 50). An analysis of trends in Australian volunteering leads Cuskelly (2005, p. 97) to conclude that volunteers have 'moved away from positions that require high individual workloads and an ongoing commitment, towards positions that might be described as episodic and low commitment volunteer work', however it is not clear if this trend is universal or more a perception (Musick & Wilson, 2008). Some (see Rochester, 2006) have characterized episodic volunteering as involving volunteers choosing an organization for personal interest, rather than a loyalty to a traditional culture; and being more pragmatic, based on a calculation of personal interest, rather than for idealistic reasons, but there is no evidence for this. Rather than reflecting a change in values, a willingness to commit only to occasional or irregular volunteering is just as likely to be a reflection of contemporary lifestyles. This is important in understanding differences between event volunteers (Downward and Ralston, 2005; Farrell et al., 1998) where commitment is intense but limited to the duration of the event, and other contexts in which commitment is more sustained, such as volunteers in museums (Holmes and Edwards, 2008), sports clubs (Nichols et al., 2005) or youth organizations (Nichols and King, 1999).

Newham Volunteers is able to match opportunities with the time volunteers want to give, both the amount of time and when they can give it. This means that the program can appeal to volunteers in a wide range of circumstances. People in full-time paid work that may involve shifts or irregular hours can fit volunteering around their work commitments and students can fit it around their college work. Those with dependant children can fit it around their children's time at school, while retired people or those who are unemployed can volunteer on more occasions but still value being able to decide themselves how much time they give and which events they volunteer for: 'I like to look a couple of months ahead, see when I'm free and go for it' (volunteer, retired from paid work). One volunteer described how, although he was retired and did not live in the Newham area, he could fit volunteering around the many other activities in his life-style and combine it with visiting relatives. While some volunteers might only help at two events a year, others may help at 20 or 30.

Thus Newham Volunteers allows volunteers flexibility of commitment and therefore overcomes one of the most significant barriers to volunteering. This flexibility in the use of volunteers is the approach advocated by Lockstone, Smith, & Baum (2007). However, flexibility of volunteer commitment has to be balanced against event managers' need for reliability, which is a major concern, especially when working with volunteers (Getz, 2005):

> The biggest worry at the bottom of your mind is that, am I actually gonna get these people? Potentially you could lose 20/30 volunteers who wake up, see it lashing down with rain...whereas if...you're paid for it, you're going to try to find your way there. (Event Manager)

To ensure reliability, Newham Volunteers hold preevent briefings for each event. Once a volunteer has committed to help at an event it is made clear that they have a responsibility to attend. If they fail to attend two events they have committed to they are dropped from the program.

Giving volunteers clear expectations

Clear and comprehensive information for volunteers is important in establishing shared expectations of what volunteers will contribute to an event and what they will receive. It contributes to the psychological contract (Rousseau, 1995) between volunteers and event managers; the combination of explicit and implicit obligations and rewards that constitute a bargain of mutual expectations. A study of the 2002 Manchester Commonwealth Games volunteers (Ralston et al., 2004) concluded that the contract was based largely on trust at the initial stages of involvement. Clearly before an event, the volunteers have to trust the event managers to tell them what they will need to do and what rewards they will receive, and the event manager has to trust the volunteers to deliver a service. However, Ralston et al. found volunteers had a 'fine line between perceptions of a breach in the contract and violation' (p. 24). In understanding volunteer management, the concept of a psychological contract helps emphasize the significant unwritten elements of the relationship, the need to understand it from both sides and the differences and similarities between the situation of volunteers and paid employees (Smith, 2004; Starnes, 2007). Keeping volunteers well informed makes as much of the psychological contract as explicit as possible.

In the case of Newham Volunteers, the contract between the volunteers and the Newham Volunteers organization is developed through the volunteer induction workshop and agreement to a written code of conduct. This code of conduct is similar to that adopted by other organizations, which involve a large number of volunteers, such as the National Trust in the United Kingdom. It tells volunteers what they can expect from the organization and what the organization expects them to contribute. However, the relationship between Newham Volunteers and the volunteers still has to be maintained through sensitive management, discussed further below.

The relationship between the volunteers and the event managers is mediated by Newham Volunteers. Prior to an event, Newham Volunteers staff discuss with the event manager how they can match volunteers to their requirements and what they should provide for the volunteers. These details are then conveyed to the volunteers in a preevent briefing. Briefings include: the nature of the event and the organization, where it is, how to get there and details of transport provided, how long volunteers will be working for, if any special clothing is required, if volunteers will be outside for long periods of time, if food and drink will be provided and if volunteers will receive any other rewards, such as souvenirs or T-shirts.

While these briefings are as comprehensive as possible, volunteers are very sensitive to perceived transgressions of the contract or where a briefing has missed out important points. Examples include not being given protective clothing when painting, not being given vouchers for food, or there being no toilet facilities. However, it is impossible for briefings to cover everything and one seasoned volunteer commented that: 'I accept now, that wherever I go, I'm not gonna really know what I'm doing 'til I get there'. For this volunteer coping with the unexpected was an attraction. A comprehensive briefing gives volunteers sufficient details of an event such that they could answer questions from competitors and the public, and take as full a part in the event as possible. This adds to volunteers' rewards of involvement and the feeling they can make a contribution. It allows volunteers to be ambassadors for particular events. For example, while marshaling on a charity bike ride for the Stroke Association, volunteers would be able to give the public basic information about this particular charity.

As a social construction, the psychological contract is continually changing. For example, an event manager recalled that she suddenly had to find a new supply of T-shirts because the volunteers had noticed other people were getting them and they wanted one too:

*When the volunteers got there, they saw that we did have a few
extra T-shirts, they all suddenly wanted T-shirts and we didn't have
enough. We said that we were told that they didn't want the T-shirts
in the first place...*

Another reported that she had to make unexpected arrangements for subsistence when it was apparent the volunteers expected more than had been planned for. These points illustrate not only that the contract changes with experience, but also that volunteers can be demanding, possibly more so than paid employees.

Giving event managers clear expectations and encouraging good practice

Newham Volunteers managers and staff are keen to promote good practice to the event managers they work with. As noted above, prior to an event they meet the event manager to discuss details of the activities they want volunteers to do and what the volunteers can expect in return. Experienced managers realize the value of this and provide Newham Volunteers staff with this information without prompting:

*When I book I send a briefing note, which includes when to arrive,
and what to wear and it also includes what they will be doing and
then when they arrive onsite, a further briefing, making sure they're
comfortable and also that they know things like, that's where the
loo is, you can put your coats and bags there, there's a tab lined up
at the café so you don't have to pay for your tea and coffee, it's one
of those things that the more they know in advance, whether that's
through the prebriefings or the sort of written briefing that I'll send
to Newham Volunteers the more they'll be able to help and I won't
need to, sort of micro-manage... (Event Manager)*

Of course, these considerations would need to be discussed in more detail with new event managers using Newham Volunteers for the first time. To promote good practice event managers are provided with a 'registration manual', which gives specific guidance on:

- break entitlements: for example, 10–15 minutes every two hours,

- refreshments: including what is appropriate for different lengths
  of volunteering and allowance for particular dietary requirements
  (as Newham is one of the most ethnically diverse boroughs in
  London the need to cater for different requirements is particularly
  important),

- a no smoking policy,

- a policy on the circumstances in which volunteers can drink alcohol (although this is not encouraged),

- reimbursement of travel expenses or any other relevant costs incurred as a result of volunteering,

- health and safety procedures: such as on-site first aid points, access to drinking water, sunscreen if working outside and

- the need to insure volunteers.

However, the manual goes beyond this to cover attitudes toward volunteers, for example, it states you must not:

- expect a volunteer to do what you would not do yourself. Volunteers are not free labor for mediocre jobs, or substitutes for paid staff,

- discriminate against any volunteer,

- use offensive language (volunteers are people too and should be respected and spoken to in a polite manner),

- force the volunteers to do something against their wishes and

- use volunteers as a promotional aid to sell your brand.

Thus, the manual is explicit in promoting not only details of good practice but also an attitude in which the volunteers are seen as more than 'cheap labor' and respected as people and for what they can add to the event.

In addition to a registration manual, event managers are provided with: a health and safety assessment form (a check list of health and safety practices that should be in place); an accident/incident form; an event registration form (covering what is required of volunteers and details of the event); an organizer's evaluation form (providing feedback to Newham Volunteers) and a 'Using Newham's Volunteers checklist' – a 'to do list' of what to do when. These all reflect Newham Volunteer's aim of promoting good practice in volunteer management.

Management style – 'program management' or developing volunteers through the program?

Cuskelly, Hoye, & Auld (2006, p. 82) contrast a 'program management' and a 'membership management' approach to managing volunteers (Meijs & Hoogstad, 2001). The first approach involves an event manager planning the tasks required to run an event and then allocating volunteers to them.

The second approach starts from the motivations and attributes of the volunteers, and allocates them to tasks accordingly. Characteristics of 'program management' (among others) include the volunteer being flexible to fit the task, a weak organizational culture, volunteers who do not usually know each other, motivations are goal-oriented and concerned with external status, and management expectations are explicit. By contrast, 'membership management' is characterized by the task being adapted to the volunteer, a strong organizational culture, volunteers who know each other very well and are motivated by social rewards, and status within the organization and management expectations are implicit.

Event managers tend to adopt the first approach. Their starting point is to analyze the work that needs to be done and therefore how many people are required. These people being present are critical to the success of the event, as these Event Managers state:

> *For health and safety reasons they have to be there. Without having 126 [volunteers], which is like bare minimum, you know, we're in trouble.*

> *The event requires approximately 150 volunteers for the event to run. …we have to have a certain number, we talked this through with Health and Safety and we need to have people in certain positions so for example, if someone did fall off their bike, you know, who's there?*

This is also the starting point for mega events, such as the Olympics or Commonwealth Games, which exhibit characteristics of a program management approach. For example, at in the 2002 Manchester Commonwealth Games volunteers did not know each other well before they came together for the event, a strong motivation was to make the event a success for Manchester, the status of the event was important for volunteers, and tasks were explicitly defined (Downward & Ralston, 2005). This is not surprising as Meijs and Hoogstad's descriptive classification (2001, p. 50) of associated program management is of organizations whose main aim is to deliver a service (such as an event) and are run by professional staff who manage volunteers. This is contrasted with 'membership management', typical of a mutual support organization such as a sports club run by its own members, where the main aim is to promote a collective enthusiasm, to the extent that such organizations are 'managed' at all.

The point of Meijs and Hoogstad's descriptive classification (2001) of management styles is that while one approach might predominate, it can learn from the other. Thus, event managers using the Newham Volunteers program might adopt some of the characteristics of membership management, for example, if they wanted to develop greater commitment from volunteers to the event and thus enable the same people to be used in successive years and build on their experience. One of the events Newham Volunteers help with regularly is a triathlon. The triathlon manager has immense respect and admiration for the volunteer's contribution and is keen to make them feel part of the event: 'we constantly preach to them that this event would not happen without you, so they really feel that they're part of something and they're making the event run smoothly'. So in this respect, he is trying to gain some of the advantages of membership management by promoting the volunteers' commitment to the event. But on the other hand, the main reason he uses Newham Volunteers is because it is an easy way to recruit a lot of volunteers and he can delegate their management reliably to a member of the Newham Volunteers management team. This gives him spare capacity to deal with the inevitable unanticipated problems.

> *The main advantages for us, rather than for any other group, is that they have a volunteer coordinator and they manage their team away from us. On event day, my job is an operations person, so I have [to deal with] any other issue that happens on the course, so if I've got 128 volunteers to look after at the same time, then it's too much.*

So an event manager might adopt elements of a membership management approach, but given the major service delivery objective of running the event well and that paid staff are managing volunteers, a program management approach is always likely to predominate. This is especially so for large events with a big public profile. For event managers, the choice of management approach is based on the assumption that management's objectives drive the organization\and this typifies human resource management theory. Both approaches are a means to an end, and the 'end' is defined by management (Pinnington & Lafferty, 2003). Thus management style is led by the objectives of the organization. The style of management promoted by Newham Volunteers, stressing the respect that should be given to volunteers as people, that they should not be exploited and that the experience of volunteering should be developmental, reflects Newham Volunteers' strategic objectives of building the capacity of individuals to enhance community cohesion and neighborhood participation. This is balanced with the event managers' objective of making sure the event runs well 'on the day'.

CONCLUSION

Newham Volunteers is an innovative program because they have the capacity to offer opportunities for volunteers to contribute the amount of time they want to give, when they want to give it. This flexibility of commitment allows the program to meet the needs of a wide range of volunteers, including those who might be regarded as 'episodic' or 'sustained', and with a wide range of motives. Newham Volunteers try to be a role model of good practice by being clear and specific about what they expect the volunteers to contribute and what Newham Volunteers will provide for them; in other words, making the psychological contract as explicit as possible. This applies to the relationship between Newham Volunteers and the volunteers, and between volunteers and the individual event managers. Newham Volunteers regard their role as not only to develop the social capital of volunteers through their involvement in the program, but to promote good practice amongst event managers through clear guidelines on volunteer management. Thus while event managers might naturally adopt a 'program management' style, reflecting their priorities of delivering an event, the approach of Newham Volunteers is much more developmental.

DISCUSSION QUESTIONS

Q17.1   What are the advantages for an event manager of involving volunteers from a pool program such as Newham Volunteers? Are there any disadvantages with this source of volunteers?

Q17.2   What is the role of the preevent briefing for volunteers? For an event with which you are familiar, what details would you include in a briefing for volunteers?

Q17.3   How does a program management approach to managing volunteers differ from a membership management approach and why is program management preferred by event managers?

FURTHER INFORMATION

Newham Volunteers Program: www.newham.gov.uk/Services/Volunteering/

CHAPTER 18

BTCV International Conservation Holidays, Lesotho

Developing Short-term Volunteer Vacations in International Development

Andy Jefferies

BTCV, United Kingdom, a.jefferies@btcv.org.uk

KEY POINTS

- BTCV is a UK-based not-for-profit organization whose volunteering programs include short-term (two- to three-week) international conservation holidays.

- Since 2004, BTCV has worked in Semongkong, Lesotho with their local partner Katleho 'Moho Association to run volunteer holidays with conservation, tourism and community development objectives.

- Conservation holidays are led by a Volunteer Leader and volunteers pay to participate.

- Successfully managing volunteer leaders on these international holidays involves ensuring leaders have appropriate experience; providing appropriate training and effective support; and giving leaders a sense of ownership.

- Volunteer holiday participants come with varied expectations and preconceptions, which are managed through provision of information in briefings and orientation; experienced leaders; and promotion of close contact with local volunteers.

CONTENTS

- Conservation holidays are intensive short-term volunteering experiences, but there is often a demand from volunteers for a longer-term relationship with projects, partner organizations, places and people.

OVERVIEW OF BTCV

BTCV, formerly the British Trust for Conservation Volunteers, is a UK-based not-for-profit nongovernment organization (NGO) that aims to involve people in directly improving their physical, natural and by extension, social environments. Founded in 1959 to recruit volunteers to help with the practical management of nature reserves, BTCV is now the United Kingdom's largest environmental volunteering organization assisting 130,000 people to volunteer in some capacity each year. BTCV has about 600 employees, and around 400 'Key Volunteers' who work within a structured support system at all levels within the organization. Significantly, and unusually for an environmental organization, BTCV does not own any land itself but achieves its work through small-scale local organizations and individuals. The concept of volunteering and practical action therefore lies at the heart of all BTCV's work.

The organization's activities are diverse and include: supporting local volunteer groups with advice, training, equipment and services; providing vocational skills training for the long-term unemployed; promoting physical and mental health through constructive physical activity; and advocating on behalf of volunteers and volunteering. In addition, BTCV's directly managed programs include 'traditional' environmental volunteering in the form of day and longer-term opportunities for volunteers to assist on nature reserves and other areas of environmental value. Residential opportunities, generally between three days and three weeks, but up to four months, are promoted to the public through the 'Conservation Holidays' (vacations) program.

Originally a solely UK-based organisation, BTCV developed an international dimension initially in response to interest in its activities from non-UK bodies. Since the late 1980s, an international department represents the organization and acts as a conduit for BTCV skills and experience outside the United Kingdom, working with local partners including community organizations, local and national NGOs, statutory bodies and government departments. BTCV's work with international partners includes training in organizational development, support in developing volunteer programs and volunteer support systems and promoting regional and global networking.

International Conservation Holidays can provide a unique mechanism for complementing and supporting BTCV's international development activities. This case study focuses on the International Conservation Holidays volunteer program model, with particular reference to its application in Lesotho, Southern Africa.

OVERVIEW OF BTCV'S INTERNATIONAL CONSERVATION HOLIDAY PROGRAM

BTCV provides around 300 places on up to 30 International Conservation Holidays annually, working directly with between 15 and 20 partners worldwide. The holiday projects are designed as group events with volunteers involved as paying participants, as project leaders and in program development and administration. The program is managed by BTCV's UK-based International Department, which consists of two permanent staff, occasional project-related staff, up to two full-time volunteers working within BTCV's Key Volunteer structure, and receives administrative support from the wider organization. The department manages a team of around 50 'International Leaders', most of whom have extensive experience with BTCV, are professionals in their own fields and give around two weeks each annually to volunteering with BTCV.

Although branded as 'holidays', the main focus of projects within this volunteer program is on practical physical environmental improvement work, with volunteers expecting to spend around five days per week engaged in the volunteering activity. Paying participation in the program is available to volunteers between the ages of 18 and 80. Fees range from £380 and £760 for a two-week project with travel to the destination meeting point the volunteer's responsibility. No previous skills are expected of participants and the activities are planned and managed to enable as wide participation as possible. Beyond the age limitations, there is no proactive selection of paying volunteers by BTCV, but self-selection based on information provided about the nature of individual projects is expected.

The volunteer program is built around BTCV's existing partnerships, with volunteer projects initiated where they can complement or enhance the value of wider development activities by either or both organizations. As well as contributing to specific 'on-the-ground' environmental improvements such as tree planting, access works (footpath construction, interpretation) or habitat management, the projects can act as vehicles promoting less obvious outcomes. For example:

- Where BTCV's partner is developing its own volunteer programs, the projects may be used to test and practice new organizational skills in volunteer and practical project management;

- They can provide a focus for local interest in environmental improvement and can build momentum far beyond the individual holiday project; and

- They can be used as a 'pioneer' tourism test-bed, actively engaging participants as 'tourists' and locals as 'hosts' in the development of small-scale sustainable tourism infrastructure.

In addition, other outcomes of BTCV's use of International Conservation Holidays to support development work have been observed:

- By engaging directly in the development process, returning participants have a far greater understanding of the realities and challenges faced in the areas they have visited;

- Through involvement directly in the direction of the project, participants feel a greater sense of being a part of it and are better able to communicate to others the issues involved;

- The deeper relations fostered by this approach can lead to further independent involvement by participants; and

- The extra publicity of having a group of visitors in an area can attract the attention of other communities and groups, promoting the development of local networks centered on BTCV's original partner.

With a small core staff, the volunteer program is closely linked to the BTCV international department's development work. The volunteer program manager is directly involved with training, fund-raising and other activities associated with partner relationships. The potential for use of volunteer projects in enhancing the relationship is assessed alongside other needs and where appropriate included in longer-term planning.

Once the partnership relationship is set up, the management of individual volunteer projects becomes the responsibility of volunteer leaders. Established guidance ensures compliance with in-house standards for safety management, British Standard 8848:2007 (Specification for the provision of visits, fieldwork, expeditions and adventurous activities, outside the United Kingdom) and UK package travel legislation (The Package Travel, Package Holidays and Package Tours Regulations 1992), but allows freedom for dynamic review and to adapt projects 'on-the-hoof' in conjunction with partners and volunteer participants.

OVERVIEW OF BTCV VOLUNTEER CONSERVATION HOLIDAYS IN LESOTHO

Key issues regarding volunteer management of International Conservation Holidays can be demonstrated using the case study of BTCV projects in Semonkong, Lesotho. Lesotho's position is unusual in that it is completely surrounded by South Africa, the continent's largest economy. The population is estimated at 2.2 million, about 58% of whom are classed as very poor and some 25% chronically undernourished. HIV/AIDS rates in adults stood at 23.4% in 2004 – the third highest in the world (Department for International Development, 2008).

BTCV has worked in Lesotho since 2004 with a community group, the Katleho 'Moho Association (KMA). KMA has been active since 2000 successfully completing small-scale health and agricultural improvement projects in the remote community of Semonkong in Lesotho's highlands. Working with the community's youth, KMA identified an opportunity to develop small-scale community tourism enterprises that would capitalize on the area's unique natural resources – notably a landscape of great botanical interest that includes the Maletsunyane Falls, the highest in Southern Africa. Initial contact with BTCV was made by a long-term 'professional' volunteer development worker with KMA, recruited by Skillshare, who had previously been a participant on a BTCV International Conservation Holiday in Japan.

The development of a three-week BTCV volunteer project in 2005 was considered a useful first step, with the relatively modest aims of:

- acting as a catalyst for a working relationship between KMA and BTCV in the absence of other viable funding for extensive meetings;

- achieving essential and uncontentious improvements to footpath access to the base of the waterfall; and

- establishing a focus for positive action toward their identified goals by local youth.

The project was integrated into BTCV's International Conservation Holidays program and targeted at the general public with participating volunteers paying around £700 for two weeks, excluding travel to a meeting point in Johannesburg, South Africa.

Following this, a second volunteer project was developed for 2006, which in addition to building on previous work and implementing a botanical survey of the area, directly engaged volunteers, as tourists, in KMA's future planning. Volunteers were surveyed by questionnaire in advance of the project on their expectations and preconceptions. After two days in Semonkong that included visits to the town, outlying villages, the waterfall, local food outlets and shops and a meeting with the local council, their 'first impressions' were captured in a workshop session facilitated by a BTCV volunteer leader. Toward the end of the three-week period in Semonkong, after having worked alongside and talked with local volunteers, seen more of the area, its people and their lives, the visiting volunteers' views, opinions and impressions were captured in a second workshop. The gathered information was distilled and presented in writing and at a public meeting attended by volunteers and community representatives.

Using this information to inform their planning, KMA, with assistance from BTCV, developed a proposal for a community-run rare plant, vegetable and tree nursery designed to preserve biodiversity, provide the materials to improve agricultural conditions, provide a source of fresh food for the community and a long-term income for KMA. In partnership with BTCV, funding for the nursery project was successfully obtained from the UK-based Rufford Small Grants Foundation. Volunteer projects continue to play a high-profile role in KMA's community initiatives with volunteers helping with the nursery construction and 'testing' new small-scale tourism developments including homestays and guides.

KEY ISSUES FOR VOLUNTEER MANAGEMENT

The politics of development work

Operating in this development context there is potential for unexpected problems. These can make the management of volunteer projects especially complex and expose volunteers to the reality of their work. One example from an early BTCV volunteer project in Lesotho demonstrates this.

In the week prior to the first Lesotho conservation holiday project in 2005, several meetings were held with KMA and other stakeholder organizations in the capital, Maseru, hosted by Skillshare Lesotho. Very early, in almost the first of these meetings, it became apparent that there was a potential local political issue, which could compromise the volunteer project. Lesotho had recently adopted a local government structure and across the country new councils had been formed only two weeks before. Previously there had been no such functioning body, and consequently the local development vacuum was filled by community-based organizations such as KMA. Now suddenly there was a new level of local decision-making with which to develop relationships. It became apparent too that there was concern within the council that KMA members would be benefiting personally and financially from the long-term project. With no training in their new roles, a questioned election process beforehand, and some confusion over rights and responsibilities, the council's response was to determine that it could not possibly let the footpath project, the core volunteer activity, go ahead. By their part, KMA's management had their political differences with the local council members and had refused to attempt to consult the new body when it was formed. Despite the earlier BTCV scoping project and significant work in the community and with KMA by Skillshare Lesotho, the local political landscape had changed and the new situation was threatening not just the holiday project but all of KMA's activities.

In this event, the combined weight of Skillshare Lesotho and BTCV International enabled the two organizations to take a mediating role and bring the two parties together. This was sufficient to break the deadlock, allow the immediate work to continue and persuade KMA and the council to cooperate on future development. A final meeting was held in Semonkong with the council on the project's orientation day and volunteers were witness to the council's u-turn. Having necessarily been briefed on the local political issue, volunteers already felt themselves to be part of the development process.

Volunteer leader skill and responsibility levels

BTCV leaders are themselves volunteers, and play a key role in ensuring the success of volunteer projects and by extension the continuing effectiveness of BTCV's relationship with partners. When volunteer projects occur in a development setting, as in Lesotho, this entails a high level of responsibility and requires significant experience and a very varied range of skills. Typically, on any BTCV volunteer project the leader will be responsible for: health and safety management; volunteer welfare; ensuring a quality experience for volunteers, including the social experience; crisis management; managing the relationship between volunteers and partner organization and community; maintaining the reputation of the partner organization in its own community and BTCV in general; and ensuring the aims of the specific project are met. The leader will need 'people' skills; an ability to appreciate the project's wider context; to communicate safety critical and some complex and subtle information; and often technical skills. The role can be physically, mentally and emotionally demanding and requires complete reliability.

In Lesotho and with other projects in the development context the leader also needs an advance awareness of the wider impacts and influence of the project, the volunteers and the leader can have on the local community. Their role can include mentoring the partner organization (e.g.

in financial management), they can find themselves being viewed as an expert in everything and have the potential through misunderstanding to place great stress on the partner organizations' resources.

Four factors have been identified as key to managing volunteer leaders in this demanding role:

- Ensuring leader experience
- Providing appropriate training
- Providing effective support
- Giving leaders a sense of ownership.

Experience is a prerequisite for becoming a BTCV International Leader. This includes experience of practical environmental volunteer projects, and international leaders are able to gain this within BTCV's other volunteer programs within the UK day-volunteering projects and BTCV UK Conservation Holidays. Almost all international leaders are already involved with BTCV. Overseas travel experience is a general requirement, with more specialized experience (e.g. of travel in a particular region) often specified. Further technical or other experience may be required for specific projects. BTCV's International Conservation Holidays program is varied and offers opportunities for gaining experience through leading more straightforward holidays before 'graduating' to the more complex projects.

Training in leadership and supporting skills such as First Aid and risk assessment are provided throughout a leader's journey in BTCV. A skills and training framework defines minimum training requirements at different stages and appropriate courses are developed and delivered generally within BTCV. International Leaders are initially 'qualified' following a training and selection weekend and attend two refresher training weekends annually. These events provide updates on changes to relevant procedure and legislation and an opportunity to share techniques and experience with other leaders.

Support is made available to volunteer leaders through a number of means:

- A step-by-step framework in workbook form is used to support risk and safety management. While leaders are trained in risk assessment, the framework provides an assurance that all relevant factors have been considered and, importantly, a means by which to share the process, techniques and responsibility with the partner organization.

- A written and personal briefing is given to all leaders in advance of the project in which the historical and wider development contexts of the project are discussed.

- Extensive online materials are accessible by leaders where computer access is available. This includes specialized risk management aids, procedural and policy guidance and technical guides.

- Leaders have 24-hour access to BTCV staff in the event of emergencies. While leaders are expected to be able to deal with most eventualities, this can provide at the minimum, moral support for decisions made or, in more serious cases, allow the leader to focus on the immediate situation, knowing that other functions such as communication are taking place.

- A mentor system is in place providing any leader that wants it with an appropriate mentor from within the leader pool.

A sense of ownership of the project, the partner relationship and even of BTCV's work is a crucial motivator. After a project has been established by BTCV staff, the leader takes over all aspects of liaison with the partner. The process includes finalizing the details of the work activities and other activities and enables the partner and leader to begin building their own relationship. Leaders are in contact with participating volunteers in advance of the project and are recognized by default as the face of BTCV. Leaders have the authority to modify projects as necessary, in conjunction with partners and if relevant participant volunteers. This helps to make BTCV volunteer projects more responsive to partner and volunteer needs and allows leaders to make the best use of individual specialist skills they or the participating volunteers may have. For BTCV, there is a consequent conflict when allocating volunteer leaders between having leaders specializing in projects with a particular partner and promoting wider experience and greater variety with circulation of leaders between partnerships.

Leaders are encouraged to get involved with other aspects of BTCV's international activities. These can include training (new leaders or partner organisations); site-visiting and project setup; promotion and publicity (e.g. representing BTCV at public events); developing leader support materials and systems; and managing leader meetings and training events. The relationship between BTCV staff and individual leaders is close, and biannual training events are intentionally sociable promoting a strong sense of 'family'.

Managing volunteer expectations

Volunteers' expectations and preconceptions of a volunteer project can be varied. Ensuring expectations are realistic or managing unrealistic expectations is therefore an important factor in ensuring the project is a success for the individual and by extension overall. Volunteers disappointed or unsettled by the unexpected are more likely to compromise the overall effectiveness of the project.

Approximately 61% of International Conservation Holiday volunteers are joining a BTCV project for the first time, with the remaining 39% having previous experience as a volunteer on BTCV projects in the United Kingdom or overseas. At the simplest level, participant volunteers joining any BTCV International Conservation Holiday have a general expectation that they will be carrying out physical environmental improvement alongside local volunteers, that this will be planned and managed effectively and safely and that they will have some kind of new experience. Information available before booking reinforces these expectations and provides as much accurate detail as possible on activities and itineraries. The volunteer projects are marketed as 'holidays' and their two to three-week timescales are designed to fit the holiday periods available to many working people. International volunteer projects, environmental and otherwise, are an established part of the tourism landscape, and the structure of the projects ensures that most fall within tourism legislation. Thus it could be concluded that volunteer participants can also be expected to enjoy the experience.

With many volunteer projects and particularly those operating in the development context there can be other factors which may or may not be considered by the individual volunteer and for which special consideration may need to be given in managing the volunteers' expectations. Volunteers may need to be prepared to face emotional challenges through exposure to poverty and poor health including HIV/AIDS. In Lesotho, volunteers are in constant and direct contact with these issues when working with local volunteers and interacting with the wider community. Begging by young children is common and volunteers are actively discouraged from acceding to their demands to prevent reinforcing this behavior. It is often necessary to be clear that their own contribution in activity, time and money, will not in itself 'save the world' and they should be helped to see their impact as an important part of a wider development program.

It may be necessary for the volunteer to 'play the game', meeting local decision-makers and people of influence. Participants on BTCV's volunteer projects in Lesotho are routinely expected to visit the local council and land controlling chiefs before work can commence. This is a necessary part of operating in the area, but if unexpected, can give an appearance of poor project preparation. Similarly, volunteers may face open local opposition to their activities. Volunteers may justifiably expect that their involvement is welcomed. The example of the Semonkong local council's veto demonstrates that this can be politically motivated and occur despite the best planning by the project organizers. Diplomatic solutions to local issues can be made significantly harder with the additional need for diplomacy with volunteers.

The need to be able to cope with flexibility in programs, timings, work activities and many other aspects of the 'advertised' project is essential, particularly when working, as BTCV does all the time, with partner organizations whose primary consideration is not the volunteer's experience. One of BTCV's roles, facilitated by the volunteer leader, in all projects is to act as a 'buffer' between the partner's and volunteers' expectations, recognizing that the volunteer input remains an essential part of achieving the overall project goals.

Female, older and younger volunteers, those with disabilities and volunteers from particular ethnic groups may face further challenges that may not be apparent in their home environment. In Lesotho, it has been particularly challenging for female leaders, with local people, including the partner's representatives, struggling to accept the leader's authority, instead deferring to the nearest male participant volunteer.

BTCV employs four key tools in managing volunteer expectations:

- Information through written and verbal briefings;
- Orientation;
- Experienced leaders; and
- Promotion of close local contact with volunteers.

Information is provided in promotional materials accessible prior to the volunteer making a commitment to participate. As well as the proposed plans for the project, information on the long-term partnership between BTCV and partner is provided, including a history and reports from previous projects. Volunteer leaders are in contact with all participants before departure and seek to address any concerns. A full briefing on all aspects of the project, the area, the community and the partner is given at the earliest practical point at commencement of the project. Usually this would be on the first evening upon meeting the volunteers and would involve BTCV and partner representatives. In the case of Lesotho, a 'soft' introduction is given with the first night in the capital city and a briefing at that point. This is partly driven by practicalities as there is a further five hours of difficult travel onwards, itself requiring some expectation management, effectively delaying on-site briefing until the next morning. Given the value of the briefing, this is an undesirable delay.

Orientation usually involves at a minimum, a tour of the volunteer site(s). It is an opportunity for further, more informal briefing and an early introduction to the wider area. Partner representatives usually lead this, and it can provide a deeper insight for volunteers into the partner's wider work. This can be a half or full day and, where appropriate, can function as a resting period following travel. In Lesotho, a full day is programmed for orientation and, in addition to serving the above functions, includes formal visits to the local council and two relevant land-owning chiefs. The meetings are relatively informal but are essential courtesies before practical activities can commence.

Experienced leaders are considered key to successfully managing volunteer expectations. Starting with the leader's initial contact with volunteers, leaders are able to anticipate where participants may require information or preparation and make this available. During the project, timing and organization of briefings and orientation and managing exposure to particular situations can assist the volunteer in developing and satisfying expectations. In the development context of BTCV's projects in Lesotho this has even included initiating discussions on philosophical and moral issues to further aid the process.

Co-working with local volunteers is a feature of most BTCV volunteer projects. It is usually a necessary feature of BTCV's work with the partner, often serving a training role for local volunteers and leaders. The experience is generally appreciated by both local and visiting volunteers and provides an invaluable opportunity for learning by both. It can serve to assist in managing volunteers' expectations, by giving them a greater opportunity to appreciate local realities and understand better the context in which the project and their personal contribution is valued.

Continuing the relationship

Even given their short duration, BTCV International Conservation Holidays in a development context can provide an intensity of experience, which leaves a lasting impression on the volunteer. This can create a bond between the volunteer and the people, partner organization, place or work that they experienced and in some cases the desire to continue their involvement. Personal initiatives have later developed leading to twinning of schools, private fund-raising and further longer-term volunteering. One volunteer with BTCV in Lesotho has now set up a UK-registered charity supporting women's weaving projects in the area. These outcomes can be positive, but there is also the possibility that misguided, poorly informed actions can have a negative impact. Such initiatives represent an impact of volunteering that is difficult to quantify and difficult to control. BTCV as the original volunteer project organizer has limited influence beyond ensuring that the initial project experience provides sufficient exposure to and appreciation of the complex issues surrounding working in these situations.

CONCLUSION

Any development intervention is necessarily sensitive and subject to a range of subtle factors. Introducing tourists in the form of volunteers adds a significant layer of complexity to the equation. High levels of sensitivity and a wide range of skills are required in the organization and management of such volunteer projects. The expectations of volunteers and hosts, both reasonable and unrealistic, need to be considered and managed carefully, with some situations being beyond the direct control of the managing body. BTCV's approach focuses heavily on developing the role of volunteer leaders in managing the relationship between local partners and participating volunteers, capitalizing on seams of commitment and professionalism sometimes only expressed through an individual's volunteering.

DISCUSSION QUESTIONS

Q18.1 What are the key factors in successfully managing relationships with all the partners in the volunteering projects in Lesotho?

Q18.2 What potential tensions are there between the expectations of the project and the expectations of the volunteer tourists?

Q18.3 How do you think the motivation for the volunteer project leaders differs from the volunteer tourists?

FURTHER INFORMATION

BTCV: www2.btcv.org

Katleho 'Moho Association: www2.btcv.org.uk/display/katlehomoho

CHAPTER 19

Greenforce Andros Marine Conservation Project, The Bahamas

Developing Gap Year Volunteering Programs and Supporting Volunteers

Siobhan White[1] and Karen A. Smith[2]

[1]*Greenforce, UK, siobhan14@googlemail.com*
[2]*Victoria University of Wellington, New Zealand, karen.smith@vuw.ac.nz*

KEY POINTS

- Greenforce is a not-for-profit organization specializing in volunteer conservation projects in remote locations for young people on a post-school or post-university gap year.

- The Andros Marine Conservation Project in The Bahamas is one of the longest running Greenforce projects; each year four groups of volunteer tourists spend 10 weeks learning to dive then surveying the barrier reef to collect baseline biodiversity research data.

- Greenforce has responded to a changing market for youth gap year volunteering by diversifying their projects (including new destinations, development aid as well as conservation projects and paid work placements) and target markets (school and college groups, and career breakers and retirees).

- The gap year industry as a whole has attracted some negative media coverage; Greenforce has countered this through membership of international organizations, working as part of the UK's Year Out Group (YOG), partnering with respected external agencies and communities in its destinations and promoting positive news stories.

CONTENTS

Managing Volunteers in Tourism
Copyright © 2009 Elsevier Ltd. All rights reserved.

■ Keeping volunteer tourists motivated throughout a project is a challenge and involves clearly managing the volunteers' expectations pre-departure and responding to changing conditions on site.

OVERVIEW OF GREENFORCE

Greenforce is a 'gap year' provider, focusing on providing volunteer tourism placements to teenagers between school or college and university, or to recent university graduates taking a break before employment or further study. Their projects offer the opportunity to volunteer, usually for up to three months, in remote, often developing world, locations.

A UK-registered not-for-profit organization, Greenforce was founded in 1997 in response to an outcome of the 1992 Rio Earth Summit. The summit called for all participating countries to assess the level of biodiversity within their borders. Countries were to undertake survey work and data collection to create baseline knowledge so that they could then work toward protecting these biodiversity levels. This research work is often expensive, which contributes to making it a low priority for many economically less developed countries. However, it is often these countries that have such important and rich biodiversity that needs recognizing and protecting. Hence, a recommendation was added to the Summit Declaration suggesting that international agencies should be enlisted to help. Greenforce was created as such an agency and it specializes in volunteer conservation projects in developing countries.

A country's government will often have its own internal agency to work on baseline data biodiversity projects or perhaps work with an international agency (e.g. WWF). However, baseline data collection is often long and tedious work so these agencies may enlist an organization such as Greenforce to assist with the survey work. It is through this layer system that Greenforce becomes involved in a specific country, and also how it is able to use potentially inexperienced people to help collect this data. The data collectors do not need to be scientists, rather they require basic training and supervision so that they understand which data they are collecting to try to minimize the margin of error in the data. By using repetitive groups in an area on a longitudinal basis it is possible to compile fairly accurate data.

Since its conception 11 years ago, the locations that Greenforce works in have changed and grown in number, from just Zambia and Fiji in 1998 to over 20 projects across the world in 2008. The principles that Greenforce employed when they first started still hold true: all volunteer projects are set up in response to a 'call for help' from the host country or a national agency; projects aim to include local residents as much as possible, as long as it is not too much of a disruption to their lives; and the aim is always to minimize the negative environmental impacts as much as possible. While initial volunteer projects were conservation based, Greenforce's scope has expanded and its volunteer program now includes development aid projects. They also offer study abroad programs for schools and colleges, and American students can use their participation as college credits through a college partnership. Greenforce is part of a wider range of gap year offerings from Gapforce. As well as Greenforce's global volunteering programs, other Gapforce brands have enabled the introduction of paid work and internship programs, including Ozforce working holidays, Skiforce instructor training and Medforce volunteer and paid medical placements. Acquisition of another gap year provider, Trekforce, in 2008 has further diversified the business by extending its extreme expeditions programs.

OVERVIEW OF GREENFORCE'S VOLUNTEER PROGRAM

Volunteer involvement is crucial in Greenforce's work as it provides the labour to undertake conservation and other projects. Volunteer tourists can experience a very different side of life and projects provide them with opportunities to learn life skills for personal growth and at the same time help out with the conservation of important natural locations. While Greenforce has primarily been a gap year organization for young people, more recently, especially with the introduction of shorter stay projects (between 4 and 10 weeks), Greenforce has seen a shift in the age profile of volunteers and now includes students, recent graduates, people on career breaks or extended leave and retirees.

The structure of Greenforce's projects varies depending on the location and project objectives. The four main volunteer tourism projects (Bahamas, Fiji, Tanzania and Ecuador) run in four 10-week phases a year, starting in January, April, July and October. Each project has a local partner organization but the camps are run by a permanent Greenforce field staff, usually from the United Kingdom, who are based at the destination. Field staff hold long-term voluntary positions with Greenforce providing international flights, food, accommodation, medical insurance, a stipend and the Greenforce Bonus Program (annual awards which can be used to help fund postgraduate study or other training). In other locations, Greenforce links up with locally based charities and conservation projects. These ongoing projects often operate throughout the year, so there is more flexibility in terms of the length of volunteering and the start and finish dates; it also means that there may be only one Greenforce volunteer on each project during any period.

Volunteers need no previous experience before joining Greenforce projects, however, in line with other gap year programs, volunteers do pay to take part. As a not-for-profit organization, Greenforce aims to keep these costs as low as possible. The fee covers the volunteers' costs out-on-camp (including staff costs) and their training, with a small percentage going to office overheads and administration. Typically, 15 to 20 volunteers will participate in each phase of the main projects, however, if the number of volunteers participating in a phase is particularly big and a surplus is made, this is reinvested into the project or other Greenforce projects. Reinvestments include moving a campsite and the erection of new buildings or investments in the local community, such as the building of a local school. Due to the nature of the projects, volunteers are encouraged to fund-raise their fees as much as possible.

OVERVIEW OF ANDROS MARINE CONSERVATION PROJECT, THE BAHAMAS

The Bahamas is made up of over 700 islands and 2400 cays in the Atlantic Ocean off the coast of Florida and the world's third largest barrier reef runs through the archipelago. The Bahamas National Trust is a nongovernmental, not-for-profit organization mandated with the conservation of the Bahamas' natural and historical resources and the management of the National Parks system. In 2001, the Bahamas National Trust wanted to start collecting baseline data on the barrier reef in order to set up Marine Protected Areas and potential 'no-take' fishing zones to preserve the reef environment. Greenforce was invited to start this work and set up a project based on Andros, the largest of the Bahamian islands.

The Andros Marine Conservation Project is a marine conservation holiday that runs four times a year. Volunteers pay £2,500 for the 10-week project, plus a dive-training fee that differs depending on their level of experience (e.g. volunteers who have never dived before pay £300). Once trained and dive certified, Greenforce volunteers participate in underwater marine surveys that involve charting the coral with the use of global positioning system (GPS), identifying fish and marine movements and locating breeding and feeding grounds.

The Bahamas sit in a hurricane belt and the original Greenforce Marine Research Station was a tented camp that could be quickly dismantled. The camp had basic facilities, limited running cold water and no electricity except for a generator to run the office computer (to record research data) and the dive air compressor. Wooden structures were subsequently added for a dining shelter and office. In January 2008, the camp was moved to 'Coconut Grove' to begin the next phase of surveying. A new higher-standard camp was built; this includes permanent structures (kitchen/dining, office and sleeping quarters), electricity and flushing toilets.

The Bahamas camp is run by a Field Staff of three: an expedition leader, chief scientist and assistant scientist. The expedition leader is also the dive instructor and Greenforce looks for someone with leadership and expedition experience and a dive instructor qualification. The chief scientist is responsible for the scientific survey work and leads and trains the team of inexperienced volunteers. They require survey experience and at least a Masters degree in Marine Biology or similar qualification. The requirements for the assistant scientist role are less stringent and often this person will hold an undergraduate degree in Marine Science and want practical field experience in preparation for postgraduate study. The assistant may also be a second dive instructor and in this case they may not have a formal marine science qualification but could be a past volunteer who has a relevant interest and some experience in conservation.

Volunteers contribute to the running of the camp and upon arrival they are put into a schedule of chores, all done in pairs, such as firewood collection, cooking, cleaning and boat duty. Every Thursday, staff and volunteers visit the local primary school and teach the children various aspects of conservation and marine life. The teaching part of the project began in 2003 and remains very popular with both the volunteers and local children.

KEY ISSUES FOR VOLUNTEER MANAGEMENT

Over the last few years there have been several key issues concerning the wider gap year industry that have affected the running of Greenforce volunteer projects, including a drop in gap year numbers and negative press coverage of some gap year programs. The Bahamas' project also illustrates some of the operational challenges of managing volunteers on longer-duration projects, including training and keeping participants motivated.

Changing market for gap year volunteering

While it is accepted that tourism volunteering has grown rapidly, particularly since 1990 (Tourism Research and Marketing, 2008), and volunteer gap year placements are now at an all-time high (YOG, 2008), there have also been periods where the demand for gap year volunteering has been less stable.

In the United Kingdom, during the mid-2000s there were pressures on many gap year providers and a number of organizations within the sector closed or reduced their operations. This coincided with increases in university fees and appears to have meant some students have reconsidered gap year volunteering, either because they could not afford it and decided to go straight to university or they spent their gap year in paid employment to earn money for their education. Another challenge facing providers has been more competition from an increasingly professionalized gap year industry offering ever more placements (Tourism Research and Marketing, 2008).

Greenforce's response to this changing market has been to diversify and offer new projects in new destinations, as well as extending the scope of some existing projects. These projects move beyond Greenforce's traditional focus on conservation to include humanitarian aid, animal rescue, teaching and paid work placements. They have also adapted their marketing to target school and college groups as well as individuals and promoted their programs at a wider demographic than their traditional young gap year students, including career-breakers and retirees. Although there has been a slight increase in the older demographic, reflecting the maturing volunteer tourism market more generally (Tourism Research and Marketing, 2008), young people (both postschool and postuniversity) remain the key volunteers for Greenforce.

Any drop in volunteers is a concern as it means less work can be done if places on projects are not filled and consequently the sustainability of individual projects and the wider organization could be at risk. In Greenforce's case, the increase in project opportunities has proved successful and their volunteer numbers have recovered. There have also been positive outcomes in terms of the quality of work undertaken as young people who are still choosing a volunteer-based gap year appear to be more selective and are demonstrating a strong interest in the conservation and aid work that Greenforce offers.

Negative press for gap year programs

Media coverage will obviously influence the decision to take a gap year, what to do (volunteer, travel, paid employment and study) and where and, if relevant, which organization and project to sign up to. Volunteer gap year programs have seen some negative press coverage in recent years and although Greenforce has not been involved directly, there has been criticism of the gap year industry in general. For example, in 2007 the critical comments of Judith Brodie, Director of international development charity VSO, were widely reported in the UK media:

While there are many good gap year providers we are increasingly concerned about the number of badly planned and supported schemes that are spurious – ultimately benefiting no one apart from the travel companies that organise them. Young people want to make a difference through volunteering, but they would be better off travelling and experiencing different cultures, rather than wasting time on projects that have no impact and can leave a big hole in their wallet. (VSO, 2007)

This followed previous criticism that gap years could create 'new colonialists', where the needs of volunteers are put above those of the communities they claim to support (Frean, 2006). While volunteer tourism can be a popular media travel story, reports also suggest that gap year volunteer programs can do more harm than good (for examples of media coverage, see Bennett, 2007; Ward, 2007; Womack, 2007). They criticize projects where untrained volunteers may damage the environment or development projects which negatively impact on a local community's way of life.

Gap year volunteer tourism is big business; annually an estimated 200,000 Britons take a gap year, including 130,000 school leavers (YOG data; see VSO, 2007). A review of gap year provision for the UK Government's Department of Education and Skills (Jones, 2004) found more than 800 organizations that provide overseas volunteering, with the average fees then ranging from £500 to £2000. The industry includes both not-for-profit organizations (such as Greenforce) and commercial companies (e.g. i-to-i, part of TUI Travel plc). Further negative publicity has focused on the high fees charged by some companies and the low percentage of the fees that reach the projects and communities supposedly benefiting. While the headline 'Gap agencies charge up to 600% mark up' (Haslam, 2007) is based on one example of a work-camp project in Ghana, the sentiment that some gap year companies are profiting at the expense of participants and beneficiaries is more widespread in the media coverage.

Reputable gap year providers have undertaken a number of strategies to address this negative publicity. Voluntary sector organizations such as Greenforce stress their not-for-profit foundations and demonstrate how the participant's fee both covers costs and benefits the communities and destinations in which they volunteer. Greenforce is a member of various umbrella organizations who work to improve the standards of gap year programs. The Year Out Group (YOG) is an association of 35 providers that aims to 'promote[s] the concept and benefits of well-structured year out programs, to promote models of good practice and to help young people and their advisers in selecting suitable and worthwhile projects' (www.yearoutgroup.org).

As a member, Greenforce complies with the YOG's Member's Charter and Code of Conduct, proves their financial stability (including holding public liability insurance) and has a crisis and risk policy supported by trained staff in the United Kingdom and overseas (YOG, 2008). This ensures that that all volunteers will work in safe environments, be fully looked after and properly trained and protected; this is in line with good practice recommendations by bodies such as Tourism Concern (see Power, 2007).

Greenforce and the YOG provide information not only to potential gap year participants but also for parents and career advisors who can be key influences on the decision to take a gap year and which organization and project to choose. Greenforce run pre-departure training briefings for volunteers and briefings are included for parents and faculty too for school and college group projects. Greenforce highlights its use of external safety and security guidelines, including UK Foreign and Commonwealth Office advice and British Standards Institute BS8848 Specifications (which covers the provision of visits, fieldwork, expeditions and adventurous activities outside the United Kingdom). This is supported by experienced and trained British staff permanently in each destination, who are able to identify and manage risks appropriately. Greenforce also work with respected host partners including governments and international bodies such as UNESCO and the International Red Cross.

Greenforce ensures the scientific value of its work through membership of organizations such as the World Conservation Union (IUCN) and the Marine Conservation Society. It emphasizes the role of its field staff, with all scientific work and volunteers being overseen and monitored by trained scientists. All Greenforce's conservation work also includes a strong community participation role, which meets its sustainable development objectives. All projects involve a host country partner and all contact with communities is at the local residents' initiation. The Bahamas' project illustrates how volunteers can get involved in education and community programs. Greenforce also offer training to upskill local residents, often with the long-term objective of them taking ownership of a project. In Greenforce's first Fijian project, local residents were trained as PADI Divemasters and the campsite and equipment were ultimately given to the local village to run as a Marine Research Station, ensuring the long-term viability of the project and research.

In 2008 Greenforce attracted significant positive media coverage of perhaps its largest scale community project when they organized for six Maasai warriors to run in the London Marathon. Greenforce had run a conservation project in Eluai, Tanzania, in partnership with the African Wildlife Foundation. From their experiences working with Greenforce volunteers, the Maasai had initiated a plan to raise money to build a borehole in their village. Greenforce supported the fund-raising campaign and organized the Maasai's participation in the London Marathon. The project proved a huge success, with more than enough money raised for the borehole project, as well as highlighting the contributions of Greenforce and its volunteers to the environment and communities.

Structuring volunteer training

Greenforce projects typically require volunteers to develop a range of skills to ensure the accuracy of the scientific data collected and to adapt to an environment which is very different to their home life. In the Andros Marine Conservation Project in the Bahamas, dive skills are essential to carry out the survey work and while some volunteers come fully or partly dive-trained, for many this is their first experience of diving. During the first four weeks, the qualified field staff will train all volunteers up to PADI Advanced Open Water Diver level as well as training them in Emergency First Response.

At the same time, the volunteers will learn basic survey skills (such as carrying out transects and quadrants) as well as learning to identify the fish, coral and invertebrates found in the area. They are also taught about the geography and geology of the islands, the formation of reefs and their importance to the protection of the land, the local people and the biodiversity levels of the oceans. Field staff have to be confident that volunteers can carry out the survey work accurately and safely and they undertake monitoring and supervision of the volunteers as their confidence and skills develop.

Keeping volunteers motivated throughout the project

Swarbrooke, Beard, Leckie, & Pomfret (2003) found that Greenforce volunteers are driven by a combination of four main motivations: personal development, excitement and risk, spiritual motivations, and wildlife seeking; and Harlow & Pomfret (2007) identified environment and conservation as the primary motivation of Greenforce volunteers on a Zambian expedition. While gap year providers do offer longer-duration projects, the 10 weeks of a typical Greenforce project (such as the Andros Marine Conservation Project) is still a significant length of time for volunteers to be involved. The enthusiasm and motivations of volunteers may change over the project and managing these fluctuations can be a challenge for project leaders.

Managing volunteers' expectations is the initial step and this begins when a potential volunteer first makes contact with Greenforce. The web site (www.greenforce.org) contains advice on what a project involves, including a video of the site and a typical day and photographs and reports from completed trips. Once a booking is made volunteers receive a briefing pack (which includes an equipment list, medical advice, travel advice from the UK Foreign and Commonwealth Office, country history and project information and a Greenforce polo shirt) and an invitation to the Meet Your Team briefing day and barbecue in Central London. This is an opportunity to meet the other volunteers on their project and includes training in basic first aid and the first of the 'science lectures', typical of the training they will receive in the destination. Greenforce spends considerable time making the volunteers aware of what life will be like on camp, often using ex-volunteers in their training days so that the new volunteers can talk to others who have already been out there and experienced it. This comprehensive preproject briefing is in line with advice offered by organizations such as YOG and Tourism Concern (Power, 2007).

The first four weeks of a project like the Andros Marine Conservation Project are hard work as volunteers learn new skills and adapt to a very different way of life. Yet this is also a fun and exciting time as volunteers are busy learning things, discovering the area and getting to know their group. Surveying can be exciting when you spot a rare fish or see a shark close up, but survey work is also repetitive and can become mundane and tedious once the novelty starts to wear off. Motivating volunteers during the midsection of the project can be a challenge, particularly if a period of bad weather sets in. Poor weather conditions halt diving and survey work and camp chores, while fun when they are a new experience, can soon become burdensome.

In their free time volunteers have access to books, games and a home-made gym and they are encouraged to carry out projects to improve the camp. However, once bad weather strikes, volunteers discover that living without the luxuries they are used to at home can become quite hard and with no diving to fill the day, the abovementioned amenities soon become inadequate. On no-dive days, field staff will organize trips to the Blue Holes – local naturally formed deep 'lakes' where everyone can go swimming and enjoy being away from camp. There are also opportunities to visit the local towns and craftspeople to experience the island and its culture. Despite field staff's best attempts, it can be hard to keep the volunteers motivated as the bad weather can create listlessness and a longing for the 'creature comforts' of home. It has, however, been found that when more favorable weather conditions return, volunteer motivation for the survey work increases as it is a chance to get back to the core task they have come to do.

It only rarely occurs that a volunteer is so unhappy out on camp that they choose to leave early, with many volunteers actually wanting to spend longer out in location and often repeating a similar experience later in their lives. Greenforce encourages this ongoing relationship by organizing reunion parties back in the United Kingdom and keeping in touch with volunteers via the Greenforce Blog and Facebook pages for the organization and individual holidays. Some participants go on to take Field Staff positions with Greenforce and at the end of each 10-week phase, one volunteer is selected to stay on as a 'trainee' for the next project intake. This involves no extra cost to the volunteer and gives them the opportunity to learn more about marine science as well as further develop diving and leadership skills. For Greenforce, it is also a way of rewarding enthusiastic, hardworking volunteers and provides an additional trained team member to contribute to the running of the subsequent holiday.

CONCLUSION

This case study has demonstrated how an individual volunteer tourism provider has responded to developments in the wider gap year industry. Greenforce has evolved beyond its conservation origins but still highlights its not-for-profit status, its commitment to sustainable development and the local partnerships and involvement of the host communities with which it works. It has widened its market from postschool and postuniversity gap year students, to include those taking a year out later in life (career break or retirees) and also tailored projects to school and college groups as well as individuals. Greenforce also strives to follow good practice in preparing volunteers for placements and ensuring it meets industry standards. The case study has also illustrated some of the operational challenges faced by those managing volunteers on longer-duration projects in remote locations and the developing world. This includes the need to train and motivate participants in an environment that can be very different from home.

ACKNOWLEDGMENT

The authors thank Greenforce for its assistance in the development of this case study and for its continuing support in Siobhan's academic and career development.

DISCUSSION QUESTIONS

Q19.1 How has the market for gap year volunteer tourism changed in the United Kingdom?

Q19.2 What steps does Greenforce take to follow good practice in managing their volunteers and projects?

Q19.3 What are the key factors in keeping volunteer tourists motivated over the course of a 10-week project?

FURTHER INFORMATION

Greenforce: www.greenforce.org

Gapforce: www.gapforce.org

Greenforce's support for Maasai Warriors' London Marathon fundraising project: www.maasaimarathon.org

Year Out Group (of which Greenforce is a member): www.yearoutgroup.org

CHAPTER 20

WWOOF Network, New Zealand

Motivations, Expectations and Experiences of Volunteers and Hosts

Alison J. McIntosh

University of Waikato, New Zealand, mcintosh@waikato.ac.nz

KEY POINTS

■ WWOOF is a worldwide membership network of farms that allows volunteers to live and work on an organic farm and learn about organics.

■ WWOOF is a tourism venture; however, unlike commercial farm stay operations, the WWOOF experience is voluntary.

■ Volunteers join WWOOF to: learn about organic farming; meet and stay with local New Zealanders and experience their everyday life; travel around New Zealand; experience farm life; experience an alternative lifestyle; work outdoors; and do volunteer work.

■ WWOOF hosts tend not to share the financial motives of their commercial farm tourism counterparts; instead, WWOOF hosts are primarily motivated by the desire to farm organically for health, environmental or ethical reasons and they tend to hold very strong environmental attitudes and practice proenvironmental behaviors.

■ The success of the WWOOF experience depends on the mutual cooperation of hosts and WWOOFers; that is, that hosts provide their hospitality and share their knowledge, while WWOOFers provide their enthusiasm and assistance with farm duties.

Managing Volunteers in Tourism
Copyright © 2009 Elsevier Ltd. All rights reserved.

OVERVIEW OF THE WWOOF NETWORK

WWOOF is a worldwide network of organizations that share a common philosophy to promote the organic movement and provides a contact point for volunteers who want to live, work and gain hands-on learning experience on organic properties/farms around the world. WWOOF can stand for 'Willing Workers on Organic Farms', although since 2000 the international WWOOF organization has used 'World Wide Opportunities on Organic Farms'. This change was made to avoid confusion caused by the word 'work' when WWOOFers are volunteers and not migrant workers. Some WWOOF groups still prefer to use the old version of the name, but more generally, the movement is simply referred to as WWOOFing. WWOOF volunteers ('WWOOFers') offer their help on the farm and in return they learn knowledge and experiences about organic farming and receive food and lodging. The opportunity to meet people and learn about different cultures is also an important part of the WWOOF exchange. Therefore, WWOOF is a network that brings benefits to communities all around the world, is recognized as an important vehicle for travel, as well as having an important contribution toward the wider organic movement by bringing more people into direct contact with organic growers and practices. Organic farming aims to:

> work in a way that is environmentally friendly and ethical with
> regard to animals, including, for example, appropriate land
> management practices, composting, crop rotation, growing a diverse
> range of crops to help soil fertility, excluding the use of chemicals,
> the humane treatment of farm animals in a 'free range' environment
> and using natural pest and disease control systems.
> (Strange and Strange, 1999, cited in McIntosh and Campbell,
> 2001, p. 112)

Organic farming is the primary activity of WWOOF hosts; however, there are variations of this based on the sustainable ethos of ecological, social and economic responsibility. For example, some hosts around the world operate health and healing centers, arts and crafts ventures, building and restoring buildings, organic cafes and restaurants, dealing with animals, eco-villages, brewing and production of foods and centers for the environment.

WWOOF began in the United Kingdom in the early 1970s; it originally stood for 'Working Weekends on Organic Farms' and its original mission was to offer the chance for people working in cities to escape to the countryside for the weekend enjoying their WWOOF experiences while also learning organic skills. As such, while the primary focus of the WWOOF venture is organic farming, hosting volunteer travelers is a secondary objective. Indeed, individuals from other countries who had enjoyed WWOOFing in the United Kingdom took the idea home and, with a little help from UK WWOOF, set up a national WWOOF in their own home country. As the phenomenon grew, the scheduled weekend holidays were replaced with a comprehensive membership booklet to facilitate direct contact and longer stays between volunteers and farms. WWOOF is now essentially a tourism venture, however, unlike commercial farm stay operations, the WWOOF experience is voluntary; that is, services or work in lieu of payment is offered instead of payment for accommodation using money.

There are now WWOOF farms worldwide, including Europe, North America, South America, Africa, Asia and the South Pacific. Each WWOOF group around the world is an independent organization networking together. The International WWOOF Association (IWA) is a not-for-profit company that provides international support and promotion for WWOOF organizations operating separately and independently in each country. WWOOF operates on a fairly informal basis by consensus. Meetings with hosts and WWOOFers, usually at a host's property over a weekend, are a good chance to hear how the exchange is working and discussing feedback and ideas.

In New Zealand, there are over 1000 WWOOF farms around the country promoted by the WWOOF NZ organization. WWOOF NZ began in 1974 when Dick Roberts put together a list of six organic farms interested in having people come to stay and help on the farm. WWOOF NZ's core role is, 'To encourage volunteers to learn biological farming techniques and promote this way of producing food and resources' and 'By enabling people to participate in an intercultural exchange WWOOF NZ promotes greater understanding and cultural awareness, which leads to peace' (www.wwoof.co.nz). To achieve this role, WWOOF NZ has the mission to:

- give people the opportunity to learn first hand organic growing techniques;

- provide everyone with the opportunity to experience living and working on a farm;

- improve communication within the organic movement;

- help individuals develop the confidence to become self-sufficient;

- bring together people from all walks of life, forming new friendships and making useful contacts. (www.wwoof.co.nz)

OVERVIEW OF THE WWOOF VOLUNTEER PROGRAM IN NEW ZEALAND

WWOOF NZ aims to offer an efficient, low-cost service to its members. Throughout New Zealand, WWOOFing opportunities exist on farms and small holdings which offer the chance to work with organic growers, eco-builders, willow weavers, on market gardens, vineyards, home orchards, dairy farms, ventures in self-sufficiency and in gardens of remembrance. No money changes hand between WWOOFers and hosts; instead, WWOOFers give their time and energy to helping on the farm and in return the host provides meals and accommodation and shares knowledge about organics. The nature of the work that WWOOFers do depends on what the hosts need at the time; this may include general farm and garden work such as planting, weeding, harvesting, feeding animals, building work, as well as household duties and childminding. The length of each WWOOF experience is agreed in advance between the WWOOFers and hosts and depends on the work available and the availability of the WWOOFer. Many WWOOFers stay for one to three weeks, while some hosts take WWOOFers for longer periods. As it takes time to get the volunteer's accommodation ready and show them how the farm operates, many hosts like to have a minimum stay period. Some WWOOF hosts continually host WWOOFers throughout the year, while others schedule gaps so that they and their families get a break or, conversely, may only host WWOOFers when they have a particular project on. WWOOFing generally takes place all year round.

Typically, WWOOFing is based on half a day's help (usually four to five hours) in return for meals and accommodation. In addition to this, hosts often ask WWOOFers to help out in the home including chores like cooking, helping with lunch, cleaning the dishes, just as any other house guest would do. As WWOOFers are predominantly visitors to the region/country, it is usual for hosts to provide their guests with travel information in their local area. However, the primary motivation for WWOOFers is usually to experience and learn about life on organic farms, meet families and have a homely environment while they are traveling; thus, WWOOFers tend to undertake fewer tourist activities in the vicinity (McIntosh & Campbell, 2001). Anyone over the age of 16 years can go WWOOFing and WWOOFers volunteering in New Zealand will usually require a student or working holiday visa as the New Zealand Immigration Department consider volunteering while getting food and accommodation to be a form of 'work'. Most WWOOF farms do not accept children due to safety issues on the farm and lack of accommodation.

Autonomous WWOOF groups in different countries have differing ways of organizing but, generally, all WWOOF hosts must pay an application fee to officially become a member of the WWOOF organization. Before a host can accept a volunteer, that volunteer must also become a member of WWOOF. Once a member, the volunteer will receive a WWOOF membership book detailing all the WWOOF farms in New Zealand. A WWOOFer is expected to contact their host to arrange their stay. WWOOF membership lasts for 12 months and can be arranged through an agent or through completion of an online application form. WWOOF NZ provides dual access to the host list, printed and online. There is often no additional charge for two members joining if they are traveling together; thus, WWOOFing can be a cheap travel option.

The difference between WWOOFing and commercial farm stays was noted by McIntosh and Campbell in their (2001) study of WWOOF farms in four regions (Otago, Southland, Timaru/Oamaru and Christchurch) of the South Island of New Zealand. McIntosh and Campbell concluded that WWOOF farms exhibit characteristics that render them distinct from conventional farm tourism ventures, especially with regard to their small-scale nonseasonal nature, their atypical nature and the dominant role of the woman in relation to farm duties. Indeed, the study found that typically, WWOOF organic farms are small-scale ventures, including herb farms and orchards, with almost half of the farms supplementing their income with off-farm employment; most farming on organic farms was seen as a means of self-sufficiency or alternative living. For example, some of the WWOOF hosts lived in an atypical design of house such as a self-built mud brick house or a bush hut, some had particular diets, others practiced holistic healing techniques, used sustainable energies in the home, followed alternative or home schooling methods or grew rare crops or kept alternative livestock (e.g. llamas). In this way, the type of food and accommodation offered at WWOOF farms varies. More women in the household were found to be responsible for the organic farming duties. Most farm hosts were aged between 30 and 50 years, most were educated to tertiary or postgraduate level, with almost one half of the respondents reporting that they had dependent children living at home. Just over 40% of the WWOOF hosts in McIntosh and Campbell's (2001) study indicated that they received volunteers all year round on a part-time basis; over 13% stated that they received workers on a full-time yearly basis and 24% received volunteers seasonally.

For the most part, although WWOOF is a venture that has been in New Zealand for over 30 years, McIntosh and Campbell's study found that hosting on organic farms is a recent venture; the mean number of years spent hosting visitors was six years, with the least amount of time being one year and the most time being 22 years. Most WWOOF hosts do not advertise or market their WWOOF venture and therefore, most people hear about the organization through word-of-mouth or through basic information given in some travel guide books (e.g. *Lonely Planet*) As such, WWOOFing was also not found to be coordinated in the same way as the marketing of commercial farm stays and is thus not commercially orientated. In addition to the volunteer and exchange nature of the stay, McIntosh and Bonnemann (2006) note that the hosted experience on an organic farm is notably different from that provided at a commercial farm stay with four key dimensions making the WWOOF experience distinct: the rurality of the experience; the opportunity to learn about organics; the personal meaningfulness of the experience; and the element of sincerity in the experience. In this way, McIntosh and Bonnemann argue that the WWOOF experience may have the ability to heighten understanding between people from different cultural, social, or ideological backgrounds, 'endear' visitors to rural regions in support of wider economic development initiatives, engender or raise appreciation, care and concern for the natural environment, support for the organic movement or an alternative lifestyle and encourage self-reflection and personal development among volunteers.

KEY ISSUES FOR VOLUNTEER MANAGEMENT

The need for mutual cooperation between hosts and volunteers

WWOOFing brings together a diverse range of people from different cultures, so it requires trust and respect from everyone involved if it is to promote actively cultural awareness and understanding; it is seen to offer a more meaningful way to learn about different communities. WWOOF is a practical way of getting involved in the organic movement and sees plenty of devoted followers, which transcends nationality, gender, age and class. However, the success of the exchange depends on the mutual cooperation of hosts and WWOOFers; that is, that hosts provide their hospitality and share their knowledge, while WWOOFers provide their enthusiasm and assistance with farm duties. Many hosts who are considering hosting longer-term WWOOFers, for example, will consider what skills and knowledge they have to share, what projects they have to be worked on and, often, may have a trial period of three nights with a WWOOFer. This allows them to consider the impact of hosting and to get to know their guest before making a commitment. It is important for hosts to communicate expectations at the start of the stay, including confirmation of arrangements for the working day, meal times and any house rules. Hosts are encouraged to talk to the WWOOFer when they phone to determine their suitability to their situation; hosts have the right to decline accommodation at their discretion.

Matching the motivations of hosts and volunteers

This can be important because WWOOF hosts are unique in relation to the organic principles they operate (i.e. practice permaculture, biodynamics, or simply organic) and may have specific interests or lifestyle (e.g. vegetarian, organics). In particular, WWOOF hosts tend not to share the financial motives of their commercial farm tourism counterparts; instead, WWOOF hosts are primarily motivated by the desire to farm organically for health, environmental or ethical reasons and they tend to hold very strong environmental attitudes and practice proenvironmental behaviors in relation to energy conservation, recycling and composting (McIntosh & Campbell, 2001). While this may be seen to heighten care for the environment and support for organics through farm tourism, occasionally, these motives and behaviors could be found to be in contrast to those of WWOOFers who are not always found to be as interested in organics, thereby leading to disappointment among hosts (McIntosh & Campbell, 2001) and complaints among volunteers, for instance, over the number of hours work expected (McIntosh & Bonnemann, 2006). Indeed, McIntosh and Bonnemann (2006) caution that the nature of the WWOOF experience may have undergone a 'shift', becoming more focused perhaps on alternative living and becoming increasingly viewed by volunteer visitors as a more sincere cultural travel experience and thus a stay on a WWOOF farm may not be as 'organic' in nature as the aims of the WWOOF organization might imply. For this reason, McIntosh and Campbell (2001) advocate a matching of host and volunteer/visitor values and motivations to minimize the potential for conflict in the host–volunteer encounter. They suggest that this can be achieved through modifications to the WWOOF hosting experience, the implementation of mechanisms to ensure a better degree of compatibility in the experience provided (e.g. by requiring volunteers to work fewer hours per day) or by introducing screening mechanisms to ensure a better host/volunteer 'fit'.

McIntosh and Bonnemann (2006), in their analysis of over 2000 WWOOF NZ application forms received by WWOOF NZ in 2001, revealed the profile and motivations of visitors applying to stay on a WWOOF farm in New Zealand in that year. Almost all the applicants had no previous experience of WWOOF in New Zealand or overseas. Reasons for wanting to join WWOOF included an interest in learning about organic farming; to meet and stay with local New Zealanders and experience their everyday life; to travel around New Zealand; to experience farm life; to experience an alternative lifestyle; to work outdoors; and to do volunteering. The study found that the majority of applicants were international visitors to New Zealand, with the largest proportions from Europe (mainly Germany and the United Kingdom), North America, and East Asia (mainly Japan). The mean age of applicants was 26.7 years, the majority were female, mainly students or those employed in professional or semiprofessional occupations, with more that half of the applicants intending to stay in New Zealand for more than three months and the majority were traveling alone. This profile somewhat contrasts with that found for visitors to commercial farm stays in New Zealand where domestic and younger visitors, those traveling as a family or couple and shorter duration stays are predominant. As such, McIntosh and Bonnemann (2006) concluded that WWOOFers may share more similar demographic characteristics with the profile of long-term budget travelers, such as backpackers, than the profile of commercial farm stay tourists.

The importance of good communication between hosts and volunteers

The communication of host and volunteer expectations is therefore pivotal to the success of WWOOFing. Expectations of WWOOF hosts and volunteers are promoted on WWOOF organization web sites. For example, according to the WWOOF NZ web site (www.wwoof.co.nz), the obligations of WWOOFers are the following:

- Arrange your stay first. Do not just turn up at the host's door.

- Let the host know if you cannot make it by the arranged date. If you don't show up, they will be concerned about what has happened to you.

- Because you are in the host's home, you must show respect for their way of life and be willing to be adaptable.

- Help out on the property for the agreed period each day.

The obligations of WWOOF hosts are stated as follows:

- Be able to provide experiences in a variety of organic techniques.

- Be able to provide a welcoming and safe environment for their WWOOFers.

- Aim to provide organic food.

- Aim to make literature available to WWOOFers to back up the practical experience gained on the farm.

- Aim to include WWOOFers in daily farm life.

Of course, the network witnesses disagreements and the occasional 'rogue' WWOOFer or WWOOF host who has not understood the WWOOF ethos; however, the inclusive network of the WWOOF system generally works. Indeed, the majority of hosts in McIntosh and Campbell's (2001) study stated that conflict between hosts and volunteers was not a major problem relating to hosting. In addition, the umbrella of the IWA provides a collective but neutral international web site for the many WWOOF organizations where developments, experiences and difficulties can be shared and new schemes and policies discussed. In fact, most WWOOF hosts agree that the social and ethical benefits derived from hosting far outweigh any minor problems. Specifically, hosts in McIntosh and Campbell's study (2001, p. 122) reported that: 'the need for labour on the farm, the exchange of organic philosophies, the stimulation from friendships and enjoyment from the company of other people and the chance for cultural exchange' were the main reasons why they continue to be WWOOF hosts.

CONCLUSION

The WWOOF volunteer program remains an important contribution to New Zealand tourism, local communities and the wider organic movement. Volunteering on a WWOOF farm provides a unique activity in which the work and leisure dimensions of the volunteer experience are centered within the philosophy and practice of organic farming.

DISCUSSION QUESTIONS

Q20.1 Discuss the differences between the nature of the hosted experience on a WWOOF farm and that provided on a commercial farm tourism venture.
Examples of commercial farm tourism ventures include:
www.ruraltourism.co.nz
www.ruralholidays.co.nz

Q20.2 Critically discuss whether farm tourism on a WWOOF farm could be considered a more sustainable form of tourism than more commercial forms of farm tourism.

Q20.3 Consider and outline management options that WWOOF hosts might take to minimize potential conflict and/or tensions between host and volunteer on the WWOOF farm.

FURTHER INFORMATION

WWOOF New Zealand: www.wwoof.co.nz

WWOOF International: www.wwoof.org or www.wwoofinternational.org/

References

ABS. (2007). *Voluntary work, Australia*. Australian Bureau of Statistics.

Adams, D. (2005). First stop Geelong. *The Age, 30 April*(Suppl.), 6.

Agency for Cultural Affairs. (2003). *Bunka Borantia no Suishin ni Mukete: Bunka Borantia Jissensya Anke-to Cyousa Kekka tou*. Agency for Cultural Affairs.

Amis, J., Slack, T., & Berrett, T. (1995). The structural antecedents of conflict in voluntary sport organisations. *Leisure Studies, 14*(1), 1–16.

Andersen, R. K. (1996). Motiver for frivillig innsats i Norges Røde Kors. Rapport 96:2. Institutt for samfunnsforskning (ISF).

Anderson, E., & Cairncross, G. (2005). Understanding and managing volunteer motivation: Two regional tourism cases. *Australian Journal on Volunteering, 10*, 7–17.

Andrew, J. (1996). Motivations and expectations of volunteers involved in a large scale sports event: A pilot study. *Australian Leisure, 7*, 21–25.

Art Gallery New South Wales. (2007). *Art Gallery New South Wales Annual Report 2007*. Art Gallery New South Wales.

Atwood, C., Singh, G., Prime, D., et al. (2003). *2001 Home Office Citizenship Survey: People families and communities. Home Office Research Study 270*. Home Office.

Australian Museum. (2007). *Australian Museum Annual Report 2006–2007 Summary Report*. Australian Museum Trust.

Australian Sports Commission. (2000a). *Volunteer management program: Managing event volunteers*. Australian Sports Commission.

Australian Sports Commission. (2000b). *Volunteer management program: Recruiting volunteers*. Australian Sports Commission.

Australian War Memorial. (2007). *Australian War Memorial Annual Report 2006–2007*. Australian War Memorial.

BAFM. (1998). *Heritage volunteer training project: Stage one report*. British Association of Friends of Museums.

Baum, T., & Lockstone, L. (2007). Volunteers and mega sporting events: Developing a research framework. *International Journal of Event Management Research, 3*, 29–41.

273

Bennett, R. (2007). Gap-year students told to forget aid projects. *The Times Online, 18 August.*

Bindloss, J., & Hindle, C. (2005). *The gap year book: The definitive guide to planning and taking a year out.* Lonely Planet Publications.

Boezemen, E. J., & Ellemers, N. (2008). Pride and respect in volunteers' organisational commitment. *European Journal of Social Psychology, 38*(1), 159–72.

Boniface, B., & Cooper, C. (2005). *Worldwide destinations: The geography of travel and tourism.* Butterworth-Heinemann.

Bowen, P. (2002). *Family volunteering: A discussion paper.* Volunteer Canada.

Bowgett, K., Dickie, K., & Restall, M. (2002). *The good practice guide: For everyone who works with volunteers.* National Centre for Volunteering.

Broad, S. (2003). Living the Thai life: A case study of volunteer tourism at the Gibbon Rehabilitation Project, Thailand. *Tourism Recreation Research, 28,* 63–72.

Broad, S., & Jenkins, J. (2008). Gibbons in their midst? Conservation volunteers' motivations at the Gibbon Rehabilitation Project, Phuket, Thailand. In K. Lyons & S. Wearing (Eds.), *Journeys of discovery in volunteer tourism: International case study perspectives* (pp. 72–85). CABI.

Brown, M. (2006). Unhappy games volunteers quit. *The Sydney Morning Herald, 9 January,* 3.

Brown, S., & Lehto, X. (2005). Travelling with a purpose: Understanding the motives and benefits of volunteer vacationers. *Current Issues in Tourism, 8,* 479–96.

Brown, S., & Morrison, A. (2003). Expanding volunteer vacation participation: An exploratory study on the mini-mission concept. *Tourism Recreation Research, 28,* 73–82.

Brudney, J. (Ed.). (2005). Emerging areas of volunteering. *ARNOVA occasional paper series, 1(2).*

Bruyere, B., & Rappe, S. (2007). Identifying the motivations of environmental volunteers. *Journal of Environmental Planning and Management, 50,* 503–16.

Bryen, L., & Madden, K. (2006). *Bounce-back of episodic volunteers: What makes episodic volunteers return? Working Paper No. CPNS 32.* Queensland University of Technology.

Caldwell, L. L., & Andereck, K. L. (1994). Motives for initiating and continuing membership in a recreation-related voluntary association. *Leisure Sciences, 16,* 33–44.

Callanan, M., & Thomas, S. (2005). Volunteer tourism: Deconstructing volunteer activities within a dynamic environment. In M. Novelli (Ed.), *Niche tourism: Contemporary issues, trends and cases* (pp. 183–200). Butterworth-Heinemann.

Campbell, L. M., & Smith, C. (2006). What makes them pay? Values of volunteer tourists working for sea turtle conservation. *Environmental Management, 38,* 84–98.

Cassell, C. (2001). Managing diversity. In T. Redman & A. Wilkinson (Eds.), *Contemporary human resource management* (pp. 404–31). Pearson Education.

Christensen, A., Rowe, S., & Needham, M. D. (2007). Value orientations, awareness of consequences, and participation in a whale watching education program in Oregon. *Human Dimensions of Wildlife, 12,* 289–93.

Clary, E. G., Snyder, M., Ridge, R. D., et al. (1998). Understanding and assessing the motivations of volunteers: A functional approach. *Journal of Personality and Social Psychology, 74,* 1516–30.

Clary, E. G., Snyder, M., & Stukas, A. A. (1996). Volunteers' motivations: Findings from a national survey. *Nonprofit and Voluntary Sector Quarterly, 25,* 485–505.

Cnaan, R. A., Handy, F., & Wadsworth, M. (1996). Defining who is a volunteer: Conceptual and empirical considerations. *Nonprofit and Voluntary Sector Quarterly, 25,* 364–83.

Coghlan, A. (2006). Choosing your conservation-based volunteer tourism market segment with care – part 1 www.voluntourism.org. *The Volun Tourist, Jan.*

Coghlan, A. (2008). Exploring the role of expedition staff in volunteer tourism. *International Journal of Tourism Research, 10,* 183–91.

Commission on the Future of Volunteering. (2008). *Report of the Commission on the Future of Volunteering: Manifesto for change.* Volunteering England.

Courne, L. (2009). Is voluntourism a dirty word? *Boots n All.* www.bootsnall.com

Cousins, J. A. (2007). The role of UK-based conservation tourism operators. *Tourism Management, 28,* 1020–30.

Coyne, B. S., & Coyne, E. J. (2001). Getting, keeping and caring for unpaid volunteers for professional golf tournament events. *Human Resource Development International, 4,* 199–214.

Cunningham, I. (1999). Human resource management in the voluntary sector: Challenges and opportunities. *Public Money and Management,* 19–25.

Cuskelly, G. (2005). Volunteer participation trends in Australian sport. In G. Nichols & M. Collins (Eds.), *Volunteers in sports clubs* (pp. 87–104). Leisure Studies Association.

Cuskelly, G., Hoye, R., & Auld, C. (2006). *Working with volunteers in sport: Theory and practice.* Routledge.

Cuskelly, G., Taylor, T., Hoye, R., & Darcy, S. (2006). Volunteer management practices and volunteer retention: A human resource management approach. *Sport Management Review, 9,* 141–63.

Davis Smith, J. (1996). Should volunteers be managed? In D. Billis & M. Harris (Eds.), *Voluntary agencies: Challenges of organisation and management* (pp. 187–99). Macmillan.

Davis Smith, J. (1998). *The 1997 National Survey of Volunteering*. National Centre for Volunteering.

Davis Smith, J., & Chambers, D. (1997). *Volunteering with the National Trust: Survey report*. National Centre for Volunteering.

Davis Smith, J., Ellis, A. & Brewis, G. (2005). Cross-national volunteering: A developing movement? In: J. L. Brudney (Ed.), *Emerging areas of volunteering: ARNOVA occasional paper series, 1(2)* (pp. 63–75).

DEMOS. (2003). *Towards a strategy for workforce development*. DEMOS and Resource.

Department for International Development (2008). *Country profile, Lesotho.* [Online] www.dfid.gov.uk/countries/africa/lesotho.asp.

Destination Marketing Association International. (2007). *Profile of a destination marketing organization*. Destination Marketing Association International.

dev-zone. (2008). Special issue on good intentions: The ethics of volunteering. *Just Change, 11.*

Downward, P., & Ralston, R. (2005). Volunteer motivation and expectations prior to the XVII Commonwealth Games in Manchester, UK: A quantitative study. *Tourism and Hospitality: Planning & Development, 2*(1), 17–26.

Downward, P., Lumsdon, L., & Ralston, R. (2005). Gender differences in sports event volunteering: Insights from Crew 2002 at the XVII Commonwealth Games. *Managing Leisure, 10,* 219–36.

Earl, C., Parker, E., Edwards, M., & Carpa, M. (2004). Capacity building and public health and emergency management for volunteers at outdoor music festivals. *Australian Journal on Volunteering, 9,* 19–24.

Edwards, D. (2004). Defining field characteristics of museums and art museums: An Australian perspective. In M. Graham & R. A. Stebbins (Eds.), *Volunteering as leisure/leisure as volunteering: An international assessment* (pp. 137–50). CABI Publishing.

Edwards, D. (2005a). It's mostly about me: Reasons why volunteers contribute their time to museums and art museums. *Tourism Review International, 9,* 21–31.

Edwards, D. C. (2005b). *Understanding the organization of volunteers at visitor attractions*. University of Western Sydney.

Edwards, P. (2005c). Now to sign up the force of volunteers. *The Age, 30 April*(Suppl.), 1.

Elstad, B. (1997a). *Organisering og ledelse av frivillige. En studie av Kongsberg Jazzfestival. Working paper no. 45/1997*. Lillehammer College.

Elstad, B. (1997b). Volunteer perception of learning and satisfaction in a mega event: The case of the XVII Olympic Winter Games in Lillehammer. *Festival Management and Event Tourism, 4*(3/4), 75–83.

Elstad, B. (2003). Continuance commitment and reasons to quit: A study of volunteers at a jazz festival. *Event Management, 8,* 99–108.

Esmond, J. (2001). *'Boomnet': Capturing the baby boomer volunteers: A research project into baby boomers and volunteering*. Department for Community Development, Government of Western Australia.

Fairley, S., Kellett, P., & Green, B. C. (2007). Volunteering abroad: Motives for travel to volunteer at the Athens Olympic Games. *Journal of Sport Management, 21,* 41–57.

Fallon, L., & Kriwoken, L. K. (2002). *Key elements contributing to effective and sustainable visitor centres: An evaluation of the Strahan Visitor Centre, Tasmania, Australia*. CRC Sustainable Tourism.

Farrell, J., Johnston, M., & Twynam, D. (1998). Volunteer motivation, satisfaction and management at an elite sporting competition. *Journal of Sport Management, 12,* 288–300.

Ferdinand, N. (2008). The benefits of using student volunteers for small businesses in the event industry: The use of student volunteers at Concert Live. *London Journal of Tourism, Sport and Creative Industries, 1,* 39–53.

Finlay, J., & Murray, M. (2005). *Possible futures: Changes, volunteering and the not-for-profit sector in Australia*. The Smith Family.

Frean, A. (2006). Gap years create 'new colonialists'. *The Times Online, 15 August*.

Fresque, J. A. (2008). *The evolution experience and drivers of collaboration in two non-profit organizations in New Brunswick, Canada*. Brock University Master's thesis.

Gaskin, K. (2003a). *A choice blend: What volunteers want from organisation and management*. Institute for Volunteering Research.

Gaskin, K. (2003b). *VIVA: The volunteer investment and value audit*. Institute for Volunteering Research.

Getz, D. (2002). Why festivals fail. *Event Management, 7,* 209–19.

Getz, D. (2008). Event tourism: Definition, evolution, and research. *Event Management, 29,* 403–28.

Goodlad, S., & McIvor, S. (1998). *Museum volunteers: Good practice in the management of volunteers*. Routledge.

Gordon, L., & Erkut, E. (2004). Improving volunteering scheduling for the Edmonton Folk Festival. *Interfaces, 34*, 367–76.

Gratton, C., Dobson, N., & Shibli, S. (2000). The economic importance of major sports events: A case-study of six events. *Managing Leisure, 5*, 17–28.

Gray, N. J., & Campbell, L. M. (2007). A decommodified experience? Exploring aesthetic, economic and ethical values for volunteer ecotourism in Costa Rica. *Journal of Sustainable Tourism, 15*, 463–82.

Green, B. C., & Chalip, L. (1998). Sports volunteers: Research agenda and application. *Sport Marketing Quarterly, 7*, 14–23.

Green, B. C., & Chalip, L. (2004). Paths to volunteer commitment: Lessons from the Sydney Olympic Games. In R. Stebbins & M. Graham (Eds.), *Volunteering as leisure/leisure as volunteering: An international assessment* (pp. 49–67). CABI.

Griffith, S. (2008). *Gap years for grown ups*. Crimson Publishing.

Hall, M., Lasby, D., Gumulka, G., & Tryon, C. (2006). *Caring Canadians, involved Canadians: Highlights from the 2004 Canada survey of giving, volunteering and participating*. Statistics Canada.

Hall, M., McKechnie, A.-J., Davidman, K., & Leslie, F. (2001). *An environmental scan on volunteering and improving volunteering*. Canadian Centre for Philanthropy.

Handy, F., & Srinivasan, N. (2004). Valuing volunteers: An economic evaluation of the net benefits of hospital volunteers. *Nonprofit and Voluntary Sector Quarterly, 33*, 28–54.

Handy, F., Cnaan, R., Brudney, J., et al. (2000). Public perception of who is a volunteer: An examination of the net-cost approach from a cross-cultural perspective. *Voluntas: International Journal of Voluntary and Nonprofit Organizations, 11*, 45–65.

Hanlon, C., & Jago, L. (2004). The challenge of retaining personnel in major sport event organizations. *Event Management, 9*, 39–49.

Harlow, S., & Pomfret, G. (2007). Evolving environmental tourism experiences in Zambia. *Journal of Ecotourism, 6*, 184–209.

Harrington, M., Cuskelly, G., & Auld, C. (2000). Career volunteering in commodity-intensive serious leisure: Motorsport events and their dependence on volunteers/amateurs. *Loisir et Societe, 23*, 421–52.

Haski-Leventhal, D., Cnaan, R., Handy, F., et al. (2008). Students' vocational choices and voluntary action: A 12-nation study. *Voluntas: International Journal for Voluntary and Nonprofit Organizations, 19*, 1–21.

Haslam, C. (2007). Gap agencies charge up to 600% mark-up. *The Sunday Times Online, 19 August.*

Hawkins, D., Lamoureux, K., & Clemmons, D. (2005). Voluntourism as a catalyst for developing the potential of tourism destinations. *TedQual, 7*, 13–17.

Hede, A.-M., & Rentschler, R. (2007). Mentoring volunteer festival managers: Evaluation of a pilot scheme in regional Australia. *Managing Leisure, 12*, 157–70.

Hegel, A., & McKechnie, A.-J. (2003). *Family volunteering: The final report.* Volunteer Canada.

Henderson, K. (1984). Volunteerism as leisure. *Journal of Voluntary Action Research, 13*, 55–63.

Hendricks, W., Ramthun, R., & Chavez, D. (2001). The effects of persuasive message source and content on mountain bicyclists' adherence to trail etiquette guidelines. *Journal of Park and Recreation Administration, 19*, 38–61.

Hindle, C. (2007). *Volunteer: A traveller's guide to making a difference around the world.* Lonely Planet Publications.

Holmes, K. (1999). Changing times: Volunteering in the heritage sector 1984–1998. *Voluntary Action, 1*, 21–35.

Holmes, K. (2002). *Volunteer and visitor interaction in the UK heritage sector.* University of Leeds PhD thesis.

Holmes, K. (2003). Volunteers in the heritage sector: A neglected audience? *International Journal of Heritage Studies, 9*, 341–55.

Holmes, K. (2006). Experiential learning or exploitation? Volunteering for work experience in the UK museums sector. *Museum Management and Curatorship, 21*, 240–53.

Holmes, K. (2008). Changing attitudes towards volunteering and the implications for tourist attractions. In S. Richardson, L. Fredline, A. Patiar, & M. Ternel (Eds.), *Tourism and hospitality research, training and practice: 'Where the bloody hell are we?' – Proceedings of the 18th annual CAUTHE conference.* Griffith University.

Holmes, K. (2009). The value of volunteering: The volunteer's story. *Australian Journal on Volunteering, 14, 6,* 1–9.

Holmes, K., & Edwards, D. (2008). Volunteers as hosts and guests in museums. In K. D. Lyons & S. Wearing (Eds.), *Journeys of discovery in volunteer tourism: International case study perspectives* (pp. 155–65). CABI.

Holmes, K., Lockstone, L., Smith, K., & Baum, T. (2007). Volunteers and volunteering in tourism: Social science perspectives. In I. McDonnell, S. Grabowski, & R. March (Eds.), *CAUTHE – Proceedings of the 17th Annual Conference.* Sydney: University of Technology.

Howlett, S., Machin, J., & Malmersjo, G. (2005). *Volunteering in museums, libraries and archives.* Institute for Volunteering Research.

Hustinx, L., & Lammertyn, F. (2004). The cultural bases of volunteering: Understanding and predicting attitudinal differences between Flemish Red Cross volunteers. *Nonprofit and Voluntary Sector Quarterly, 33,* 548–84.

Hutin, M. (2008). *Regular and occasional volunteers: How and why they help out.* Institute for Volunteering Research.

Hylton, T. (2004). *New directions in social policy: Cultural diversity for museums, libraries and archives.* Council for Museums, Libraries and Archives.

IVR. (2004). *Volunteering for all? Exploring the link between volunteering and social exclusion.* Institute for Volunteering Research.

IVR. (2005). *Volunteers in museums: Key findings and issues from the literature.* Institute for Volunteering Research.

Jago, L., & Deery, M. (2001). Managing volunteers. In S. Drummond & I. Yeoman (Eds.), *Quality issues in heritage visitor attractions* (pp. 194–217). Butterworth Heinemann.

Jago, L., & Deery, M. (2002). The role of human resource practices in achieving quality enhancement and cost reduction: An investigation of volunteer use in tourism organisations. *International Journal of Contemporary Hospitality Management, 14,* 229–36.

Johnston, M., Twynam, D., & Farrell, J. (1999/2000). Motivation and satisfaction of event volunteers for a major youth organization. *Leisure/Loisir, 24,* 161–77.

Jones, A. (2004). *Review of gap year provision.* Department for Education and Skills.

Jones, M., & Stokes, T. (2003). The Commonwealth Games and urban regeneration: An investigation into training initiatives and partnerships and their effects on disadvantaged groups in East Manchester. *Managing Leisure, 8,* 198–211.

Karkatsoulis, P., Michalopoulos, N., & Moustakatou, V. (2005). The national identity as a motivational factor for better performance in the public sector: The case of the volunteers of the Athens 2004 Olympic Games. *International Journal of Productivity and Performance Management, 54,* 579–94.

Kemp, S. (2002). The hidden workforce: Volunteers' learning in the Olympics. *Journal of European Industrial Training, 26,* 109–16.

Ker, P. (2006). Games on spur to alter habits: Survey. *The Age,* 3 July, 6.

Kitchen, S., Michaelson, J., Wood, N., & John, P. (2006). *2005 Citizenship Survey: Active communities topic report.* Department for Communities and Local Government, UK Government.

KPMG. (2006). *Economic impact study of the Melbourne 2006 Commonwealth Games: Post-event analysis.* Office of Commonwealth Games Coordination.

Kuyper, J. (1993). *Volunteer programme administration: A handbook for museums and other cultural institutions.* American Council for the Arts.

Leigh, D. (2006). Third cultured volunteer tourists and the process of re-assimilation into home environments. *Australian Journal on Volunteering, 11,* 59–67.

Lewis, D. S., French, E., & Steane, P. (1997). A culture of conflict. *Leadership and Organisation Development Journal, 18*(6), 275–82.

Lockstone, L. (2005). *Managing the volunteer workforce: Flexible structures and strategies to integrate volunteers and paid workers.* Melbourne: Victoria University PhD thesis.

Lockstone, L., & Baum, T. (2009). The public face of event volunteering at the 2006 Commonwealth Games: The media perspective. *Managing Leisure, 14*(1), 38–56.

Lockstone, L., & Smith, K. A. (2009). Episodic experiences: Volunteering flexibility in the events sector. In T. Baum, M. Deery, C. Hanlon, et al. (Eds.), *People and work in events and conventions: A research perspective* (pp. 108–24). CABI.

Lockstone, L., Smith, K., & Baum, T. (2007). Flexibility in the tourism sector: Do organisations and events need to be flexible in order to recruit and retain volunteers? *Australian Journal on Volunteering, 12*(2), 37–49.

Lorentzen, H., & Rogstad, J. (1994). *Hvorfor frivillig? Begrunnelser for frivillig sosialt arbeid. Rapport 1994:11.* Institutt for samfunnsforskning (ISF).

Low, N., Butt, S., Ellis Paine, A., & Davis Smith, J. (2007). *Helping out: A national survey of volunteering and charitable giving.* Cabinet Office.

Lynch, B. (2001). Lessons from the Olympics. In J. Noble & F. Johnston (Eds.), *Volunteering visions.* The Federation Press.

Lynn, P., & Smith, J. D. (1991). *The national survey of voluntary activity in the UK. Second series paper no. 1.* The Volunteer Center.

Lyons, K. D. (2003). Ambiguities in volunteer tourism: A case study of Australians participating in a J-1 Visitor Exchange Programme. *Tourism Recreation Research, 28,* 5–13.

Lyons, K., & Wearing, S. (2008a). All for a good cause? The blurred boundaries of volunteering and tourism. In K. D. Lyons & S. Wearing (Eds.), *Journeys of discovery in volunteer tourism: International case study perspectives* (pp. 147–54). CABI.

Lyons, K. D., & Wearing, S. (2008b). *Journeys of discovery in volunteer tourism: International case study perspectives.* CABI.

Macduff, N. (1991). *Episodic volunteering: Building the short-term volunteer program.* MBA Publishing.

Macduff, N. (2005). Societal changes and the rise of the episodic volunteer. In: J. L. Brudney (Ed.), Emerging areas of volunteering: *ARNOVA occasional paper series, 1(2)* (pp. 49–61).

MacLean, J., & Hamm, S. (2007). Motivation, commitment, and intentions of volunteers at a large Canadian sporting event. *Leisure/Loisir, 31*, 523–56.

Makoto, I. (2003). The voluntary response to the Hanshin Awaji earthquake: A trigger for the development of the voluntary and non-profit sector in Japan. In S. Osborne (Ed.), *The voluntary and non-profit sector in Japan: Time for change* (pp. 40–50). RoutledgeCurzon.

Manchester 2002. (2002). *Post games report*. Manchester 2002 The XVII Commonwealth Games.

Maslach, C., & Jackson, S. E. (1986). *Maslach burnout inventory*. Consulting Psychologists Press.

Mavin, S, & Girling, G. (2000). What is managing diversity and why does it matter? *Human Resource Development International, 3*, 419–33.

McCurley, S., & Lynch, R. (1998). *Essential volunteer management*. Directory of Social Change.

McCurley, S., & Lynch, R. (2005). *Keeping volunteers: A guide to retention*. Fat Cat Publications.

McDougall, M. (1996). Equal opportunities versus managing diversity, another challenge for public sector management. *International Journal of Public Sector Management, 9*, 62–72.

McGehee, N. G. (2002). Alternative tourism and social movements. *Annals of Tourism Research, 29*, 124–43.

McGehee, N. G., & Andereck, K. (2008). 'Pettin' the Critters': Exploring the complex relationship between volunteers and the voluntoured in Mcdowell County, West Virginia, USA, and Tijuana, Mexico. In K. Lyons & S. Wearing (Eds.), *Journeys of discovery in volunteer tourism: International case study perspectives* (pp. 12–24). CABI.

McGehee, N. G., & Norman, W. C. (2002). Alternative tourism as impetus for consciousness-raising. *Tourism Analysis, 6*, 239–51.

McGehee, N. G., & Santos, C. A. (2005). Social change, discourse and volunteer tourism. *Annals of Tourism Research, 32*, 760–79.

McIntosh, A. J., & Bonnemann, S. M. (2006). Willing Workers on Organic Farms (WWOOF): The alternative farm stay experience? *Journal of Sustainable Tourism, 14*(1), 82–99.

McIntosh, A., & Campbell, T. (2001). Willing Workers on Organic Farms (WWOOF): A neglected aspect of farm tourism in New Zealand. *Journal of Sustainable Tourism, 9*, 111–27.

McIntosh, A. J., & Zahra, A. (2007). A cultural encounter through volunteer tourism: Towards the ideals of sustainable tourism? *Journal of Sustainable Tourism, 15*, 541–56.

Meijs, L. C. P. M., & Hoogstad, E. (2001). New ways of managing volunteers: Combining membership management and program management. *Voluntary Action, 3*(3), 41–61.

Melbourne 2006 Commonwealth Games. (2006). *The official guide: The quest for gold [Brochure]*. Melbourne 2006 Commonwealth Games.

Mellor, D., Hayashi, Y., Stokes, M., et al. (2008). Volunteering and its relationship with personal and neighbourhood well-being. *Nonprofit and Voluntary Sector Quarterly, May*, 1–16.

Merrill, M. V. (2006). Global trends and the challenges for volunteering. *The International Journal of Volunteer Administration, XXIV*, 9–14.

Millar, S. (1994). Managing volunteers: A partnership approach. In R. Harrison (Ed.), *Manual of heritage management* (pp. 270–79). Butterworth-Heinemann.

Mintel. (2008). Adult gap years – International. *Travel & Tourism Analyst, 42*.

Monga, M. (2006). Measuring motivation to volunteer for special events. *Event Management, 10*, 47–61.

Monga, M., & Treuren, G. (2001). Employment relations without paid work: An exploration into the HRM and motivations of special event volunteers. In K. Spooner & C. Innes (Eds.), *Employment relations in the new economy – Proceedings of the Ninth Annual Conference of International Employment Relations Association* (pp. 445–58). University of Technology, Sydney.

MORI. (2001). *Visitors to museums and galleries in the UK*. Resource.

Musick, M. A., & Wilson, J. (2008). *Volunteers: A social profile*. Indiana University Press.

Mustonen, P. (2005). Volunteer tourism: Postmodern pilgrimage. *Journal of Tourism and Cultural Change, 3*, 160–78.

Nakajima, T., Nakano, S., Imada, S. (2004). *Waga kuni no Borantia Katsudou, "Syakai Seikatsu Kihon Chousa" no Kohyou Deta niyoru Kansatsu Kekka*, PRI Discussion Paper Series (No. 04A-24), Ministry of Finance, Policy Research Institute.

nfpSynergy. (2005). *The 21st century volunteer: A report on the changing face of volunteering in the 21st century*. nfpSynergy.

Ng, J. (2006). *Gap year volunteer: A guide to making it a year to remember*. Summersdale Publishers.

Nichols, G., & King, L. (1999). The changing motivations and frustrations facing volunteers in youth programs: A study of the Guide Association of the United Kingdom. *Journal of Applied Recreation Research, 23*(3), 243–62.

Nichols, G., Taylor, P., James, M., et al. (2005). Pressures on the UK voluntary sports sector. *Voluntas: International Journal for Voluntary and Nonprofit Organizations, 16*(1), 33–50.

Nogawa, H. (2004). An international comparison of the motivations and experiences of volunteers at the 2002 World Cup. In: W. Manzenreiter & J. Horne (Eds.), *Football goes east: Business, culture and the people's game in China, Japan and South Korea* (pp. 222–42). Routledge.

Nordhaug, O. (1993). *Human capital in organisations: Competence, training, and learning.* Scandinavian University Press.

Ockenden, N. (2007). *Volunteering in the natural outdoors in the UK and Ireland: A literature review.* Institute for Volunteering Research.

OCVS. (2007). *Mahi Aroha: Maori perspectives on volunteering and cultural obligations.* Office for the Community and Voluntary Sector.

Onyx, J., & Leonard, R. (2000). Women, volunteering and social capital. In J. Warburton & M. Oppenheimer (Eds.), *Volunteers and Volunteering* (pp. 113–24). Federation Press.

Orr, N. (2006). Museum volunteering: Heritage as 'serious leisure'. *International Journal of Heritage Studies, 12,* 194–210.

Osborne, K. (1999). 'When they are good they are very, very good, but...': The challenge of motivating retired volunteers in small museums. In K. Moore (Ed.), *Museum Management* (pp. 149–84). Athlone Press.

Pazanski, T., & Pennington-Gray, L. (2008). Voluntourism at conventions www.voluntourism.org. *The VolunTourist, 4*(3).

Pearce, J. A. (1980). A volunteer worker placement model for business. *Annals of Tourism Research, 7,* 443–54.

Pearce, J. L. (1993). *Volunteers: The organizational behavior of unpaid workers.* Routledge.

Pearce, P. L. (2004). The functions and planning of visitor centres in regional tourism. *The Journal of Tourism Studies, 15,* 8–17.

Pinnington, A., & Lafferty, G. (2003). *Human resource management in Australia.* Oxford University Press.

Plummer, R. (1998). *A multiple case study of community-based water management initiatives in New Brunswick.* University of New Brunswick Master's thesis.

Plummer, R., & Arai, S. M. (2005). Co-management of natural resources: Opportunities for and barriers against working with citizen volunteers. *Environmental Practice, 7*(4), 221–34.

Power, S. (2007). *Gaps in development: An analysis of the UK international volunteering sector.* Tourism Concern.

Preston, J. B., & Brown, W. A. (2004). Commitment and performance of nonprofit Board members. *Nonprofit Management and Leadership, 15*(2), 221–38.

Putnam, D. (2000). *Bowling alone: The collapse and revival of American community*. Simon Schuster.

Ralston, R., Downward, P., & Lumsdon, L. (2003). The XVII Commonwealth Games: An initial overview of the expectations and experiences of volunteers. In G. Nichols (Ed.), *Volunteers in sport* (pp. 43–54). Leisure Studies Association.

Ralston, R., Downward, P., & Lumsdon, L. (2004). The expectations of volunteers prior to the XVII Commonwealth Games, 2002: A qualitative study. *Event Management, 9*, 13–26.

Ralston, R., Lumsdon, L., & Downward, P. (2005). The third force in events tourism: Volunteers at the XVII Commonwealth Games. *Journal of Sustainable Tourism, 13*, 504–19.

Raymond, E. (2007). *Volunteer tourism in New Zealand: The role of sending organisations in ensuring that volunteer tourism programmes 'make a difference'*. Ministry of Tourism.

Raymond, E. (2008). 'Make a Difference!': The role of sending organizations in volunteer tourism. In K. Lyons & S. Wearing (Eds.), *Journeys of discovery in volunteer tourism: International case study perspectives* (pp. 48–60). CABI.

Raymond, E. M., & Hall, C. M. (2008). The development of cross-cultural (mis)understanding through volunteer tourism. *Journal of Sustainable Tourism, 16*, 530–43.

Resource. (2002). *Volunteers in the cultural sector*. Institute for Volunteering Research & Resource.

Rhoden, S., Ineson, E. M., & Ralston, R. (2009). Volunteer motivation in heritage railways: A study of the West Somerset Railway volunteers. *Journal of Heritage Tourism, 4*, 19–36.

Richards, G. (2007). *New Horizons II: The young independent traveller*. WYSE Travel Confederation.

Ritchie, J. R. B. (2000). Turning 16 days into 16 years through Olympic legacies. *Event Management, 6*, 155–65.

Rochester, C. (2006). *Making sense of volunteering: A literature review*. Volunteering England.

Rousseau, D. M. (1995). *Psychological contract in organizations: Understanding written and unwritten agreements*. Sage.

Ryan, C., & Bates, C. (1995). A rose by any other name: The motivations of those opening their gardens for a festival. *Festival Management and Event Tourism, 3*, 59–71.

Saleh, F., & Wood, C. (1998). Motives of volunteers in multicultural festivals: The case of Saskatoon Folkfest. *Festival Management and Event Tourism, 5*, 59–70.

Sandell, R. (2001). The strategic significance of workforce diversity in museums. *International Journal of Heritage Studies, 6*, 213–30.

Sheard, J. (1995). From lady bountiful to active citizen: Volunteering and the voluntary sector. In J. Davis Smith (Ed.), *An introduction to the voluntary sector* (pp. 114–27). Routledge.

Sherraden, M. S., Lough, B., & Moore McBride, A. (2008). Effects of international volunteering and service: Individual and institutional predictors. *Voluntas: International Journal for Voluntary and Nonprofit Organizations, 19*, 395–421.

Simpson, K. (2004). 'Doing development': The gap year, volunteer-tourists and a popular practice of development. *Journal of International Development, 16*, 681–692.

SJRS. (1994). *The St. John: Portrait of a river [Brochure]*. St. John River Society.

Smith, J. (2004). What they really want: Assessing psychological contracts of volunteers. *The Journal of Volunteer Administration, 22*(1), 18–21.

Smith, K. A. (2002). Modelling the volunteer experience: Findings from the heritage sector. *Voluntary Action, 4*, 9–30.

Smith, K. A. (2003). Literary enthusiasts as visitors and volunteers. *International Journal of Tourism Research, 5*, 83–95.

Smith, K. A., & Lockstone, L. (2009). Involving and keeping event volunteers: Management insights from cultural festivals. In T. Baum, M. Deery, C. Hanlon et al. (Eds.), *People and work in events and conventions: A research perspective* (pp. 154–67). CABI.

Snyder, M., Clary, E. G., & Stukas, A. A. (2000). The functional approach to volunteerism. In G. R. Maio & J. M. Olson (Eds.), *Why we evaluate: Functions of attitudes* (pp. 365–93). Lawrence Erlbaum.

Söderman, N., & Snead, S. L. (2008). Opening the gap: The motivation of gap year travellers to volunteer in Latin America. In K. Lyons & S. Wearing (Eds.), *Journeys of discovery in volunteer tourism: International case study perspectives* (pp. 118–29). CABI.

Solberg, H. A. (2003). Major sporting events: Assessing the value of volunteers' work. *Managing Leisure, 8*, 17–27.

Stamer, D., Lerdall, K., & Guo, C. (2008). Managing heritage volunteers: An exploratory study of volunteer programmes in art museums worldwide. *Journal of Heritage Tourism, 3*, 203–14.

Starnes, B. J. (2007). An analysis of psychological contracts in volunteerism and the effect of contract breach on volunteer contributions to the organization. *The International Journal of Volunteer Administration, XXIV*, 31–41.

State of Victoria (2005). Event management: Introduction to the Commonwealth Games. [Online] www.publish.csiro.au/multimedia/projects/comm_games/content/cg_sr_event_mgmt.htm

Statistics Canada (2006). Trips by Canadians in Canada, by province and territory. [Online] 40.statcan.ca/l01/cst01/arts26a.htm

Stebbins, R. A. (1992). *Amateurs, professionals and serious leisure*. McGill-Queen's University Press.

Stebbins, R. A. (1996). Volunteering: A serious leisure perspective. *Nonprofit and Voluntary Sector Quarterly*, *25*, 211–24.

Stebbins, R. A. (1997). Casual leisure: A conceptual statement. *Leisure Studies*, *16*, 17–25.

Stebbins, R. A. (2005). Project-based leisure: Theoretical neglect of a common use of free time. *Leisure Studies*, *24*, 1–11.

Stoddart, H., & Rogerson, C. M. (2004). Volunteer tourism: The case of habitat for humanity South Africa. *GeoJournal*, *60*, 311–18.

Strigas, A., & Jackson, N. (2003). Motivating volunteers to serve and succeed: Design and results of a pilot study that explores demographics and motivational factors in sport volunteerism. *International Sports Journal*, *7*, 111–21.

Swarbrooke, J. (2002). *The development and management of visitor attractions*. Butterworth-Heinemann.

Swarbrooke, J., Beard, C., Leckie, S., & Pomfret, G. (2003). *Adventure tourism: The new frontier*. Butterworth-Heinemann.

Taylor, T., Darcy, S., Hoye, R., & Cuskelly, G. (2006). Using psychological contract theory to explore issues in effective volunteer management. *European Sport Management Quarterly*, *6*, 123–47.

The National Trust. (1998). *Volunteering with the National Trust: Summary of the findings of the 1997 survey*. The National Trust.

Topsfield, J. (2008). A country in pursuit of the vanishing tourist. *The Age, 4 June*, 3.

Tourism Research and Marketing. (2008). *Volunteer tourism: A global analysis*. ATLAS.

Tourism Victoria. (2002). *2002–2006 strategic plan*. Tourism Victoria.

Treuren, G. and Monga, M. (2002). Who are special event volunteers, and where do they from? Evidence from four South Australian Special event organisations. In G. Bamber & M. Barrett (eds.), *ANZAM/IFSAM VIth World Congress*.

Tuan, Y. (2005). Can volunteerism be promoted through government administration? *Volunteer Service Journal (China), Special English Edition*, 16–23.

Twynam, D., Farrell, J., & Johnston, M. (2002/2003). Leisure and volunteer motivation at a special sporting event. *Leisure/Loisir*, *27*, 363–77.

Uriely, N., & Reichel, A. (2000). Working tourists and their attitudes to hosts. *Annals of Tourism Research, 27,* 267–83.

Uriely, N., Reichel, A., & Ron, A. (2003). Volunteering in tourism: Additional thinking. *Tourism Recreation Research, 28,* 57–62.

Uriely, N., Schwartz, Z., Cohen, E., & Reichel, A. (2002). Rescuing hikers in Israel's deserts: Community altruism or an extension of adventure tourism? *Journal of Leisure Research, 34,* 25–36.

Van Der Westhuizen, J. (2004). Marketing Malaysia as a model modern Muslim state: The significance of the 16th Commonwealth Games. *Third World Quarterly, 25*(7), 1277–91.

VisitBritain. (2007). *Survey of visits to visitor attractions England 2006.* VisitBritain.

Volunteering Australia. (2005). *Definitions and principles of volunteering.* Volunteering Australia.

Volunteering Australia. (2006a). *Involved and valued? Findings from a national survey of Australian volunteers from diverse cultural and linguistic backgrounds.* Volunteering Australia.

Volunteering Australia. (2006b). *Subject guide: Event volunteering – take a closer look.* Volunteering Australia.

Volunteering Australia. (2006c). *Volunteering and work/life balance.* Volunteering Australia.

Volunteering Australia. (2007a). *Involving baby boomers as volunteers: Take a closer look.* Volunteering Australia.

Volunteering Australia. (2007b). *Staff recruitment, retention, satisfaction and productivity: The effects of employee volunteering programs.* Volunteering Australia.

Volunteering Australia. (2007c). *What are the real costs of volunteering?* Volunteering Australia.

Volunteering Australia. (2007d). *Young people and volunteering: Take a closer look.* Volunteering Australia.

Volunteering Australia. (2008). *National survey of volunteering issues 08.* Volunteering Australia.

Volunteering England. (2008). *Overcoming barriers to volunteering.* Volunteering England.

VolunTourism.org (2009) What is voluntourism? www.VoluntTourism.org

VSO. (2007). Ditch (un)worthy causes, VSO advises gap year students. *VSO Media Release, 14 August.*

Walker, M. P. (2002). Going for customer service gold. *T&D, May,* 62–9.

Wallace, T. (2006). Working on the train gang: Alienation, liminality and communitas in the UK preserved railway sector. *International Journal of Heritage Studies*, *12*, 218–33.

Ward, L. (2007). You're better off backpacking – VSO warns about perils of 'voluntourism'. *The Guardian Online*, *14 August*.

Warrior, B. (2007). The Commonwealth Games Pre Volunteer Programme (PVP) as a catalyst for addressing social exclusion. *Voluntary Action*, *8*, 98–108.

Wearing, S. (2001). *Volunteer tourism: Experiences that make a difference*. CABI.

Wearing, S. (2002). Re-Centering the self in volunteer tourism. In G. M. S. Dann (Ed.), *The tourist as a metaphor of the social world* (pp. 237–62). CABI.

Wearing, S. (2004). Examining best practice in volunteer tourism. In R. Stebbins & M. Graham (Eds.), *Volunteering as leisure/leisure as volunteering: An international assessment* (pp. 209–24): CABI.

Weiler, B., & Richins, H. (1995). Extreme, extravagant and elite: A profile of eco-tourists on Earthwatch expeditions. *Tourism Recreation Research*, *20*, 29–36.

Williams, P. W., Dossa, K. B., & Tompkins, L. (1995). Volunteerism and special event management: A case study of Whistler's Men's World Cup of Skiing. *Festival Management and Event Tourism*, *3*, 83–95.

Wilson, A., & Pimm, G. (1996). The tyranny of the volunteer: The care and feeding of voluntary workforces. *Management Decision*, *34*, 24–40.

Windsor, T. D., Anstey, K. J., & Rodgers, B. (2008). Volunteering and psychological well-being among young-old adults: How much is too much?. *The Gerontologist*, *48*, 59–70.

Womack, S. (2007). Gap-year students 'wasting time on projects'. *The Daily Telegraph Online*, *18 August*.

Yau, M. K., McKercher, B., & Packer, T. L. (2004). Travelling with a disability: More than an access issue. *Annals of Tourism Research*, *31*, 946–60.

Yeoman, I. (2008). *Tomorrow's tourist: Scenarios & trends*. Elsevier.

YOG. (2008). Volunteering tops poll of gap year go-getters. *Year Out Group Press Release*, *29 August*.

Yufang, S. (2005). An analysis of the characteristics and management of Olympic volunteers. *China Volunteer Service Journal, Special English Edition*, 40–9.

Zahra, A., & McIntosh, A. (2007). Volunteer tourism: Evidence of cathartic tourist experiences. *Tourism Recreation Research*, *32*, 115–19.

Zappalà, G., & Burrell, T. (2001). *Why are some volunteers more committed than others? A socio-psychological approach to volunteer commitment in community services*. The Smith Family.

Index